Reading
in
English

DOROTHY DANIELSON · REBECCA HAYDEN

Reading in English

**for students of English
as a second language**

PRENTICE-HALL, INC.
ENGLEWOOD CLIFFS, N.J.

Current printing (last digit):
20 19 18

PREFACE

This collection of readings with accompanying exercises grew out of many years of work in classes of English as a second language with students from all over the world. Selections were tested in a search for material that would be of interest and use to students. The readings included here proved to be among those most helpful in developing college-level vocabulary, in giving students ideas to discuss and to think and write about, and in encouraging further reading of contemporary writers. We have made no attempt to edit or simplify the selections beyond footnoting of certain terms, for this book was prepared for students eager to get on with the problem of reading college-level materials. Some of the selections are admittedly rather difficult in level of vocabulary and complexity of structure and thought; nonetheless, we have found that students appreciate, and profit from, the chance to read mature materials under circumstances that permit vocabulary study and a testing of comprehension.

Although we could not hope to put together a collection that would completely please everyone, we think that these selections, reflective of our own tastes, provide a stimulating glimpse of twentieth-century writing in America. More importantly, we have tried to choose selections representative of good standard English; very technical writing and dialect writing (with brief exceptions) have been ruled out. Many of the readings are short enough to be read aloud by the instructor if he considers that approach valuable to the students.

The vocabulary notes with each selection are intended to lift some of the burden of endlessly looking up words in the dictionary. The notes are hardly a substitute for the dictionary; the reader will still want to look up some words for definition and clarification. The terms footnoted represent words and phrases that required explanation when the material was used in classes. In the definitions and explanations, we have made an attempt to use words or phrases that can be directly substituted, in most cases, for the terms defined or explained.

The vocabulary quizzes at the end of the book are intended to be instructional as well as testing devices; they are purposely varied in order to give students practice in different types of test situations. The short-answer questions are designed to give practice in using the language as well as to test comprehension. The discussion questions go a step beyond and make further demands on the student to think in English and to think about questions important to his own mental development. Class discussions will provide opportunity to gain experience and facility in the use of the language, and writing essay-type answers may serve to augment what has been learned and to develop skill in writing. Finally, the listing of book titles in the headnotes preceding each selection and in the reading list at the end of the book may give students suggestions for continuing their reading beyond the scope of this book.

We wish to thank the following for their helpful criticism: James C. Austin of Southern Illinois University, Lubitsa Nenadovich Katz of the University of Illinois, Jane Kluckhohn of the University of New Mexico, and David W. Reed of the University of California. We also extend thanks to Mrs. Virginia T. Schaefer for her care in typing the manuscript.

D. D.

R. H.

ACKNOWLEDGMENTS

"Listening, Speaking, Reading, and Then Writing—the Fundamental Order in Language Learning." From *Learning a Foreign Language* by Eugene A. Nida. Copyright 1957 (revised edition) by Friendship Press, Inc. Reprinted by permission of the publisher.

"Mr. Kaplan and Vocabulary." From *The Education of Hyman Kaplan* by Leonard Q. Ross, copyright 1937, by Harcourt, Brace and Company, Inc. Reprinted by permission of Harcourt, Brace and Company, Inc., New York, and Constable & Company Ltd., London.

"How to Mark a Book" by Mortimer J. Adler. From the *Saturday Review* (July 6, 1940). Reprinted by permission of the *Saturday Review* and the author.

"The Cliché Expert Doesn't Feel Well." From *A Rock in Every Snowball* (Boston: Little, Brown and Company). Copyright 1946 by Frank Sullivan. Reprinted with permission of the author.

"University Days" by James Thurber. From *The New Yorker* (September 23, 1933). Permission by the author; Copr. © 1933 The New Yorker Magazine, Inc.

"What Every Yale Freshman Should Know" by Edmund S. Morgan. From the *Saturday Review* (January 23, 1960). Reprinted by permission of the *Saturday Review* and the author.

"Some Conclusions about Man." From Crane Brinton, John B. Christopher & Robert Lee Wolff, A *History of Civilization*, Volume I, 2nd Ed. Copyright 1955, 1960, by Prentice-Hall, Inc., Englewood Cliffs, N.J. Reprinted by permission of the publisher.

"The Half-People." From *More in Anger* by Marya Mannes. Copyright 1953, 1954, 1956, 1957 by Marya Mannes. Reprinted by permission of the publisher, J. B. Lippincott Company.

"Wonderful People." From *The Dove Brings Peace* by Richard Hagopian (New York: Farrar & Rinehart, Inc.). Copyright 1944 by Richard Hagopian. Reprinted by permission of the author.

"The Pomegranate Trees." From *My Name Is Aram*. Copyright 1937, 1938, 1939, 1940, by William Saroyan. Reprinted by permission of Harcourt, Brace and Company, Inc., New York, and Faber & Faber, Ltd., London.

"A Day's Wait." Reprinted by permission of Charles Scribner's Sons from *Winner Take Nothing* by Ernest Hemingway, copyright 1933, Charles Scribner's Sons, New York. Also with permission of Jonathan Cape Limited, London.

"The Use of Force." From *Make Light of It*. Copyright 1933, 1950, by William Carlos Williams. Reprinted by permission of McDowell, Obolensky Inc.

"Abraham Lincoln Grows Up." Chapter 13 from *Abraham Lincoln: The Prairie Years* by Carl Sandburg, copyright 1926, by Harcourt, Brace and Company, Inc.; renewed by Carl Sandburg. Reprinted by permission of the publishers.

"Man's Youth" and "Hunger to Devour the Earth." Reprinted by permission of Charles Scribner's Sons from *Of Time and the River* by Thomas Wolfe, copyright 1935, Charles Scribner's Sons (pp. 454, 455, 90-93). Also with permission of William Heinemann Ltd., London.

"The Universe and Dr. Einstein." From *The Universe and Dr. Einstein* by Lincoln Barnett, copyright 1948 by Harper & Brothers; copyright 1948, 1950, 1957 by Lincoln Barnett, by permission of William Sloane Associates, Inc., New York, and Victor Gollancz, Ltd., London.

"March 17." From *The Log from the Sea of Cortez* by John Steinbeck, copyright 1951 by John Steinbeck. Reprinted by permission of The Viking Press, Inc., New York, McIntosh and Otis, Inc., New York, and William Heinemann Ltd., London.

"Wealth from the Salt Seas." From *The Sea Around Us* by Rachel L. Carson, copyright 1950, 1951 by Rachel L. Carson. Reprinted by permission of Oxford University Press, Inc., New York, and Staples Press, London.

"The Jilting of Granny Weatherall." From *Flowering Judas and Other Stories*, copyright 1930, 1935, 1958, by Katherine Anne Porter. Reprinted by permission of Harcourt, Brace and Company, Inc., New York, and Jonathan Cape Limited, London.

"A Rose for Emily." Copyright 1930 and renewed 1957 by William Faulkner. Reprinted from *Collected Stories of William Faulkner* by permission of Random House, Inc., New York, and Chatto and Windus Ltd., London.

"Work and Play." From *The Sense of Beauty* by George Santayana, copyright 1896, 1936, by Charles Scribner's Sons. Reprinted by courtesy of Charles Scribner's Sons, New York, and by permission of Constable & Company Ltd., London.

CONTENTS

1   THE READINGS

2   THE EXERCISES

1

The Readings

EUGENE A. NIDA *(1914–)*

Eugene A. Nida, one of the foremost linguists in the United States, has specialized in the study of languages and dialects of primitive peoples. His work includes field surveys, linguistic research, and the writing of books and articles on languages, anthropology, and the science of meaning. As Secretary for the Translation Department of the American Bible Society, he has traveled to more than fifty countries, where he has worked with translators on linguistic problems of more than 120 different languages. He obtained his degrees at the University of California at Los Angeles (A.B.), the University of Southern California (M.A.), and the University of Michigan (Ph.D.); he has taught linguistics at the Universities of Michigan and Oklahoma. His books include *Customs and Cultures*, a fascinating account of strange customs and little-known cultures, and *Learning a Foreign Language* (1957), from which the following selection is taken. Here he outlines and discusses the basic order in learning a language: listening, speaking, reading, and finally writing.

Listening, Speaking, Reading, and Then Writing— the Fundamental Order in Language Learning

*T*HE SCIENTIFICALLY VALID[1] PROCEdure in language learning involves[2] listening first, to be followed by speaking. Then comes reading, and finally the writing of the language. This is just the order in which a child learns his mother tongue—first hearing, then speaking; and only after he has acquired considerable facility[3] in understanding and speaking, does he learn to read and write. However, most traditional methods of teaching languages to adults have almost completely reversed[4] this process—first comes reading, closely linked[5] with writing. Then, after one is supposed to   **10**

[1] **valid**—sound; well-grounded. [2] **involves**—includes; implies. [3] **facility**—ease in or readiness for. [4] **reversed**—turned around. [5] **linked**—joined; connected.

3

have acquired a knowledge of reading and writing, classes are offered in conversation. This major deficiency[6] in language teaching is in large measure the result of our classical tradition of Greek and Latin studies, languages which are only known to us in the dead forms of written documents. It was falsely assumed that since the classical tongues were taught exclusively[7] through the printed page, modern, living languages should be introduced the same way. A further practical reason why students in the classroom have rarely heard the language is that frequently the teacher is not capable of speaking the language fluently. Accordingly, the weight of tradition and the inexperience of teachers combine to make language learning a largely inefficient, boring,[8] and discouraging process.   20

The infrequent, clumsy,[9] oral reading of prescribed[10] sentences in the textbook can scarcely be called learning to speak a language. What actually happens in so many instances is that the student begins by writing out sentences on the basis of the grammar rules. This is done almost from the first day, certainly before one has half a chance to become acquainted with the vocabulary or the flow of the language. He soon gets involved in hundreds of intricate[11] rules, some of them purely orthographic,[12] as in French and Hebrew, and he usually ends   30 up by hating grammar and detesting[13] the language. But worst of all, he rarely learns to use the language, for though he may pass tests so as to graduate, his ability to carry on a conversation in the foreign language with a native speaker is almost nil.[14] He may spend so much time with the Masoretic pointing[15] of Hebrew vowels that he does not get a chance to read the language extensively,[16] and in the end his only contact with Hebrew may be an infrequent use of an analytical Hebrew-Chaldee lexicon.[17]

Our primary trouble is that we have tackled[18] the study of language from the wrong end. We are like the man who thinks he can learn to   40 swim merely by reading books about swimming. In actuality, we learn by doing. The grammatical rules are valuable as we plunge[19] into the language and need some assistance. In the same way, advanced instructions about swimming are helpful as we learn something from

---

[6] **deficiency**—weakness; defect; inadequacy. [7] **exclusively**—only; by shutting out all other methods. [8] **boring**—dull; uninteresting. [9] **clumsy**—awkward; not smooth or graceful. [10] **prescribed**—set (by custom or tradition). [11] **intricate**—complex; complicated. [12] **orthographic**—pertaining to spelling. [13] **detesting**—disliking intensely; hating. [14] **nil**—nothing; no amount. [15] **Masoretic pointing**—traditional system of indicating vowels in the study of Hebrew writing. [16] **extensively**—widely. [17] **lexicon** —dictionary. [18] **tackled**—undertaken; set to work on. [19] **plunge**—throw (in this case, ourselves); dive.

actual experience in the water. But reading books never makes a swimmer and learning rules never makes a practical linguist.

By setting up listening, speaking, reading, and writing in this order, we do not imply that one must be able to understand everything before beginning to speak. Certainly the child does not understand everything he hears before he begins to use the limited vocabulary which he has acquired. However, by emphasizing[20] the primary importance of listening, we clearly indicate that learning to speak is dependent upon hearing someone else speak, not upon reading orally on the basis of certain "rules of pronunciation." When we hear words and expressions from a native speaker, we should of course imitate[21] just as closely as possible, so that speaking follows immediately upon listening. Reading may begin rather soon if one is studying a language such as Spanish or German where the orthography rather consistently[22] represents the meaningful distinctions[23] in sound; but if the language is French or English, then reading traditionally spelled words is a great disadvantage at first. It is better to use some so-called "phonetic alphabet"[24] first until one has mastered several hundred phrases. Only then should one read the traditional orthography. In the case of Chinese, it is probably better to put off the reading process for several months and until such time as one has a rather good conversational ability for simple situations. Many linguists advise mastering a vocabulary of two or three thousand words before embarking[25] on the difficult and quite different task[26] of learning the Chinese symbols.[27]

Our emphasis upon the auditory perception[28] does not mean that we should set aside all the other factors in the memory process. We should listen to expressions (an auditory process), write them down (a motor process), read them (a visual process), and then pronounce them over and over (repeated motor processes). People differ in the importance which these various processes have in their memorization of materials. Some people find it very helpful to write a phrase several times. Others consider that seeing the phrase repeatedly is just as valuable for them. Still others apparently learn most rapidly by means of auditory impressions.[29] Whatever one's special aptitudes[30] are, these

20 **emphasizing**—stressing.   21 **imitate**—speak as much like the person as possible.
22 **consistently**—regularly;   constantly.   23 **distinctions**—differences.   24 "**phonetic alphabet**"—alphabet, such as the International Phonetic Alphabet, in which each symbol represents one sound only.   25 **embarking**—starting; becoming involved in.   26 **task**—job; undertaking.   27 **symbols**—characters (written or printed signs that represent words, which in turn stand for things or concepts).   28 **auditory perception**—hearing sense.
29 **impressions**—effects upon the ear and, thus, mind and feelings.   30 **aptitudes**—abilities.

should be cultivated[31] and improved. Nevertheless, one should constantly try to improve one's auditory memory. Our own civilization
does very little for us in this way, for our training is predominantly[32]
a matter of sight. We are frequently astonished to find people who
cannot read and yet who can recite from memory entire books of the
Bible. This is true of a number of people in Africa and the Orient.
The auditory memory can be developed as well as any other, and anyone learning a language will do well to concentrate in so far as possible
on improving this vital[33] factor.

[31] cultivated—developed;   cared   for.   [32] predominantly—mainly.   [33] vital—essential;
very important.

LEONARD Q. ROSS (1908 –)

The Education of H*Y*M*A*N K*A*P*L*A*N has been continuously popular since its publication in 1937. A sequel, *The Return of Hyman Kaplan,* appeared in 1959. Some curious facts about the author were revealed with the publication of the second book. "Leonard Q. Ross" had been the pseudonym for Leo Rosten, the name appearing on the title page of the later book. When the first book was published, Mr. Rosten was working for his Ph.D. degree in political science. Fearing that his professors might disapprove of his activities as a fiction writer, he adopted his now famous "pen name."

In the stories in both collections, we encounter English classes for immigrants taught by Mr. Parkhill at the American Night Preparatory School for Adults. Mr. Kaplan is perhaps the most eager, lovable, and annoying student in the class. He always signs his name in an unusual way: the letters are printed in red and outlined in blue, and between the letters are green stars. In this story, as the title suggests, we look in on the class as it takes up vocabulary study—a part of the language-learning process that continues to plague students of English as a second language.

Mr. K*A*P*L*A*N and Vocabulary

"VOCABULARY!" SAID MR. PARKHILL. "Above all, we must work on vocabulary."

He was probably right. For the students in the beginners' grade, vocabulary was a dire[1] and pressing[2] need. Spelling, after all, was not of such immediate importance to people who did little writing during their daily lives. Grammar? They needed the substance—words, phrases, idioms—to which grammar might be applied. Pronunciation? Mr. Parkhill had

---

[1] **dire**—terrible, extreme. [2] **pressing**—urgent, requiring immediate attention.

7

come to the reluctant[3] conclusion that for some of them accurate
pronunciation was a near impossibility. Take Mr. Kaplan, for example.   10
Mr. Kaplan was a willing, an earnest, aye![4] an enthusiastic pupil. And
yet, despite Mr. Parkhill's tireless tutelage, Mr. Kaplan referred to the
most celebrated of movie lovers as "Clock Gebble,"[5] who, it appeared,
showed a fine set of teeth "venever he greens."[6] Mr. Kaplan, when
asked to use "heaven" in a sentence, had replied promptly, "In
sommer, ve all heaven a fine time."[7]

"Yes, vocabulary—that, Mr. Parkhill thought, was the greatest need.
". . . And so tonight I shall write a list of new, useful words on the
blackboard. To each student I shall assign three words. Write a sentence in your notebooks using each word. Make sure you have no   20
mistakes. You may use your dictionaries, if you wish. Then go to the
board and copy your three sentences for class analysis."

The class was impressed and pleased. Miss Mitnick's ordinarily shy
expression changed to one of eager expectancy. Mrs. Moskowitz,
simple soul that she was, prepared her notebook with stolid solemnity.[8] And Mr. Kaplan, in the middle of the front row, took
out his box of crayons, smiled more broadly than ever (a chance
to use his crayons always intensified Mr. Kaplan's natural euphoria),[9]
turned to a fresh page in his notebook, and printed, slowly and with
great love: 30

VOCAPULERY[10]
(Prectice[11] in Book. Then Going to Blackb. and putting on.)
by
H*Y*M*A*N K*A*P*L*A*N

For the title he chose purple crayon; for the methodological observation in parentheses, orange; for the "by," yellow. His name he
printed, fondly, as always: in red and blue and flamboyant[12] green.
As he handled the crayons Mr. Kaplan smiled with the sweet serenity[13] of one in direct communication with his Muse.[14]

Mr. Parkhill assigned three words to each student and the be-

[3] reluctant—unwilling; disinclined. [4] aye!—yes (an exclamation). [5] "Clock Gebble"
—Clark Gable, famous movie star. (NOTE: Vocabulary notes for this story include
"translations" of speeches by Mr. Kaplan and other students that might cause some
difficulty in understanding the story.) [6] "venever he greens"—whenever he grins
(smiles). [7] "in sommer, ve all heaven a fine time"—in the summer, we all have a
fine time. [8] stolid solemnity: a) stolid—firm, calm, impassive; b) solemnity—serious·
ness. [9] euphoria—feeling of good or well-being. [10] "vocapulery"—vocabulary.
[11] "prectice . . . blackb."—practice . . . blackboard. [12] flamboyant—loud; highly colored; vivid. [13] serenity—calmness; peacefulness; tranquility. [14] Muse—in Greek
myths, one of the daughters of Zeus, who protected and encouraged the arts of poetry,
music, etc.

ginners' grade went into action. Lips pursed,[15] brows wrinkled, distant looks appeared in thoughtful eyes; heads were scratched, chins stroked,[16] dictionaries fluttered.[17] Mr. Kaplan tackled his three words with gusto:[18] *pitcher, fascinate, university.* Mr. Parkhill noticed that   40
Mr. Kaplan's cerebration[19] was accompanied by strange sounds: he pronounced each word, and tried fitting it into a sentence, in a whisper which could be heard halfway across the room. He muttered the entire process of his reasoning. Mr. Kaplan, it seemed, thought only in dialogue with his other self. There was something uncanny[20] about it.

"Pitcher . . . pitcher," Mr. Kaplan whispered. "Is maybe a pitcher for milk? Is maybe a pitcher on de vall[21]—*art!* Aha! Two minninks![22] 'Plizz[23] take milk fromm de pitcher.' Fine! 'De pitcher hengs cockeye.'[24] Also fine! Pitcher . . . pitcher."

This private colloquy[25] was not indulged in[26] without a subtle de-   50
sign,[27] for Mr. Kaplan watched Mr. Parkhill's facial expressions carefully out of the corner of his eye as he whispered to himself. Mr. Kaplan hoped to discover which interpretation of "pitcher" was acceptable. But Mr. Parkhill had long ago learned to beware of[28] Mr. Kaplan's strategies; he preserved a stern facial immobility as Mr. Kaplan's stage whispers floated[29] through the classroom.

When Mr. Kaplan had finished his three sentences he reread them proudly, nodded happily to Mr. Parkhill (who, though pretending to be watching Miss Schneiderman at the blackboard, was watching Mr. Kaplan out of the corner of *his* eye), and went to the board. He   60
whispered the sentences aloud as he copied them. Ecstasy[30] illuminated his face.

"Well," said Mr. Parkhill after all the students had transcribed their work, "let's start at this end. Mr. Bloom, I think?"

Mr. Bloom read his sentences quickly:

> She *declined*[31] the money.
> In her red hat she falt[32] *conspicuous.*[33]
> Last Saturday, I saw a *remarkable* show.

---

[15] **pursed**—drawn together rather tightly. [16] **stroked**—rubbed, usually with long strokes or movements. [17] **fluttered**—moved in a quick, light, irregular manner (as a bird "fluttering its wings"). [18] **gusto**—hearty enjoyment. [19] **cerebration**—act of thinking; thought. [20] **uncanny**—strange; unnatural; mysterious. [21] **"pitcher on de vall"**—picture on the wall. [22] **"minninks"**—meanings. [23] **"plizz"**—please. [24] **"hengs cockeye"**—hangs cockeyed (crooked). [25] **colloquy**—talk or conversation. [26] **indulged in**—enjoyed. [27] **subtle design:** *a*) **subtle**—clever, crafty, cunning; *b*) **design**—plan. [28] **to beware of**—to be cautious of. [29] **stage whispers floated:** *a*) **stage whispers**—type of whispers used on the stage (loud enough to be heard but with vocal qualities suggesting a whisper); *b*) **floated**—soared or sailed; went. [30] **ecstasy**—extreme delight. [31] **declined**—refused to accept. [32] **"falt"**—felt. [33] **conspicuous**—very noticeable.

"Excellent!" said Mr. Parkhill. "Are there any questions?" There
were no questions. Mr. Parkhill corrected "falt" and the exercise   70
continued. On the whole, all went surprisingly well. Except for those
of Mrs. Moskowitz, who worked havoc[34] with "niggardly"[35] ("It was
a *niggardly* night"), the sentences were quite good. Mr. Parkhill was
delighted. The experiment in vocabulary-building was proving a decided success. At last Mr. Kaplan's three sentences came up.

"Mr. Kaplan is next, I believe." There was a note of caution in Mr.
Parkhill's voice.

Mr. Kaplan went to the board. "Mine foist void, ladies an' gantleman,"[36] he announced, smiling (Mr. Kaplan always did things with a
certain bravado[37]), "is 'pitcher.' So de santence[38] is: 'Oh, how beauri-   80
ful is dis *pitcher.*' "

Mr. Parkhill saw that Mr. Kaplan had neatly straddled[39] two words
by a deliberately noncommittal[40] usage. "Er—Mr. Kaplan. The word
is 'p-i-t-c-h-e-r,' not 'p-i-c-t-u-r-e.' "

Too late did Mr. Parkhill realize that he had given Mr. Kaplan the
clue[41] he had been seeking.

"Mr. Pockheel," Mr. Kaplan replied with consummate[42] simplicity,
"dis void *is* 'p-i-t-c-h-e-r.' "

"But when you say, 'Oh, how *beautiful* this pitcher is,' " said Mr.
Parkhill, determined to force Mr. Kaplan to the wall,[43] "you sug-   90
gest—"

"Ah!" Mr. Kaplan murmured, with a tolerant[44] smile. "In som
houses is even de *pitchers* beauriful."

"Read your next sentence, Mr. Kaplan."

Mr. Kaplan went on, smiling. "De sacond void, ladies an' gantleman, is 'fascinate'—an' believe me is a plantyhod void! So is mine
santence: 'In India is all kinds snake-fescinators.' "[45]

"You are thinking of snake-*charmers.*" (Mr. Kaplan seemed to
have taken the dictionary's description of "fascinate" too literally.)
"Try 'fascinate' in another sentence, please."   100

---

[34] worked havoc—ruined. [35] niggardly—stingy, mean. [36] "mine foist void, ladies
an' gantleman"—my first word, ladies and gentlemen. [37] bravado—dramatic enthusiasm; showmanship. [38] "de santence . . . beauriful"—the sentence . . . beautiful.
[39] neatly straddled: *a*) neatly—cleverly; *b*) straddled—taken an indecisive position on.
[40] noncommittal—not taking one side or the other. (See *Fn.* 39.) [41] clue—hint;
piece of evidence; suggestion. [42] consummate—complete; perfect. [43] to force Mr.
Kaplan to the wall—to put him in a position where there would be no way out, so
that he would have to take a definite stand or position on the word. [44] tolerant—
patient. [45] "De sacond void . . . is a planty hod void! So is mine santence: 'In
India is all kinds of snake-fescinators.' "—The second word . . . is a plenty (very)
hard word! So is my sentence: "In India, there are all kinds of snake-charmers."

Mr. Kaplan gazed ceilingward with a masterful insouciance,[46] one eye half-closed. Then he ventured: "You *fescinate* me."

Mr. Parkhill hurried Mr. Kaplan on to his last word.

"Toid void, faller-students, is 'univoisity.' De santence usink dis void: 'Eleven yiss is married mine vife an' minesalf, so is time commink for our tvalft *univoisity.*' "[47]

It was the opportunity for which Miss Mitnick had been waiting. "Mr. Kaplan mixes up two words," she said. "He means 'anniversary.' 'University, is a high college—the *highest* college."

Mr. Kaplan listened to this unwelcome correction with a fine suf- 110
ferance.[48] Then he arched[49] his eyebrows and said, "You got right, Mitnick. Hau Kay! So I'll givink anodder santence: 'Som pipple didn't have aducation in a *univoisity*' "—he glanced meaningfully at Miss Mitnick—" 'but just de same, dey havink efter elaven yiss de tvalft annivoisery.' "[50]

With this retort[51] courteous Mr. Kaplan took his seat. Through the next few recitations he was strangely silent. He did not bother to offer a correction of Miss Kowalski's spectacular misuse of "guess." ("Turn out the guess."[52]) He did not as much as volunteer an opinion on Miss Hirschfield's "The cat omits[53] a cry." For all his proud smile 120
it was clear that Mr. Kaplan had suffered a deep hurt: like a smoldering cinder[54] in his soul lay the thought of his humiliation[55] at the mundane[56] hands of one Rose Mitnick. He smiled as bravely as ever, but his silence was ominous.[57] He seemed to be waiting, waiting. . . .

"Miss Mitnick, please," said Mr. Parkhill. A flame leaped into Mr. Kaplan's eyes.

Miss Mitnick's first sentence was "*Enamel* is used for painting chairs." Before she could read it Mr. Kaplan's voice rang out in triumph.

---

[46] insouciance—air of freedom from care; carefreeness. [47] "Toid void, faller-students, is 'univoisity.' De santence usink dis void: 'Eleven yiss is married mine vife an' minesalf, so is time commink for our tvalft univoisity.' "—The third word, fellow-students, is "university." Here is a sentence using this word: "My wife and I have been married for eleven years, so the time is coming soon for our twelfth *anniversary*." [48] sufferance—capacity to endure pain; tolerance. [49] arched—raised; made in the shape of an arch; curved upward. [50] "You . . . annivoisery"—You are right, Miss Mitnick. Okay! I'll give another sentence: "Some people haven't had a university education, but just the same, they do have the twelfth anniversary after eleven years of marriage." [51] retort—reply in answer to the comment of another person. [52] "Turn . . . guess."—Turn out the gas. [53] "omits"—emits (*omits* means "leave out"; *emits*, "makes a noise"). [54] smoldering cinder: *a*) smoldering—burning or smoking without a flame (his hurt is suppressed without outward demonstration of his feeling); *b*) cinder—small piece of wood or other matter that is partially burned out. [55] humiliation—embarrassment. [56] mundane—commonplace or ordinary; earthly or worldly as opposed to spiritual. [57] ominous—threatening.

"Mistake by Mitnick! Ha! Mit *enimals* she is painting chairs? Ha!"   130
"The word is '*enamel*,' " said Mr. Parkhill coldly. "Not 'animal.' "

Rebuffed,[58] Mr. Kaplan let Miss Mitnick's reading of that sentence, and her next, go unchallenged. But the flame burned in his eyes again when she read her final effort: "The prisoner stood in the *dock*."

"Well," suggested Mr. Parkhill, before Mr. Kaplan, squirming[59] with excitement in his chair, could offer a rash[60] correction, "that's one way to use the word. The English use it that way. But there is a—er—more common usage. Can you use 'dock' in a more familiar meaning, Miss Mitnick?"

Miss Mitnick was silent.   140

"Anyone?"

"I like roast *duck!*" cried Mr. Kaplan promptly.

"*Dock!*" Mr. Parkhill said severely. "Not *duck!*" Once again Mr. Kaplan bowed to a cruel fate.

" 'Dock' isn't hard," said Mr. Parkhill encouragingly. "I'll give you a hint, class. Each of you, in coming to America, has had *direct experience with a dock.*" He smiled almost gaily, and waited.

The class went into that coma[61] which signified thought, searching its collective memory of "coming to America." Mrs. Moskowitz closed her eyes as the recollection of her sea-sickness surged over[62] her like   150 a wave, and searched her memory no more. Mr. Kaplan, desperate to make the kill, whispered his associations tensely:[63] " 'Dock' . . . Commink to America . . . boat . . . feesh[64] . . . big vaves . . . cremps."

It was clear they were getting nowhere. (Mr. Norman Bloom, indeed, had forgotten all about "dock" in his sweet recollection of the pinochle game[65] on the boat when he had won four and a half dollars.)

"Well, I'll make it even easier," said Mr. Parkhill lightly. "Where did your boats *land?*"   160

"New York!" cried Mr. Kaplan eagerly.

Mr. Parkhill cleared his throat. "Yes—of course. But I mean—"

A cry of joy came from the lips of Hyman Kaplan. "I got him! Ufcawss! 'Dock!' Plain an' tsimple! Ha!" He shot a look of triumph toward Miss Mitnick. "I'm soprize so high-cless a student like Mit-

---

[58] **rebuffed**—checked or caught.   [59] **squirming**—moving impatiently.   [60] **rash**—hasty; not thought out.   [61] **coma**—state of prolonged unconsciousness from which it is difficult to be awakened or aroused.   [62] **surged over**—rushed or swept over.   [63] **tensely**—with tense, tight muscles (as the lips and tongue in pronouncing words).   [64] " . . . **feesh . . . cremps**"—fish . . . cramps.   [65] **pinochle game**—card game.

nick, she knows all abot fency voids like 'univoisities' and 'anni-
voiseries,' she shouldn't know a leetle void like 'dock'!"[66]

Something in Mr. Parkhill warned him. Not for a moment could
he believe that Mr. Kaplan's confidence and enthusiasm were authentic[67] indications of a correct answer. Mr. Parkhill would have   170
preferred that some other student try a sentence with "dock." But
no one volunteered.

"Very well, Mr. Kaplan," he said, staring at his fingers, as if to break
the impact[68] of Mr. Kaplan's contribution.

Mr. Kaplan rose, inspiration in his eyes.[69] His smile was so wide
that his face seemed to be one ecstatic cavern.[70] He cast majestic
glances to both sides, as if reading the tribute in the faces of his
fellow-students. Then he said, in one triumphant breath, "Hollo,
Doc!"

Peace fell upon the room. Through the windows, from far away,   180
there came the muted rumble[71] of the Third Avenue elevated.[72] The
features of Abraham Lincoln on the wall took on, somehow, a softer
understanding. But Mr. Parkhill was aware only of a strange and un-
accountable ringing[73] in his ears ("Hello, Doc!" . . . "Hello, Doc!")
and, while shaking his head sadly to show Mr. Kaplan that he was
wrong, he thought to himself with feverish persistence, "Vocabulary.
Above all, vocabulary."

[66] "I got him! . . . void like 'dock'!"—I get it! Of course! "Dock!" Plain and simple!
I'm surprised that such a good student as Miss Mitnick, who knows all about fancy
words like "universities" and "anniversaries" wouldn't know a little word like "dock"!
[67] authentic—genuine; real. [68] impact—force; crash. [69] inspiration in his eyes—
stimulation to creative effort showing in his eyes. [70] cavern—opening; hole. [71] muted
rumble—deadened or quieted noise. [72] elevated—train on tracks above the street.
[73] ringing—noise.

MORTIMER J. ADLER (1902 –   )

Mortimer J. Adler was born and raised in New York City. For many years he was Professor of Philosophy of Law at the University of Chicago. Later he became editor of *Great Books of the Western World,* and in that capacity became a leader in the movement to get people to read and discuss books that appear on the list of Great Books. Since 1952, he has served as director of the Institute for Philosophical Research in San Francisco.

Mr. Adler, in 1940, published one of the first "how to" self-help books, *How to Read a Book,* a great popular success. He extended his practical guide for readers in the *Saturday Review* magazine article that appears here; in it, he advises readers to mark books to assure active reading of them.

How to Mark a Book

*Y*OU KNOW YOU HAVE TO READ "between the lines"[1] to get the most out of anything. I want to persuade you to do something equally important in the course of your reading. I want to persuade you to "write between the lines." Unless you do, you are not likely to do the most efficient kind of reading.

I contend,[2] quite bluntly,[3] that marking up a book is not an act of mutilation[4] but of love.

You shouldn't mark up a book which isn't yours. Librarians (or   10
your friends) who lend you books expect you to keep them clean, and you should. If you decide that I am right about the usefulness of marking books, you will have to buy them. Most of the world's great

---

[1] read "between the lines"—read more into something or find more meaning in something than is actually stated in the words in print or in writing. [2] contend—argue or maintain as true. [3] bluntly—speaking plainly, or in a straightforward manner. [4] mutilation—destruction; tearing to pieces.

books are available today, in reprint editions, at less than a dollar.

There are two ways in which one can own a book. The first is the property right you establish by paying for it, just as you pay for clothes and furniture. But this act of purchase is only the prelude[5] to possession. Full ownership comes only when you have made it a part of yourself, and the best way to make yourself a part of it is by writing in it. An illustration may make the point clear. You buy a beefsteak and transfer it from the butcher's icebox to your own. But you do not own the beefsteak in the most important sense until you consume it and get it into your bloodstream. I am arguing that books, too, must be absorbed in your bloodstream to do you any good.

Confusion about what it means to *own* a book leads people to a false reverence[6] for paper, binding, and type—a respect for the physical thing—the craft of the printer rather than the genius of the author. They forget that it is possible for a man to acquire the idea, to possess the beauty, which a great book contains, without staking his claim[7] by pasting his bookplate[8] inside the cover. Having a fine library doesn't prove that its owner has a mind enriched by books; it proves nothing more than that he, his father, or his wife, was rich enough to buy them.

There are three kinds of book owners. The first has all the standard sets and best sellers—unread, untouched. (This deluded[9] individual owns woodpulp[10] and ink, not books.) The second has a great many books—a few of them read through, most of them dipped into, but all of them as clean and shiny as the day they were bought. (This person would probably like to make books his own, but is restrained[11] by a false respect for their physical appearance.) The third has a few books or many—every one of them dog-eared[12] and dilapidated,[13] shaken and loosened by continual use, marked and scribbled[14] in from front to back. (This man owns books.)

Is it false respect, you may ask, to preserve intact[15] and unblemished[16] a beautifully printed book, an elegantly bound edition? Of course not. I'd no more scribble all over a first edition of *Paradise Lost* than I'd give my baby a set of crayons and an original Rem-

---

[5] **prelude**—something that comes before.   [6] **reverence**—a feeling or attitude of deep respect, love, and awe.   [7] **staking his claim**—indicating ownership.   [8] **bookplate**—a sticker or label with one's name on it that is pasted in the front of a book.   [9] **deluded** —misled; having persuaded himself to believe what he wishes to believe.   [10] **woodpulp** —wood reduced to pulp; the substance out of which paper is made.   [11] **restrained**—held back; inhibited.   [12] **dog-eared**—corners turned down.   [13] **dilapidated**—broken down; worn out.   [14] **scribbled**—written in a careless or hasty manner so that what is written is difficult for others to read.   [15] **intact**—untouched or undamaged; complete.   [16] **unblemished**—unmarked.

brandt! I wouldn't mark up a painting or a statue. Its soul, so to speak, is inseparable from its body. And the beauty of a rare edition or of a richly manufactured volume is like that of a painting or a statue.   50

But the soul of a book *can* be separated from its body. A book is more like the score of a piece of music than it is like a painting. No great musician confuses a symphony with the printed sheets of music. Arturo Toscanini reveres[17] Brahms, but Toscanini's score of the C-minor Symphony is so thoroughly marked up that no one but the maestro himself can read it. The reason why a great conductor makes notations on his musical scores—marks them up again and again each time he returns to study them—is the reason why you should mark your books. If your respect for magnificent binding or typography gets in the way, buy yourself a cheap edition and pay your respects   60
to the author.

Why is marking up a book indispensable[18] to reading? First, it keeps you awake. (And I don't mean merely conscious; I mean wide awake.) In the second place, reading, if it is active, is thinking, and thinking tends to express itself in words, spoken or written. The marked book is usually the thought-through book. Finally, writing helps you remember the thoughts you had, or the thoughts the author expressed. Let me develop these three points.

If reading is to accomplish anything more than passing time, it must be active. You can't let your eyes glide[19] across the lines of a   70
book and come up with an understanding of what you have read. Now an ordinary piece of light fiction, like, say, *Gone with the Wind*,[20] doesn't require the most active kind of reading. The books you read for pleasure can be read in a state of relaxation, and nothing is lost. But a great book, rich in ideas and beauty, a book that raises and tries to answer great fundamental questions, demands the most active reading of which you are capable. You don't absorb the ideas of John Dewey[21] the way you absorb the crooning of Mr. Vallee.[22] You have to reach for them. That you cannot do while you're asleep.

If, when you've finished reading a book, the pages are filled with   80
your notes, you know that you read actively. The most famous *active* reader of great books I know is President Hutchins,[23] of the University of Chicago. He also has the hardest schedule of business

---

[17] **reveres**—regards with deep respect, love, and awe. (See *fn.* 6.)   [18] **indispensable**—absolutely necessary or required; essential.   [19] **glide**—move or flow easily.   [20] **Gone with the Wind**—popular novel by Margaret Mitchell, published in 1936.   [21] **John Dewey**—American philosopher and educator (1859–1952).   [22] **Mr. Vallee**—Rudy Vallee, American singer of popular music who enjoyed fame in the 1920's.   [23] **President Hutchins**—Robert Maynard Hutchins (1899–   ), president of the University of Chicago from 1929 to 1950.

activities of any man I know. He invariably reads with a pencil, and sometimes, when he picks up a book and pencil in the evening, he finds himself, instead of making intelligent notes, drawing what he calls "caviar factories" on the margins. When that happens, he puts the book down. He knows he's too tired to read, and he's just wasting time.

But, you may ask, why is writing necessary? Well, the physical act   90
of writing, with your own hand, brings words and sentences more sharply before your mind and preserves them better in your memory. To set down your reaction to important words and sentences you have read, and the questions they have in your mind, is to preserve those reactions and sharpen those questions.

Even if you wrote on a scratch pad,[24] and threw the paper away when you had finished writing, your grasp[25] of the book would be surer. But you don't have to throw the paper away. The margins (top and bottom, as well as side), the end papers, the very space between the lines, are all available. They aren't sacred. And, best of all, your   100
marks and notes become an integral[26] part of the book and stay there forever. You can pick up[27] the book the following week or year, and there are all your points of agreement, disagreement, doubt, and inquiry. It's like resuming an interrupted conversation with the advantage of being able to pick up where you left off.

And that is exactly what reading a book should be: a conversation between you and the author. Presumably he knows more about the subject than you do; naturally, you'll have the proper humility[28] as you approach him. But don't let anybody tell you that a reader is supposed to be solely on the receiving end. Understanding is a two-way   110
operation; learning doesn't consist in being an empty receptacle.[29] The learner has to question himself and question the teacher. He even has to argue with the teacher, once he understands what the teacher is saying. And marking a book is literally an expression of your differences, or agreements of opinion, with the author.

There are all kinds of devices[30] for marking a book intelligently and fruitfully. Here's the way I do it:

1. *Underlining*: of major points, of important or forceful statements.

24 **scratch pad**—note pad; a number of pieces of paper fastened together, usually without a cover, that may be used for writing notes.   25 **grasp**—understanding.   26 **integral** —essential; necessary for completeness.   27 **pick up**—begin again or resume activity.   28 **humility**—feeling that recognizes the superiority of another; feeling of unimportance either generally or in relation to another person.   29 **receptacle**—container. 30 **devices**—means; ways; techniques.

2. *Vertical lines at the margin:* to emphasize a statement already 120
underlined.

3. *Star, asterisk, or other doodad*[31] *at the margin:* to be used spar-
ingly, to emphasize the ten or twenty most important statements in
the book. (You may want to fold the bottom corner of each page on
which you use such marks. It won't hurt the sturdy[32] paper on which
most modern books are printed, and you will be able to take the book
off the shelf at any time and, by opening it at the folded-corner page,
refresh your recollection of the book.)

4. *Numbers in the margin:* to indicate the sequence[33] of points the
author makes in developing a single argument.   130

5. *Numbers of other pages in the margin:* to indicate where else in
the book the author made points relevant[34] to the point marked; to
tie up the ideas in a book, which, though they may be separated by
many pages, belong together.

6. *Circling of key words or phrases.*

7. *Writing in the margin, or at the top or bottom of the page, for
the sake of:* recording questions (and perhaps answers) which a passage raised in your mind; reducing a complicated discussion to a
simple statement; recording the sequence of major points right
through the books. I use the end papers[35] at the back of the book 140
to make a personal index of the author's points in the order of their
appearance.

The front end papers are, to me, the most important. Some people
reserve them for a fancy bookplate. I reserve them for fancy thinking. After I have finished reading the book and making my personal
index on the back end papers, I turn to the front and try to outline
the book, not page by page, or point by point (I've already done that
at the back), but as an integrated structure,[36] with a basic unity and
an order of parts. This outline is, to me, the measure of my understanding of the work.   150

If you're a die-hard[37] anti-book-marker, you may object that the
margins, the space between the lines, and the end papers don't give
you room enough. All right. How about using a scratch pad slightly
smaller than the page size of the book—so that the edges of the sheets
won't protrude?[38] Make your index, outlines, and even your notes on

---

[31] **doodad**—marking that usually has meaning only to the person who has made it.
[32] **sturdy**—hardy or strong; not fragile or delicate.   [33] **sequence**—order of appearance.
[34] **relevant**—pertinent, or to the point.   [35] **end papers**—pages without printing at the
back and front of the book.   [36] **integrated structure**—structure in which the parts are
brought into a whole.   [37] **die-hard**—person who resists vigorously to the end a new way
of doing something.   [38] **protrude**—stick out.

the pad, and then insert[39] these sheets permanently inside the front and back covers of the book.

Or you may say that this business of marking books is going to slow up your reading. It probably will. That's one of the reasons for doing it. Most of us have been taken in by the notion that speed of   160 reading is a measure of our intelligence. There is no such thing as the right speed for intelligent reading. Some things should be read quickly and effortlessly,[40] and some should be read slowly and even laboriously.[41] The sign of intelligence in reading is the ability to read different things differently according to their worth. In the case of good books, the point is not to see how many of them you can get through,[42] but rather how many can get through you[43]—how many you can make your own.[44] A few friends are better than a thousand acquaintances.[45] If this be your aim, as it should be, you will not be impatient if it takes more time and effort to read a great book than it   170 does a newspaper.

You may have one final objection to marking books. You can't lend them to your friends because nobody else can read them without being distracted[46] by your notes. Furthermore, you won't want to lend them because a marked copy is a kind of intellectual diary, and lending it is almost like giving your mind away.

If your friend wishes to read your Plutarch's *Lives,* Shakespeare, or *The Federalist Papers,*[47] tell him gently, but firmly, to buy a copy. You will lend him your car or your coat—but your books are as much a part of you as your head or your heart.   180

³⁹ **insert**—put in. ⁴⁰ **effortlessly**—with ease. ⁴¹ **laboriously**—with effort. ⁴² **get through**—read through or finish. ⁴³ **get through you**—be well understood by you. (A play on words by the author.) ⁴⁴ **make your own**—understand and thus make a part of you. ⁴⁵ **acquaintances**—persons one knows slightly or not very well. ⁴⁶ **distracted** —diverted; side-tracked; confused by having one's attention drawn away from his object of concentration. ⁴⁷ **The Federalist Papers**—set of eighty-five articles by Alexander Hamilton, James Madison, and John Jay, published in 1787 and 1788, analyzing the Constitution of the United States and urging its adoption.

FRANK SULLIVAN (1892–   )

Frank Sullivan, humorist and journalist, has lived most of his life in Saratoga Springs, New York. He has been known to say, "When Saratoga gets too quiet I go to New York and when New York gets too noisy I come back to Saratoga." While he was still in high school, he began working on his home town newspaper—something he has done from time to time ever since. Many of his humorous essays have appeared in *The New Yorker* magazine and in books such as *A Rock in Every Snowball* (1946), from which the selection here is taken. The targets of his sharp wit include everything from football to good will.

Sullivan has written a series of interviews in which Mr. Arbuthnot, "the cliché expert," answers questions on subjects such as the atom and Christmas. Mr. Arbuthnot never has to think about what he is going to say because he never runs out of clichés. The reader finds these interviews humorous because he recognizes that, although clichés are used by almost everyone in daily conversation, they become ridiculous and meaningless when they replace spontaneity and originality of expression. In this dialogue, Mr. Arbuthnot is questioned about his health—a subject discussed in clichés all over the world.

The Cliché Expert Doesn't Feel Well

Q——Mr. Arbuthnot, you are an expert in[1] the use of the cliché[2] as applied to matters of health and ill health, are you not?

A——I am.

Q——In that case, how do you feel?

A——Oh, fair to middling.[3] I suppose I can't complain.

Q——You don't sound so awfully chipper.[4]

[1] **expert in**—authority on. [2] **cliché**—expression that has been overused to the point of being dull or without freshness. (Examples: "busy as a bee" or "good Joe.") [3] **fair to middling**—not bad, not good (literally, from fairly well to a medium good feeling). [4] **awfully chipper**—very lively and happy; in very good spirits.

20

A——What's the use of complaining?[5] I hate people who are always telling their friends abouts their ailments.[6] O-o-h!

Q——What's the matter?

A——My head. It's splitting.[7] I've had one of my sick headaches[8]   10
all day long.

Q——One of your *sick* headaches, eh. What caused it?

A——I don't know. I haven't been feeling right[9] lately. My stomach has been bothering me. My knee has been bothering me. My head has been bothering me. Yesterday I had one of my dizzy spells.[10]

Q——Really? That's too bad.

A——I thought my time had come.[11]

Q——What was it? Did something you ate disagree with you?

A——Nothing I eat ever agrees with me. But I mustn't talk about myself. You'll be thinking I'm a hypochondriac.[12] You know the   20
definition of a bore[13]—a fellow who tells you how he feels when you ask him. . . . Oh, what was that?

Q——Just an auto backfiring.[14] You're rather jumpy.[15]

A——I'm nervous as a cat,[16] you know. The least little thing upsets me. I'm just about two jumps ahead of a fit[17] most of the time.

Q——I suppose you don't sleep well.

A——Why, I go to bed all tired out and then don't get a wink of sleep.[18] Don't shut my eye all night long. Just lie there and toss.[19] Least little thing wakens me. And when I get up in the morning I'm just as tired as when I went to bed. Just like a rag,[20] no good all   30
day.

Q——Have you taken anything?

A——I've taken everything but nothing seems to do me any good.[21]

Q——Maybe you're coming down with a cold.[22]

A——Oh, I always have a cold. I'm subject to colds.[23]

Q——There's certainly quite a lot of 'em[24] around.

---

5 the use of complaining—the advantage of finding fault or expressing discomfort. **6 ailments**—slight illnesses or pains.   **7 splitting**—aching severely (as if the head were splitting open).   **8 sick headaches**—severe headaches (usually accompanied by an upset stomach).   **9 haven't been feeling right**—haven't been feeling well or the way one should.   **10 dizzy spells**—faint or light-headed periods or moments.   **11 thought my time had come**—thought I was going to die.   **12 hypochondriac**—a person who is always thinking or imagining that he is ill.   **13 bore**—dull person; a person who is uninteresting to other people.   **14 backfiring**—making a loud bang from the exhaust pipe. **15 jumpy**—nervous or upset.   **16 nervous as a cat**—easily upset (see *jumpy*).   **17 two jumps ahead of a fit**—feeling ready to explode at the least little irritation.   **18 don't get a wink of sleep**—don't sleep at all.   **19 toss**—turn over and over.   **20 like a rag**—limp and lifeless.   **21 nothing seems to do me any good**—nothing seems to help me get well or relieve my discomfort or pain.   **22 coming down with a cold**—catching a cold.   **23 I'm subject to colds**—I have a tendency to catch colds easily.   **24 'em**—them (conversational form; the spelling reflects the way the word is pronounced in rapid conversation).

A——You know, I'm supposed to say that. I'm the cliché expert around here, not you.

Q——I beg your pardon, Mr. Arbuthnot.

A——Quite all right. I was merely about to say that if anything's   40
around I'll catch it. I always caught everything going.[25] I was very delicate as a child. They had quite a time raising me.

Q——Really?

A——Yes, indeed. When I was ten years old the doctors gave me six months to live. Said they wouldn't give "That!"[26] for my chances.

Q——Well, you fooled 'em.[27]

A——Sometimes I wonder. O-o-h!

Q——What's the matter?

A——That stitch[28] in my side. It's bothering me again.

Q——Maybe it's your appendix. Have you had it out?[29]   50

A——Have I! I'll never forget that experience. They had to rush me to the hospital and operate immediately. The doctor said mine was the worst case he had seen in all his practice. He came twice a day for a week. I had a day and night nurse.[30] They just took it in time.[31]

Q——You neglected it,[32] eh?

A——Oh, it doesn't pay[33] to neglect your health, I always say. And I always say that if you've got your health you don't have to worry about money.

Q——How true.   60

A——O-o-o-h!

Q——Now what's the matter?

A——My back has gone back on me[34] again. There's a crick[35] in it.

Q——Why don't you see a doctor?

A——I've seen every one in town. I've been to the best specialists.[36] None of them understands my case. They don't know what's the matter with me. They say "Cut down on your drinking and smoking, get plenty of rest, and don't worry." Don't worry, me eye![37] How's a person going to keep from worrying when his head—oh, but let's

[25] **everything going**—every disease that appeared in an epidemic or that anyone had. [26] **wouldn't give "That!"**—wouldn't give a snap of the finger. [27] **fooled 'em**—proved otherwise by staying alive. [28] **stitch**—sharp pain. [29] **had it out**—had it (the appendix) removed by surgery. [30] **a day and night nurse**—one nurse in the day and another at night. [31] **just took it in time**—removed the appendix just before it burst. [32] **neglected it**—didn't give it care. [33] **doesn't pay**—never comes to any good. [34] **gone back on me**—been troubling me again. [35] **crick**—a painful muscular spasm or cramp (a common type of crick is in the neck). [36] **specialists**—doctors who specialize in a certain branch of medicine, such as cardiology (heart) or neurology (nervous system). [37] **me eye!**—my eye (an emphatic remark that indicates disgust or scorn).

talk about something else except me. I don't want you to think I'm   70
one of those people who are always talking about their bodily ailments and so on.

Q——Oh, do go on. I love to hear other people talk about their
ailments.

A——You know this new doctor on Main Street?

Q——Yes. Quite a bright young fellow, they tell me.

A——Maybe so, but this is the experience I had with him. I went
to see him the other day. I'd tried all the others,[38] and thought I might
as well try him, too. I told him how I was all run-down[39] and he gave
me a thorough going-over.[40] And what do you think the young   80
whippersnapper[41] had the nerve[42] to tell me?

Q——What?

A——He told me there wasn't a thing the matter with me. He said
to me, "You think about yourself too much. What you need is something to occupy your mind. Why don't you take up golf?"[43] Golf!
With my heart!

Q——Oh, you have a bad heart, too?

A——Yes. A bum ticker.[44] Doctors indeed!

Q——What about 'em?

A——They're never in when you want 'em.   90

Q——What else?

A——They're all specialists nowadays. Give me the old-fashioned
family doctor.[45] Imagine telling a man with a weak heart to take up
golf.

Q——But, Mr. Arbuthnot, you look the picture of health[46] to me.

A——Nonsense. I wouldn't want my worst enemy[47] to go through
what I've been through.[48] You don't by any chance think I'm a
hypochondriac, do you?

Q——Oh, no! No, no!

A——I don't talk about my health, do I?   100

Q——No, indeed. Far from it.[49]

A——I mean to say, if you ask me how I am, I have to answer you,

---

[38] **I'd tried all the others**—I'd gone to see all the other doctors in town.   [39] **all run-down**—in a very weakened physical condition.   [40] **thorough going-over**—complete medical examination or check-up.   [41] **young whippersnapper**—inexperienced fool.   [42] **had the nerve**—had the boldness, impudence, shamelessness, or effrontery.   [43] **take up golf**—start playing golf.   [44] **bum ticker** (slang)—weak heart.   [45] **old-fashioned family doctor**—doctor who treats all types of illnesses; a general practitioner, not a specialist.   [46] **look the picture of health**—give the appearance of having perfect health.   [47] **my worst enemy**—the person I hate or dislike most.   [48] **go through what I've been through**—undergo the pain and discomfort I've experienced.   [49] **far from it** —not at all.

don't I? Well, I guess it's my turn to go in now.[50] I think the doctor's ready for me.

Q——Heaven help him.

A——I beg your pardon.

Q——I didn't say a thing. Good-by, Mr. Arbuthnot.

A——Good day, son. O-o-oh, my back!

[50] **my turn to go in**—my time to go in to see the doctor.

JAMES THURBER (1894 – 1961)

James Thurber ranks high as a humorist. For many years, he has kept people laughing with his writings and cartoons in *The New Yorker* magazine. He has also published about twenty books, including *Fables for Our Time* and *The Thurber Carnival*. While playing Indians as a boy, he was blinded in one eye, and long fought a losing battle against loss of sight in the other eye. Several years ago he was forced to give up drawing, but not writing. He is a native of Ohio, and quite often his Ohio background comes out in his stories and essays—as in "University Days," a satirical account of some of his experiences at The Ohio State University (first published in 1933 in *The New Yorker*). Like many students interested primarily in the liberal arts and the humanities, the author had difficulty in adjusting to certain courses required for graduation. Thurber humorously describes his experiences in botany, economics, physical education, and military training.

University Days

I PASSED ALL THE OTHER COURSES that I took at my University, but I could never pass botany. This was because all botany students had to spend several hours a week in a laboratory looking through a microscope at plant cells, and I could never see through a microscope. I never once saw a cell through a microscope. This used to enrage my instructor.[1] He would wander around the laboratory pleased with the progress all the students were making in drawing the involved and, so I am told, interesting structure of flower cells, until he came to me. I would just be standing   10 there. "I can't see anything," I would say. He would begin patiently enough, explaining how anybody can see through a microscope, but

[1] **enrage my instructor**—make my instructor very angry or furious; infuriate my instructor.

he would always end up in a fury,[2] claiming that I could *too* see through a microscope but just pretended[3] that I couldn't. "It takes away from the beauty of flowers anyway," I used to tell him. "We are not concerned with beauty in this course," he would say. "We are concerned solely with what I may call the *mechanics* of flars."[4] "Well," I'd say, "I can't see anything." "Try it just once again," he'd say, and I would put my eye to the microscope and see nothing at all, except now and again a nebulous[5] milky substance—a phenomenon[6]   20 of maladjustment. You were supposed to see a vivid,[7] restless clock-work of sharply defined plant cells. "I see what looks like a lot of milk," I would tell him. This, he claimed, was the result of my not having adjusted the microscope properly, so he would readjust it for me, or rather, for himself. And I would look again and see milk.

I finally took a deferred pass,[8] as they called it, and waited a year and tried again. (You had to pass one of the biological sciences or you couldn't graduate.) The professor had come back from vacation brown as a berry,[9] bright-eyed, and eager to explain cell-structure again to his classes. "Well," he said to me, cheerily, when we met in the   30 first laboratory hour of the semester, "we're going to see cells this time, aren't we?" "Yes, sir," I said. Students to right of me and to left of me and in front of me were seeing cells; what's more, they were quietly drawing pictures of them in their notebooks. Of course, I didn't see anything.

"We'll try it," the professor said to me, grimly,[10] "with every adjustment of the microscope known to man. As God is my witness, I'll arrange this glass so that you see cells through it or I'll give up teaching. In twenty-two years of botany, I—" He cut off abruptly[11] for he was beginning to quiver all over, like Lionel Barrymore,[12] and   40 he genuinely wished to hold onto[13] his temper; his scenes with me had taken a great deal out of him.[14]

So we tried it with every adjustment of the microscope known to man. With only one of them did I see anything but blackness or the familiar lacteal opacity,[15] and that time I saw, to my pleasure and

[2] **in a fury**—in a rage; in a state of violent anger.   [3] **pretended**—made believe.   [4] **flars** —flowers (the spelling indicates the instructor's pronunciation of the word).   [5] **nebulous**—cloudy; misty.   [6] **phenomenon**—unusual or extraordinary occurrence.   [7] **vivid**—bright; lively.   [8] **deferred pass**—application or request to delay or postpone completing a course.   [9] **brown as a berry**—with skin browned or tanned by the sun; with a good tan.   [10] **grimly**—sternly; harshly.   [11] **abruptly**—suddenly.   [12] **to quiver all over like Lionel Barrymore**—to shake the entire body in the manner of Lionel Barrymore (an actor who, in his later years, played the part of an explosive, hot-tempered older man).   [13] **hold onto**—keep control of.   [14] **had taken a great deal out of him**—had exhausted him and had made him impatient.   [15] **lacteal opacity**—milky substance which would not let light through, that is, not transparent.

amazement, a variegated constellation of flecks, specks, and dots.[16] These I hastily drew. The instructor, noting my activity, came back from an adjoining desk, a smile on his lips and his eyebrows high in hope. He looked at my cell drawing. "What's that?" he demanded, with a hint of a squeal[17] in his voice. "That's what I saw," I said. "You didn't, you didn't, you *did*n't!" he screamed, losing control of his temper instantly, and he bent over and squinted[18] into the microscope. His head snapped up.[19] "That's your eye!" he shouted. "You've fixed the lens so that it reflects! You've drawn your eye!"

Another course that I didn't like, but somehow managed to pass, was economics. I went to that class straight from the botany class, which didn't help me any in understanding either subject. I used to get them mixed up.[20] But not as mixed up as another student in my economics class who came there direct from a physics laboratory. He was a tackle[21] on the football team, named Bolenciecwcz. At that time Ohio State University had one of the best football teams in the country, and Bolenciecwcz was one of its outstanding stars. In order to be eligible[22] to play it was necessary for him to keep up in his studies, a very difficult matter, for while he was not dumber than an ox[23] he was not any smarter. Most of his professors were lenient[24] and helped him along. None gave him more hints, in answering questions, or asked him simpler ones than the economics professor, a thin, timid[25] man named Bassum. One day when we were on the subject of transportation and distribution, it came Bolenciecwcz's turn to answer a question. "Name one means of transportation," the professor said to him. No light[26] came into the big tackle's eyes. "Just any means of transportation," said the professor. Bolenciecwcz sat staring[27] at him. "That is," pursued the professor, "any medium, agency, or method of going from one place to another." Bolenciecwcz had the look of a man who is being led into a trap.[28] "You may choose among steam, horse-drawn, or electrically propelled vehicles," said the instructor. "I might

50

60

70

---

[16] **variegated constellation of flecks, specks, and dots**—variety of very small marks, lines, and dots in an arrangement or formation like a constellation of stars. [17] **hint of a squeal**—suggestion of excited annoyance (*squeal* describes a particular sound, usually high pitched, caused by great annoyance or great surprise or pleasure). [18] **squinted** —looked with eyes partially closed in order to improve vision or the ability to see. [19] **his head snapped up**—he raised his head quickly or suddenly, almost with a jerk. [20] **mixed up**—confused. [21] **tackle**—one of the players on a football team. [22] **eligible** —qualified by meeting the requirements set down (in this case, academic requirements). [23] **dumber than an ox**—stupider than an ox, the animal considered to be extremely stupid. [24] **lenient**—very easy or gentle in treatment; not severe or harsh. [25] **timid**— shy; nonaggressive. [26] **no light**—no look or gleam of understanding. [27] **staring**— looking or gazing without blinking the eyes. [28] **led into a trap**—led into a place from which there is no escape.

suggest the one which we commonly take in making long journeys across land." There was a profound[29] silence in which everybody stirred uneasily, including Bolenciecwcz and Mr. Bassum. Mr. Bassum abruptly broke this silence in an amazing manner. "Choo-choo-choo,"   80 he said in a low voice, and turned instantly scarlet. He glanced appealingly around the room. All of us, of course, shared Mr. Bassum's desire that Bolenciecwcz should stay abreast of[30] the class in economics, for the Illinois game, one of the hardest and most important of the season was only a week off. "Toot, tooot, too-toooooooot!" some student with a deep voice moaned, and we all looked encouragingly at Bolenciecwcz. Somebody else gave a fine imitation of a locomotive letting off steam. Mr. Bassum himself rounded off[31] the little show. "Ding, dong, ding, dong," he said, hopefully. Bolenciecwcz was staring at the floor now, trying to think, his great brow furrowed,[32] his huge hands   90 rubbing together, his face red.

"How did you come to college this year, Mr. Bolenciecwcz?" asked the professor, "*Chuf*fa, chuffa, *chuf*fa chuffa."

"M'father sent me," said the football player.

"What on?" asked Bassum.

"I git an 'lowance,"[33] said the tackle, in a low, husky voice, obviously embarrassed.

"No, no," said Bassum. "Name a means of transportation. What did you ride here on?"

"Train," said Bolenciecwcz.   100

"Quite right," said the professor. "Now, Mr. Nugent, will you tell us—"

If I went through anguish[34] in botany and economics—for different reasons—gymnasium work was even worse. I don't even like to think about it. They wouldn't let you play games or join in the exercises with your glasses on and I couldn't see with mine off. I bumped into[35] professors, horizontal bars, agricultural students, and swinging iron rings. Not being able to see, I could take it but I couldn't dish it out.[36] Also, in order to pass gymnasium (and you had to pass it to graduate) you had to learn to swim if you didn't know how. I didn't   110

[29] profound—deep.   [30] stay abreast of: *a*) abreast of—side by side; *b*) stay abreast of—to keep up with.   [31] rounded off—completed.   [32] brow furrowed: *a*) brow—portion of the face from the eyebrows to the hairline; *b*) furrowed—creased or lined, resembling the furrows made in the soil by a plow; *c*) brow furrowed—brow heavily creased or lined.   [33] 'lowance—allowance (a sum of money).   [34] went through anguish—experienced great distress.   [35] bumped into—knocked into; ran into.   [36] I could take it but I couldn't dish it out—I could stand or bear up under whatever punishment was given me, but I couldn't give back the same treatment.

like the swimming pool, I didn't like swimming, and I didn't like the swimming instructor, and after all these years I still don't. I never swam but I passed my gym work anyway, by having another student give my gymnasium number (978) and swim across the pool in my place. He was a quiet, amiable[37] blonde youth, number 473, and he would have seen through a microscope for me if we could have got away with it,[38] but we couldn't get away with it. Another thing I didn't like about gymnasium work was that they made you strip[39] the day you registered. It is impossible for me to be happy when I am stripped and being asked a lot of questions. Still, I did better than a   120 lanky[40] agricultural student who was cross-examined[41] just before I was. They asked each student what college he was in—that is, whether Arts, Engineering, Commerce, or Agriculture. "What college are you in?" the instructor snapped at[42] the youth in front of me. "Ohio State University," he said promptly.

It wasn't that agrcultural student but it was another a whole lot like him who decided to take up journalism, possibly on the ground that when farming went to hell he could fall back on newspaper work.[43] He didn't realize, of course, that that would be very much like falling back full-length on a kit of carpenter's tools.[44] Haskins didn't seem   130 cut out for journalism,[45] being too embarrassed to talk to anybody and unable to use a typewriter, but the editor of the college paper assigned him to the cow barns, the sheep house, the horse pavilion, and the animal husbandry department generally. This was a genuinely big "beat,"[46] for it took up five times as much ground and got ten times as great a legislative appropriation as the College of Liberal Arts. The agricultural student knew animals, but nevertheless his stories were dull and colorlessly written. He took all afternoon on each of them, on account of having to hunt for each letter on the type-writer. Once in a while he had to ask somebody to help him hunt.   140 "C" and "L," in particular, were hard letters for him to find. His

---

[37] **amiable**—friendly; pleasant.   [38] **could have got away with it**—had been able to do something without being caught or discovered.   [39] **made you strip**—made you take off all your clothes.   [40] **lanky**—tall and lean or slender (usually awkward or clumsy rather than graceful).   [41] **cross-examined**—questioned; in court language, the process whereby a witness is examined or questioned by one attorney and then turned over to the at-torney representing the opposing side for cross-examination.   [42] **snapped at**—sharply or abruptly asked.   [43] **on the ground that when farming went to hell he could fall back on newspaper work**—on the basis that when farming was no longer profitable and one couldn't make a living from farming he would have newspaper work to rely on.   [44] **like falling back full-length on a kit of carpenter's tools**—figuratively, like falling back on a case of saws, hammers, and other sharp objects. (The implication is that newspaper work would be more difficult than farming.)   [45] **didn't seem cut out for**—didn't seem suited by talent or natural ability for.   [46] **"beat"**—the area or territory assigned to a newspaper man for coverage.

editor finally got pretty much annoyed at the farmer-journalist because his pieces were so uninteresting. "See here, Haskins," he snapped at him one day, "Why is it we never have anything hot[47] from you on the horse pavilion? Here we have two hundred head of horses on this campus—more than any other university in the Western Conference[48] except Purdue—and yet you never get any real low-down[49] on them. Now shoot over[50] to the horse barns and dig up[51] something lively." Haskins shambled out[52] and came back in about an hour; he said he had something. "Well, start it off snappily,"[53] said the editor. "Something people will read." Haskins set to work and in a couple of hours brought a sheet of typewritten paper to the desk; it was a two-hundred word story about some disease that had broken out among the horses. Its opening sentence was simple but arresting.[54] It read: "Who has noticed the sores on the tops of the horses in the animal husbandry building?"

Ohio State was a land grant university[55] and therefore two years of military drill was compulsory. We drilled with old Springfield rifles[56] and studied the tactics[57] of the Civil War[58] even though the World War was going on at the time. At 11 o'clock each morning thousands of freshmen and sophomores used to deploy over the campus, moodily creeping up on the old chemistry building. It was good training for the kind of warfare that was waged at Shiloh[59] but it had no connection with what was going on in Europe. Some people used to think there was German money behind it,[60] but they didn't dare say so or they would have been thrown in jail as German spies. It was a period of muddy thought[61] and marked, I believe, the decline of higher education in the Middle West.

As a soldier I was never any good at all. Most of the cadets were

[47] **we never have anything hot**—we never get an interesting, timely story. [48] **Western Conference**—association of athletic teams of western universities. [49] **real low-down**—really basic information that will be the basis of a sensational story. [50] **shoot over**—hurry over. [51] **dig up**—find. [52] **shambled out**—walked out with shuffling or dragging of the feet. [53] **start it off snappily**—begin the story in such a way as to attract the attention of the reader. [54] **arresting**—startling; eye-catching. [55] **land grant university**—university established with income from land given to the state for that purpose by the federal government. (All such grants made to states carried the stipulation that all male students who were citizens of the United States would be subject to two years of military training.) [56] **drilled with Springfield rifles**—practiced with Springfield rifles (the brand name for a certain type of gun). [57] **tactics**—methods of warfare. [58] **Civil War**—the war fought between the northern and southern sections of the United States (1861–1865). [59] **waged at Shiloh**—fought at Shiloh (the place where a major battle of the Civil War took place). [60] **there was German money behind it**—that the Germans were paying for the training of soldiers in antiquated methods of warfare. [61] **muddy thought**—confused, unclear thinking.

glumly indifferent soldiers,[62] but I was no good at all. Once General 170
Littlefield, who was commandant of the cadet corps, popped up[63] in
front of me during regimental drill and snapped, "You are the main
trouble with this university!" I think he meant that my type was the
main trouble with the university but he may have meant me individu-
ally. I was mediocre at drill, certainly—that is, until my senior year.
By that time I had drilled longer than anybody else in the Western
Conference, having failed at military[64] at the end of each preceding
year so that I had to do it all over again.[65] I was the only senior still in
uniform. The uniform which, when new, had made me look like an
interurban railway conductor, now that it had become faded and too 180
tight[66] made me look like Bert Williams[67] in his bellboy act. This had
a definitely bad effect on my morale. Even so, I had become by sheer
practice[68] little short of wonderful at squad manoeuvres.[69]

One day General Littlefield picked our company out of the whole
regiment and tried to get it mixed up by putting it through[70] one
movement after another as fast as we could execute them: squads
right, squads left, squads on right into line, squads right about, squads
left front into line, etc. In about three minutes one hundred and nine
men were marching in one direction and I was marching away from
them at an angle of forty degrees, all alone. "Company, halt!" 190
shouted General Littlefield, "That man is the only man who has it
right!" I was made a corporal[71] for my achievement.

The next day General Littlefield summoned me to his office. He
was swatting[72] flies when I went in. I was silent and he was silent too,
for a long time. I don't think he remembered me or why he had sent
for me, but he didn't want to admit it. He swatted some more flies,
keeping his eyes on them narrowly before he let go with the swatter.
"Button up your coat!" he snapped. Looking back on it now I can
see that he meant me although he was looking at a fly, but I just
stood there. Another fly came to rest on a paper in front of the gen- 200
eral and began rubbing its hind legs together. The general lifted the
swatter cautiously. I moved restlessly and the fly flew away. "You

---

[62] **glumly indifferent soldiers**—gloomily or moodily uninterested soldiers; that is, the
cadets were not interested in being soldiers and were low in spirits as a result.
[63] **popped up**—appeared suddenly.   [64] **having failed at military**—since I had not succeeded at military training.   [65] **to do it over again**—to repeat the course in military
training.   [66] **had become faded and too tight**—had lost color and become too snug-
fitting.   [67] **Bert Williams in his bellboy act**—Bert Williams was a very popular stage
comedian who did song and dance specialties.   [68] **by sheer practice**—by practice alone;
by practice only.   [69] **squad manoeuvres**—drills or movements by a squad, usually ten
soldiers.   [70] **by putting it through**—by having the regiment perform.   [71] **made a corporal**—promoted in rank to corporal.   [72] **swatting**—hitting or squashing.

startled him!" barked General Littlefield, looking at me severely.[73] I said I was sorry. "That won't help the situation!" snapped the General, with cold military logic. I didn't see what I could do except offer to chase some more flies toward his desk, but I didn't say anything. He stared out the window at the faraway figures of co-eds crossing the campus toward the library. Finally, he told me I could go. So I went. He either didn't know which cadet I was or else he forgot what he wanted to see me about. It may have been that he wished to apol-   210 ogize for having called me the main trouble with the university; or maybe he had decided to compliment me on my brilliant drilling of the day before and then at the last minute decided not to. I don't know. I don't think about it much any more.

[73] severely—sternly.

EDMUND S. MORGAN (1916 –   )

Edmund S. Morgan is a professor of history at Yale
University. He obtained his degrees (A.B., Ph.D.) at
Harvard. Before joining the Yale faculty, he had taught
at the University of Chicago and Brown University.
His special field of interest is early American history,
and he has written several books (including *The Puritan
Dilemma*, 1958), as well as numerous articles and re-
views for historical journals. The following selection
was originally given as a speech to the 1959 freshman
class at Yale. What he had to say to the Yale students
should be of interest to students everywhere. In his
talk he told the students that scholarship begins in
curiosity but ends in communication. He also said that
curiosity and communication do not come about simply
by wanting them, but by questioning and seeking
answers and by disciplining oneself to communicate
through writing and speaking.

What Every Yale Freshman Should Know

THE WORLD DOES NOT MUCH LIKE
curiosity.[1] The world says that curiosity killed
the cat.[2] The world dismisses[3] curiosity by
calling it idle, or *mere* idle, curiosity[4]—even
though curious persons are seldom idle.[5] Parents do their best to
extinguish[6] curiosity in their children, because it makes life difficult to
be faced every day with a string of[7] unanswerable questions about
what makes fire hot or why grass grows, or to have to halt junior's
investigations[8] before they end in explosion and sudden death. Children whose curiosity survives parental discipline and who manage to   10
grow up before they blow up[9] are invited to join the Yale faculty.
Within the university they go on asking their questions and trying to
find the answers. In the eyes[10] of a scholar, that is mainly what a uni-

[1] curiosity—the desire to know or to learn about something. [2] curiosity killed the
cat—an expression, usually given as a warning that being curious may lead to serious
trouble. [3] dismisses—rejects or puts aside. [4] mere, idle curiosity—pointless or useless
curiosity. [5] idle—unoccupied; not busy. [6] extinguish—put out; wipe out; bring to an
end. [7] a string of—a series of. [8] to halt junior's investigations—to stop junior (a
young son is often referred to as "junior") from experimenting with fire and other dangerous materials. [9] blow up—kill themselves by their investigations. [10] in the eyes—
from the point of view.

33

versity is for. It is a place where the world's hostility to curiosity can be defied.

Some of the questions that scholars ask seem to the world to be scarcely worth asking, let alone[11] answering. They ask about the behavior of protons, the dating of a Roman coin, the structure of a poem. They ask questions too minute[12] and specialized for you and me to understand without years of explanation.   20

If the world inquires of one of them why he wants to know the answer to a particular question, he may say, especially if he is a scientist, that the answer will in some obscure[13] way make possible a new machine or weapon or gadget.[14] He talks that way because he knows that the world understands and respects utility and that it does not understand much else. But to his colleagues and to you he will probably not speak this language. You are now part of the university, and he will expect you to understand that he wants to know the answer simply because he does not know it, the way a mountain climber wants to climb a mountain simply because it is there.   30

Similarly a historian, when asked by outsiders why he studies history, may come out with a line of talk[15] that he has learned to repeat on such occasions, something about knowledge of the past making it possible to understand the present and mold[16] the future. I am sure you have all heard it at one time or another. But if you really want to know why a historian studies the past, the answer is much simpler: he wants to know about it because it is there. Something happened, and he would like to know what.

All this does not mean that the answers which scholars find to their questions have no consequences.[17] They may have enormous conse-   40
quences; they may completely alter the character of human life. But the consequences seldom form the reason for asking the questions or pursuing the answers. It is true that scholars can be put to work answering questions for the sake of the consequences, as thousands are working now, for example, in search of a cure for cancer. But this is not the primary function of the scholar. For the scholar the consequences are usually incidental[18] to the satisfaction of curiosity. Even for the medical scholar, the desire to stamp out[19] a dreaded[20] disease may be a less powerful motive than the desire to find out about the

---

[11] **let alone**—not to mention.   [12] **minute** (adj.)—very small; tiny.   [13] **obscure**—hidden; not obvious; not clearly seen.   [14] **gadget**—mechanical device.   [15] **come out with a line of talk**—use an explanation, designed to conceal his real motives.   [16] **mold**—shape; give direction to.   [17] **consequences**—results; acts or facts that follow an action or argument.   [18] **incidental**—by chance or in addition to something else; subordinate.   [19] **stamp out**—wipe out; get rid of.   [20] **dreaded**—feared.

nature of living matter. Similarly Einstein did not wish to create an 50 atomic bomb or to harness atomic energy. He simply wanted to find out about energy and matter.

I said that curiosity was a dangerous quality. It is dangerous not only because of incidental effects like the atomic bomb but also because it is really nothing more or less than a desire for truth. For some reason this phrase sounds less dangerous than curiosity. In fact, the desire for truth sounds rather respectable. Since so many respectable people assure us that they have found the truth, it does not sound like a dangerous thing to look for. But it is. The search for it has again and again overturned institutions and beliefs of long standing, in 60 science, in religion, and in politics. It is easy enough to see today that these past revolutions brought great benefits to mankind. It was less easy to see the benefits while the revolutions were taking place, especially if you happened to be quite satisfied with the way things were before. Similarly it is not always easy today to see that the satisfaction of a scholar's curiosity is worth the disruption of society that may result from it. The search for truth is, and always has been, a subversive activity.[21] And scholars have learned that they cannot engage in it without an occasional fight.

You may therefore find them rather belligerent[22] toward any threat 70 to the free pursuit of curiosity. They are wary[23] of committing themselves to institutions or beliefs that might impose limitations on them or deliver ready-made answers to their questions. You will find them suspicious of loyalty oaths, religious creeds, or affiliations[24] with political parties. In particular they will try to preserve their university as a sanctuary[25] within whose walls *any* question can be asked.

This wariness of commitment can sometimes degenerate[26] into a scholarly vice,[27] a vice that paralyzes curiosity instead of preserving it. A scholar at his worst sometimes seems to be simply a man who cannot make up his mind. Every classroom from here to Melbourne 80 has echoed with the feeble[28] phrases of academic indecision: "There are two schools of thought on this question, and the truth probably lies halfway between them." When you hear this sentence repeated, or when you are tempted to repeat it yourself, remember that the truth may lie between two extremes, but it assuredly does not lie

---

[21] **subversive activity**—activity tending to cause overthrow or downfall of a particular institution or established belief. [22] **belligerent**—hostile; warlike. [23] **wary**—cautious; careful; on guard. [24] **affiliations**—associations; memberships. [25] **sanctuary**—refuge or shelter where one is free from cares or fears (often a holy or sacred place). [26] **degenerate**—deteriorate; decline in mental or moral qualities. [27] **vice**—fault; defect. [28] **feeble**—weak.

halfway between right and wrong. Don't short-circuit[29] your curiosity
by assuming you have found the answer when you have only made a
tidy[30] list of possible answers.

Dedication[31] to curiosity should not end in indecision. It should, in
fact, mean willingness to follow the mind into difficult decisions. 90

A second quality that makes a scholar has no apparent relation to
the first and yet is inseparably connected to it. It is a compulsion[32]
to communicate. A scholar is driven by a force as strong as his curiosity, that compels him to tell the world the things he has learned.
He cannot rest with learning something: he has to tell about it. Scholarship begins in curiosity, but it ends in communication. And though
scholars may in a university take refuge[33] from the world, they also
acknowledge responsibility to the world, the responsibility to communicate freely and fully everything that they discover within the
walls of their sanctuary. The search for truth needs no justification, 100
and when a man thinks he has found any part of it, he cannot and
ought not to be silent. The world may sometimes not care to listen,
but the scholar must keep telling it until he has succeeded in communicating.

Now, there are only two methods of communication for scholars,
writing and speaking. The scholar publishes his discoveries in books
and articles and he teaches them in the classroom. Sometimes one
or the other method will satisfy him, but most of us feel the need
for both. The scholar who merely writes books falls into the habit of
speaking only to the experts. If he works at his subject long enough, 110
he reaches the position where there is no one else quite expert enough
to understand him, and he winds up writing to himself. On the other
hand, if he writes not at all, he may become so enamored[34] of his own
voice that he ceases to be a scholar and becomes a mere showman.

Communication is not merely the desire and the responsibility of
the scholar; it is his discipline, the proving ground[35] where he tests
his findings against criticism. Without communication his pursuit of
truth withers into eccentricity.[36] He necessarily spends much of his
time alone, in the library or the laboratory, looking for the answers to
his questions. But he needs to be rubbing constantly against[37] other 120

29 **short-circuit**—stop short; cut off too soon. 30 **tidy**—neat. 31 **dedication**—state of
giving oneself over to something. 32 **compulsion**—compelling act; strong impulse to
carry out a certain act—in this case, to communicate. 33 **refuge**—protection or shelter
from danger or trouble. (See *fn.* 25.) 34 **enamored of**—captivated by; charmed by.
35 **proving ground**—place where tests are made or where the genuineness of facts or
ideas is established. 36 **withers into eccentricity**—shrivels or fades into strangeness or
peculiarity. 37 **to be rubbing constantly against**—to be in continual contact with.

minds. He needs to be tested, probed,[38] and pushed around.[39] He needs to be made to explain himself. Only when he has expressed himself, only when he has communicated his thoughts, can he be sure that he is thinking clearly.

The scholar, in other words, needs company to keep him making sense. And in particular he needs the company of fresh minds, to whom he must explain things from the beginning. He needs people who will challenge him at every step, who will take nothing for granted.[40] He needs, in short, you.

You may have various purposes in coming here, and you may fulfill them: you may play football or tennis or the trombone; you may sing in the glee club, act in plays, and act up[41] on college weekends. But what the faculty expects of you is four years of scholarship, and they will be satisfied with nothing less. For four years we expect you to join us in the pursuit of truth, and we will demand of you the same things we demand of ourselves: curiosity and communication.

Curiosity, of course, is not something you get simply by wishing for it. But it is surprisingly contagious.[42] The curiosity we expect is more than a passing interest. We will not be satisfied by your ability to ask an occasional bright question, nor yet by your assimilation[43] of a lot of predigested information. The accumulation[44] of information is a necessary part of scholarship, and unfortunately the part most likely to be tested on examinations, especially those wretched ones called "objective examinations" where the truth is always supposed to lie in answer space A, B, C, D, or E, but never apparently in X, Y, or Z. But the curiosity we expect of you cannot be satisfied by passing examinations or by memorizing other people's answers to other people's questions. We do not wish to put you through a mere course of mental gymnastics. We want you to be content with nothing less than the whole truth about the subject that interests you. Which means that we want you to be forever discontent with how little you know about it and with how little we know about it. We want you to back us into corners,[45] show us up,[46] make us confess we don't

130

140

150

---

[38] **probed**—examined thoroughly; questioned closely or deeply, not superficially. [39] **pushed around**—pressed hard; challenged. [40] **take nothing for granted**—assume nothing; accept nothing without questioning it. [41] **act up**—cut up or behave in a reckless or foolish manner. [42] **contagious**—infectious (curiosity has a tendency to spread from one person to another). [43] **assimilation**—absorbing of a lot of predigested information (that is, information treated before presentation to make it easier to digest or to comprehend). [44] **accumulation of**—gathering of; getting of. [45] **back us into corners**—force us backward into difficult places to get out of (in this case, into positions or arguments that are hard to defend or uphold). [46] **show us up**—reveal or show us what we don't know; show publicly the extent of our knowledge).

know. Does this sound formidable?[47] It is not. We may tell you what we know with great assurance, but push us and you will find the gaps.[48]

Follow your own minds into the gaps. Follow your minds where curiosity takes them. You will not get the whole truth, not about protons, not about the structure of a poem, not even about a Roman coin. Nobody does. But if you learn anything, it ought to change your [160] minds, and hopefully it will change ours too. It will be a sign that we have both wasted four years if you leave here thinking pretty much the same way that you do now or if you leave us thinking the same way *we* do now.

We expect of you, then, that you will be curious for the truth. We also expect that you communicate whatever truth you find, and that you do it both in speech and in writing. Many people suppose that they know something if they can stammer out[49] an approximation[50] of what they mean in speech. They are mistaken. It is extremely un- likely that you have thought clearly if you cannot express yourself [170] clearly, especially in writing. Writing is more than an instrument of communication. It is an instrument of thought. You should have acquired some competence[51] in its use by now. I suspect from past ex- perience that you have not. But even if you have, you have a great deal more to learn about it. And if you do not know much more about it four years from now, it will again be a sign that we have failed in part of our job, the job of making you communicate clearly.

Communication is a two-way process, and a university is a com- munity of scholars, where questions are asked and the answers communicated, your answers to us, ours to you. For the next four [180] years we will be engaged as scholars together in this community. After the four years are over, most of you will leave Yale, but if our community is a successful one, if we really do communicate with each other, I believe that you will continue to be in some sense scholars, asking new questions, looking for new answers, and communicating them to the world.

[47] formidable—of alarming difficulty; like something to be dreaded or feared; overawing. [48] gaps—blank spaces in knowledge; the things the scholar does not know. [49] stammer out—say with great difficulty and with many breaks and pauses. [50] approximation— closeness or nearness; sufficient closeness for the purpose. [51] competence—capability; skill.

CRANE BRINTON (1898 –)
JOHN B. CHRISTOPHER (1914 –)
ROBERT LEE WOLFF (1915 –)

The three authors of this selection are professors of history—Brinton and Wolff at Harvard University, and Christopher at the University of Rochester. They have contributed numerous scholarly works to their fields of special interest: Brinton to the history of ideas and the nature of revolution, Christopher to the study of civilization, and Wolff to research on the Balkans. The senior author, Crane Brinton, is such a popular lecturer that his early morning classes have been labeled by the students as "breakfast with Brinton." He has also gained a wide audience through books that have appealed to the general but serious reading public—books that are highly respected for their urbanity, sharp analysis, and readability, such as *Ideas and Men: A Story of Western Thought* and *A History of Western Morals*.

A History of Civilization (1955), from which "Some Conclusions about Man" is taken, is a widely adopted textbook that tells the history of man with vigor, completeness, and authority. In this brief section, the authors give some conclusions based upon their survey of prehistory. Their final conclusion is that, while possessing great potentialities, men are torn by the paradox that they are "creatures of custom reluctant to change, yet quite unable to take this world as they find it."

Some Conclusions About Man

FROM THIS BRIEF SURVEY[1] OF PREhistory,[2] then, our most useful conclusion is that even thousands of years ago men in society displayed[3] that great variety of behavior which is always the despair of the dogmatic simplifiers[4] of human nature. We may now list a few more positive conclusions, with

---

[1] **survey**—general view. [2] **prehistory**—the period before recorded history or before the events of history were written down. [3] **displayed**—showed. [4] **despair of the dogmatic simplifiers:** *a*) **despair**—loss of hope; *b*) **dogmatic**—opinionated; *c*) **simplifiers**—persons who simplify; *d*) **dogmatic simplifiers of human nature**—persons who state in a positive, authoritative manner that human nature is simple.

the caution that in this field, even more than in that of written history, the experts disagree.

First, the study of these millennia[5] definitely puts man in the general evolutionary history of the primates, a subdivision of the mammals. The old question of man's descent[6] is so well settled that no trained scientist would find much sense in the once familiar fighting words, "Man is (or is not) descended from[7] the monkeys." Even the problem of the "missing link"[8] no longer bothers[9] the scientist. *Homo sapiens* is clearly the product of a long development. Although the exact relation between his family tree[10] and that of such apes as the chimpanzee is not clear, there is pretty general agreement that man branched off[11] the primate stock[12] at a different point from that at which any ape branched off. The apes are, as it were, our cousins many times removed[13] rather than our ancestors. Just as the scientific doctrine of the immense age of the earth does not invalidate[14] many arguments for the existence of God, so the zoological cataloguing of *homo sapiens* does not destroy theological doctrines which insist that man has a soul and is thus not *merely* an animal.

Second, man is unique[15] among animals in two broad[16] ways. Man seems alone among animals to have the ability to use words, and therefore to communicate his thoughts—and, indeed, to *have* thoughts that separate out individual experiences and enable him to list, to compare, and to remember these experiences. And in some sense related to this power of thinking, man alone seems able to pass on to his young in the form of education certain ways of living—ways that we can loosely[17] call culture.

Third, over the long ages of prehistory material culture unquestionably shows what we call *progress*. Man progressively secured[18] more food, better housing, and fuller satisfaction of his physical wants. Indeed, the very names that we give to the various ages—stone, bronze, and iron—suggest that man's tools progressed from the very simple to the more elaborate.[19] They suggest the increasing adaptation[20] of means to ends that we are familiar with today as technolog-

---

[5] millennia—thousands of years. [6] descent—lineage; line of ancestry. [7] descended from—come down from certain ancestors, the monkeys in this case. [8] "missing link"—the unknown stage between man and the apes; hypothetical animal that connects man and the apes. [9] bothers—worries or gives trouble to. [10] family tree—line of ancestors; line of descent. [11] branched off—went off in another direction from; forked off; diverged. [12] stock—type from which certain animals or plants are derived. [13] many times removed—very distantly related. [14] invalidate—render false; destroy. [15] unique—the only one of a kind; unequaled. [16] broad—very general. [17] loosely—very generally. [18] secured—obtained. [19] elaborate—complex. [20] adaptation—modification; adjustment.

ical improvement. Again, all this can be treated quite separately from   40
man's moral and spiritual improvement or progress. We may or may
not be more virtuous than the Magdalenians;[21] we may or may not be
"happier" than they; a modern painting may or may not be better
than a Magdalenian cave painting. There is, however, no doubt that
our modern tools are better tools than those of Magdalenian man,
just as Magdalenian tools were better than those of Neanderthal man
thousands of years before him.

Fourth, man has long existed on this earth as a single species.[22]
Apparently throughout human wanderings separate groups of men
have stayed long enough in a given area to produce the kind of   50
subspecies called a race. Thus white, yellow, and Negro races developed, but, since they did not remain "pure," they did not become
separate species. Or, put in another way, man is and long has been
a mongrel.[23] Hardly does he get started breeding a variant[24] that
might become a new species when others come into the group, or
else the group forces itself onto others, and the process is ended.
Most of the variations that stand out in human achievement seem to
be individual variations rather than group variations. Thus great
artistic or athletic ability is a matter of individual gift and skill, not
one of the marks[25] of the subspecies or race. Prehistory, like history,   60
does not back up[26] modern notions of racism, the doctrine that one
race is as a whole "superior" to another. As we shall see later, terms
like Semitic and Aryan that racists use so frequently refer properly not
to well-defined races, "superior" or "inferior," but only to families of
human languages.

Finally, to return to a point made already, the abiding[27] impression
one gets from a study of prehistory is of the great range of potentialities[28] in human beings and in human cultures. Above all, one is
aware of a basic paradox of human behavior:[29] men are creatures of
custom, reluctant[30] to change, yet quite unable to take this world as   70
they find it. They will daydream another world, if nothing better
comes up. Ever since the first rude,[31] manlike creature banged off a

21 **Magdalenians**—people who lived in the Old World Stone Age, named from the
discoveries in La Madeleine, France. 22 **species**—class of individuals having some
common characteristics or qualities. 23 **mongrel**—mixture of races. 24 **breeding a
variant**: *a*) **breeding**—producing; *b*) **a variant**—a different form or characteristic.
25 **marks**—signs; evidences; distinctive features. 26 **back up**—support. 27 **abiding**—
permanent; lasting; continuing. 28 **potentialities**—undeveloped possibilities; latent
powers or qualities. 29 **basic paradox of human nature**—basic contradiction or incon-
sistency in human behavior. 30 **reluctant**—hesitant; unwilling. 31 **rude**—unrefined;
uncultured.

few awkward protuberances[32] from his eolithic fist hatchet,[33] some men have always been dissatisfied with things as they are. Man is no doubt much more, but at a minimum he is the inventive animal. That is, he changes his environment[34]—his tools, his society, his art, his religion. He does not, as far as we know, greatly change his body. Man's ability to change his environment without altering his body is the most extraordinary of his inventions, something no other animal has ever attained. Other land mammals have indeed learned to fly and   80 to live in the water, but only by becoming bats or whales.[35] Twentieth-century man—*homo sapiens*, still anatomically[36] almost identical with our Magdalenian of thousands of years ago—flies in airplanes and sails in ships.

[32] **banged off a few awkward protuberances:** *a)* **banged off**—knocked off; broke off; *b)* **awkward**—clumsy; ungraceful; *c)* **protuberances**—rounded projections; bulges that stick out beyond the surrounding surface. [33] **eolithic fist hatchet:** *a)* **eolithic**—belonging to or characteristic of the earliest stage of human culture when stone implements were used; *b)* **fist hatchet**—stone ax or hatchet, held in the fist rather than by a handle. [34] **environment**—surroundings. [35] **bats or whales:** *a)* **bats**—mouse-like mammals that fly; *b)* **whales**—fish-like mammals that live in the sea. [36] **anatomically**—from the standpoint of anatomy.

MARYA MANNES (1904 –   )

Marya Mannes, a native New Yorker, was the daughter of musicians, and she grew up in a home atmosphere that fostered creativity and humanity. Although she did not attend a university, she received a disciplined education in a New York private school and a broad education from living, working, reading, and traveling. She is an author, editor, wife, and mother, and has been on the staff of *The Reporter* magazine for about ten years. Her books include a novel, *Message for a Stranger*, a collection of satirical verse, *Subverse*, and a book of essays, *More in Anger* (1953), in which "The Half-People" is found. She is also widely known through her television program, "I Speak for Myself."

Miss Mannes has her own ideas about everything from politics to art, and some of them are expressed in *More in Anger*. She wrote the book, as explained in the introduction, because she was angry with the waste in American culture resulting from fear, softness, and complacency. She wrote in the mood of one willing to stand up and say what she thought. What she says is lively and, as one reviewer put it, "not a gloomy but a sparkling anger." The little essay here suggests that cars have changed people by bestowing motion but removing dignity, and by breeding a race of half-people who are moving along in a direction that they have not necessarily chosen.

The Half-People

*P*EOPLE ON HORSES LOOK BETTER than they are. People in cars look worse than they are. On any of our highways this last observation, unfortunate as it may be, is inescapable. For the car, by bisecting[1] the human outline, diminishes[2] it, producing a race of half-people in a motion[3] not of their own making.[4]

---

[1] bisecting—cutting in half.   [2] diminishes it—makes it less.   [3] in a motion—going in a direction.   [4] not of their own making—not directed by themselves.

43

Automobiles can be handsome things, particularly if they are foreign, but they bestow[5] none of their power and beauty on their passengers. It is not only that the people in them face in one direction,[6] like gulls in a wind[7] or curious penguins,[8] but that the sleekness[9] and brightness of the cars' exterior makes them look shabby[10] if not downright sordid.[11] It also in some mysterious way accentuates[12] the baser[13] characteristics. Boys under twenty in cars look delinquent;[14] men over thirty shifty[15] and gross.[16] Most middle-aged women look bad-tempered, and most young women hard.[17] Children in cars are either asleep or unmanageable,[18] jumping up and down in the back seat, leaning over the front seat, or pressing dirty faces against the rear window.[19] Only dogs, I think, preserve[20] their charm; there is nothing more attractive than the canine[21] face shoved out[22] of the window inhaling the sharp breeze and the myriad[23] smells it carries.

Cars do something sinister[24] to the relationship of the sexes. I do not know what is more disturbing: the husband and wife in the front seat facing forward, speechless, with set mouths, as if their destination were doomed[25] and their communications broken; or the young couple intertwined and two-headed,[26] the delinquent driving with one hand and half a mind.[27] On a bench their closeness would be endearing;[28] on a highway it is alarming.

Cars have bestowed motion but removed dignity. And if they have given us one sort of freedom, they have become also small prisons, in which a group of people are locked within steel walls, motionless in movement, changeless during change, and borne inexorably[29] in a direction which is not always of their choosing.

Get a horse.

---

[5] **bestow on**—give to. [6] **face in one direction**—are looking in the same direction. [7] **gulls in the wind**—birds, like seagulls, that fly in a flock. [8] **curious penguins**—birds, usually found in the Southern Hemisphere, that walk upright (in this case, in a group carried forward in the same direction by curiosity in wanting to find out something). [9] **sleekness**—smoothness. [10] **look shabby**—have a poor appearance. (In contrast to the shiny cars, the people look worn.) [11] **downright sordid:** a) **downright**—actually; absolutely; b) **sordid**—vulgar. [12] **accentuates**—emphasizes; stresses. [13] **baser**—lower or more vulgar. [14] **delinquent**—like juvenile criminals. [15] **shifty**—untrustworthy. [16] **gross**—fat, heavy. [17] **hard**—not soft and feminine. [18] **unmanageable**—undisciplined. [19] **rear window**—back window of car. [20] **preserve**—maintain; keep. [21] **canine**—doglike; pertaining to dogs. [22] **shoved out of**—stretching or hanging out of. [23] **myriad**—many; varied. [24] **sinister**—bad; evil. [25] **doomed**—expected to fail. [26] **intertwined and two-headed**—sitting close together and with arms around each other so that they look like one body with two heads. [27] **half a mind**—half of one's attention. [28] **endearing**—touching. [29] **inexorably**—relentlessly; not to be stopped or changed under any circumstances.

RICHARD HAGOPIAN (1914 -   )

Richard Hagopian was born near Boston in Revere, Massachusetts, where he grew up in an Armenian-Italian neighborhood. Gifted with a fine tenor voice, he first thought of becoming a singer and studied for some time at the New England Conservatory of Music. Eventually, while on a concert tour in Maine, he met Robert P. Tristram Coffin, the poet, and showed him some short stories he had written. The poet encouraged Hagopian to complete a book of stories, which was published in 1944 under the title *The Dove Brings Peace*. Since then he has written many stories for magazines like the *Atlantic Monthly*, and two novels, *Faraway the Spring* and *Wine for the Living*. Most of his stories, as well as his novels, are peopled by Armenian and Italian characters who live and work in communities near Boston. These people struggle against poor conditions, but are possessed of a richness in responding to life—celebrating joyously or mourning deeply as the occasion demands.

"Wonderful People"—included in *The Dove Brings Peace*—is somewhat different; it is a love story, very briefly sketched, with which almost anyone can identify himself. The author seems to say that sometimes unlike people may fall in love, change, and part, and, although never meeting again, grow to be more like each other as time goes by.

Wonderful People

I SAW HER AND LIKED HER BECAUSE she was not beautiful. Her chin was not just right and something about her nose fell short of perfection. And when she stood up, well, there wasn't much to see but her tallness, the length from her hips to her feet, and the length from her hips to her shoulders. She was a tall girl and that was all. She was the first tall girl I had ever liked, perhaps

45

because I had never watched a tall girl get up from a table before; that is, get up the way she did, everything in her rising to the art of getting up, combining to make the act look beautiful and not like just another casual[1] movement, an ordinary life motion.   **10**

Maybe I liked her because when I talked to her for the first time I found that she had tall ideas too, ideas which like her chin and nose did not seem just right to me, but like her getting up were beautiful. They hung together.[2] They were tall ideas, about life and people, morals and ethics.[3] At first they seemed shockingly loose[4] to me, but when I saw them all moving together, like her body, they hung together. They looked naturally beautiful. They had the same kind of pulled-out poetry[5] that sometimes defies[6] the extra-long line and hangs together; hangs together when you see the whole thing finished,   **20** when you've scanned it up and down[7] and seen all the line endings melt into a curious kind of unity, which makes strange music— strange because everything is long yet compact.[8] She was music. I see it now, her getting up impressed[9] me at the time because for the first time I felt poetry in a person rising—music in body parts moving in natural rhythms. I liked the tall girl.

By stature[10] I was not tall. I was built almost too close to the ground. Perhaps that is why I had old-fashioned[11] ideas, ideas as simple and as pure as the good soil. Maybe my eyes saw more in the ground than other people's because I was closer to it. I was what you   **30** might call compact. Everything was knitted together strongly,[12] like my ideas about life, morals and ethics, all squeezed[13] together, rhyming easily, making music of a strong, dominant[14] sort. Call it smugness[15] if you wish. But I really couldn't move far without taking along everything I had. My ideas were like that too. I could take a radical fling[16] once in a while, but sooner or later, mostly sooner, the rest of me ganged up[17] and compressed[18] the wild motion with one easy squeeze.

We were a funny pair, the tall girl and I, funny because we were

---

[1] casual—unplanned; without plan; caused by chance; incidental; indifferent or unconcerned.   [2] hung together—fitted; harmonized.   [3] ethics—moral principles.   [4] shockingly loose: a) shockingly—disturbingly; surprisingly; b) loose—undisciplined; unprincipled.   [5] pulled-out poetry—free verse as distinguished from traditional strict verse.   [6] defies—challenges.   [7] scanned it up and down—looked it over; examined it closely.   [8] compact—packed together tightly or closely.   [9] impressed—deeply affected.   [10] by stature—from the standpoint of height.   [11] old-fashioned—traditional; not new or modern.   [12] knitted together strongly—tightly interwoven.   [13] squeezed —pressed.   [14] dominant—controlling; ruling. (In classical music the dominant key is the key in which a movement begins and ends, and it suggests completeness or balance.)   [15] smugness—self-satisfaction.   [16] a radical fling—a wild departure from the traditional or customary.   [17] ganged up on—got together against.   [18] compressed—pressed closely together.

so different in everything. She was a slow walker and I had to hold   40
back. She talked in long lines and I used the short one. She ate easily
and I ate hard and fast. We were different.

The tall girl and I fell in love with each other. Why, I do not know.
We just did, that's all. We did crazy things:[19] tall things and compact
things, like running madly up and down a beach laughing and feeling
loose and free, or like sitting down and knitting our minds together[20]
to feel after a piece of music or a problem. Something made us agree.
We couldn't figure out what, but we agreed. And after looking at each
other and seeing our bodies and the stuff[21] behind them, we couldn't
quite understand, but we accepted our good luck and we called our-   50
selves wonderful people.

After a while we talked about marriage, children, and a home. For
a few months we didn't agree on a couple of things, but, as I said, we
were wonderful people, and one day we decided to get married.

But the tall girl and I didn't get married. For one moment somewhere I think we stopped being wonderful people, and she must have
felt her tallness for the first time, and maybe the ground came up too
close to my face. But that was all; it was the end. Something had come
between the tall girl and me. I don't know what it was, but something died and with it went all the funny music and poetry in people.   60

Many years have passed and sometimes I get a strange feeling—I
mean about walking and getting up. I don't seem to hang together as
I used to. Only last week my best friend told me to pull myself together.[22] And when I looked around, I'll be damned if I wasn't just all
pieces and parts, going this way and that, down and . . . up. Up!
That was it. I felt taller. And I felt good. I liked the freedom. I could
reach for an idea now without straining[23] everything in me to hold
it; and I didn't care about the rest of me. What music there was left
in me, what music I heard in others, was the strange kind one finds in
long-line poetry. It made me happy.   70

Sometimes I think of the tall girl; but she doesn't seem tall any
more. She just seems natural—arms, legs, ideas, and everything. I
wonder what I thought was *tall?* Sometimes I wonder if she is the
same girl I first saw rising from a table. I don't know. But people grow
taller, I know that. Perhaps they grow shorter and more compact
too. Maybe that's what makes us wonderful people.

19 crazy things—wild, unusual things. 20 knitting our minds together—putting our
minds together. 21 stuff—things; substance or background. 22 to pull myself together—to get hold of myself; to bring myself under control. 23 straining—putting
great pressure on; stretching to the maximum limit; extending to the utmost; forcing.

WILLIAM SAROYAN (1908 –   )

William Saroyan's parents and relatives were Armenian immigrants who settled in the farm area around Fresno, California. Saroyan left school at fifteen and went to work doing odd jobs. During this time he read widely and began writing in his distinctive natural style. By the late 1930's his many short stories, novels, and plays had established him as a writer. His play *The Time of Your Life* was awarded the 1940 Pulitzer Prize,[1] which he refused to accept. Many of his stories have grown out of his experiences in the Armenian community around Fresno. He writes in a simple, flowing style about characters that are generally warm-hearted, life-loving people—sometimes, as in "The Pomegranate Trees," carried away by fantastic dreams of glory. The story first appeared in a collection of stories entitled *My Name Is Aram*, published in 1937.

The Pomegranate Trees

*M*Y UNCLE MELIK WAS JUST ABOUT[2] the worst farmer that ever lived. He was too imaginative and poetic for his own good.[3] What he wanted was beauty. He wanted to plant it and see it grow. I myself planted over one hundred pomegranate trees[4] for my uncle one year back there in the good old days[5] of poetry and youth in the world. I drove a John Deere[6] tractor too, and so did my uncle. It was all pure esthetics, not agriculture. My uncle just liked the idea of planting trees and watching them grow.

Only[7] they wouldn't grow. It was on account of the soil. The soil   10

---

[1] **Pulitzer Prize**—annual prize initiated by Joseph Pulitzer, a newspaper owner, who left a large sum of money to the School of Journalism at Columbia University for prizes to be awarded for outstanding journalistic, literary, and musical works. [2] **just about** (colloquial)—almost; very nearly. [3] **for his own good**—for his benefit. [4] **pomegranate trees**—small trees that yield a fruit with a tough skin, usually red, covering many small seeds. [5] **one year back there in the good old days**—a year in my childhood with its many fond memories. [6] **John Deere**—brand name of a tractor. [7] **only**—but; except that.

was desert soil. It was dry. My uncle waved at the six hundred and eighty acres of desert he had bought and he said in the most poetic Armenian anybody ever heard, "Here in this awful desolation[8] a garden shall flower, fountains of cold water shall bubble out of the earth, and all things of beauty shall come into being."[9]

"Yes, sir," I said.

I was the first and only relative to see the land he had bought. He knew I was a poet at heart, and he believed I would understand the magnificent impulse[10] that was driving him to glorious ruin.[11] I did. I knew as well as he that what he had purchased was worthless[12] desert land. It was away over to hell and gone,[13] at the foot of the Sierra Nevada Mountains.[14] It was full of every kind of desert plant that ever sprang out of dry hot earth. It was overrun with prairie dogs, squirrels, horned toads, snakes, and a variety of smaller forms of life. The space[15] over this land knew only the presence of hawks, eagles, and buzzards. It was a region of loneliness, emptiness, truth, and dignity. It was nature at its proudest, driest, loneliest, and loveliest.

My uncle and I got out of the Ford roadster in the middle of his land and began to walk over the dry earth.

"This land," he said, "is my land."

He walked slowly, kicking into the dry soil. A horned toad scrambled[16] over the earth at my uncle's feet. My uncle clutched[17] my shoulder and came to a pious[18] halt.

"What is that animal?" he said.

"That little tiny lizard?" I said.

"That mouse with horns," my uncle said. "What is it?"

"I don't know for sure," I said. "We call them horny toads."

The horned toad came to a halt about three feet away and turned its head.

My uncle looked down at the small animal.

"Is it poison?" he said.

"To eat?" I said. "Or if it bites you?"

"Either way," my uncle said.

"I don't think it's good to eat," I said. "I think it's harmless.[19] I've

---

[8] **awful desolation**—terrible, uninhabited, lonely, barren land.   [9] **shall come into being** —shall be realized.   [10] **magnificent impulse**—splendid or glorious inner urge or motivation.   [11] **glorious ruin**—complete but magnificent downfall or loss.   [12] **worthless**— without value.   [13] **away over to hell and gone**—far out, away from civilization.   [14] **Sierra Nevada Mountains**—a mountain range in eastern California.   [15] **space**—sky.   [16] **scrambled**—went hurriedly; crawled quickly.   [17] **clutched**—grabbed, grasped, seized.   [18] **pious**—reverent.   [19] **harmless**—not dangerous.

caught many of them. They grow sad in captivity,[20] but never bite. Shall I catch this one?"

"Please do," my uncle said.

I sneaked up on[21] the horned toad, then sprang on it while my uncle looked on.

"Careful," he said. "Are you sure it isn't poison?" 50

"I've caught many of them," I said.

I took the horned toad to my uncle. He tried not to seem afraid. "A lovely little thing, isn't it?" he said. His voice was unsteady.

"Would you like to hold it?" I said.

"No," my uncle said. "You hold it. I have never before been so close to such a thing as this. I see it has eyes. I suppose it can see us."

"I suppose it can," I said. "It's looking up at you now."

My uncle looked the horned toad straight in the eye. The horned toad looked my uncle straight in the eye. For fully half a minute they looked one another straight in the eye and then the horned toad 60 turned its head aside and looked down at the ground. My uncle sighed with relief.

"A thousand of them," he said, "could kill a man, I suppose."

"They never travel in great numbers," I said. "You hardly ever see more than one at a time."

"A big one," my uncle said, "could probably bite a man to death."

"They don't grow big," I said. "This is as big as they grow."

"They seem to have an awful eye for such small creatures," my uncle said. "Are you sure they don't mind being picked up?"

"I suppose they forget all about it the minute you put them down," 70 I said.

"Do you really think so?" my uncle said.

"I don't think they have very good memories," I said.

My uncle straightened up, breathing deeply.

"Put the little creature down," he said. "Let us not be cruel to the innocent creations of Almighty God. If it is not poison and grows no larger than a mouse and does not travel in great numbers and has no memory to speak of, let the timid little thing return to the earth. Let us be gentle toward these small things which live on the earth with us." 80

"Yes, sir," I said.

I placed the horned toad on the ground.

[20] in captivity—when imprisoned. [21] sneaked up on—moved quietly toward.

"Gently now," my uncle said. "Let no harm come to this strange dweller on my land."[22]

The horned toad scrambled away.

"These little things," I said, "have been living on soil of this kind for centuries."

"Centuries?" my uncle said. "Are you sure?"

"I'm not sure," I said, "but I imagine they have. They're still here, anyway." My uncle looked around at his land, at the cactus and brush[23] growing out of it, at the sky overhead.

"What have they been eating all this time?" he shouted.

"I don't know," I said.

"What would you say they've been eating?" he said.

"Insects, I guess."

"Insects?" my uncle shouted. "What sort of insects?"

"Little bugs, most likely," I said. "I don't know their names. I can find out tomorrow at school."

We continued to walk over the dry land. When we came to some holes in the earth my uncle stood over them and said, "What lives down there?"

"Prairie dogs," I said.

"What are *they*?" he said.

"Well," I said, "they're something like rats. They belong to the rodent family."

"What are all these things doing on my land?" my uncle said.

"They don't know it's your land," I said. "They've been living here a long while."

"I don't suppose that horny toad ever looked a man in the eye before," my uncle said.

"I don't think so," I said.

"Do you think I scared it or anything?" my uncle said.

"I don't know for sure," I said.

"If I did," my uncle said, "I didn't mean to. I'm going to build a house here some day."

"I didn't know that," I said.

"Of course," my uncle said. "I'm going to build a magnificent house."

"It's pretty far away," I said.

"It's only an hour from town," my uncle said.

90

100

110

120

---

22 **dweller on my land**—animal that dwells or lives on my land; inhabitant. 23 **cactus and brush**—desert plants and ground covering, usually brown and dry.

"If you go fifty miles an hour," I said.

"It's not fifty miles to town," my uncle said. "It's thirty-seven."

"Well, you've got to take a little time out for rough roads," I said.

"I'll build me the finest house in the world," my uncle said. "What else lives on this land?"

"Well," I said, "there are three or four kinds of snakes."

"Poison or non-poison?" my uncle said.

"Mostly non-poison," I said. "The rattlesnake is poison, though."

"Do you mean to tell me there are *rattlesnakes* on this land?" my uncle said.   130

"This is the kind of land rattlesnakes usually live on," I said.

"How many?" my uncle said.

"Per acre?" I said. "Or on the whole six hundred and eighty acres?"

"Per acre," my uncle said.

"Well," I said, "I'd say there are about three per acre, conservatively."[24]

"Three per acre?" my uncle shouted. "Conservatively?"

"Maybe only two," I said.

"How many is that to the whole place?" my uncle said.

"Well, let's see," I said. "Two per acre. Six hundred and eighty   140 acres. About fifteen hundred of them."

"Fifteen hundred of them?" my uncle said.

"An acre is pretty big," I said. "Two rattlesnakes per acre isn't many. You don't often see them."

"What else have we got around here that's poison?" my uncle said.

"I don't know of anything else," I said. "All the other things are harmless. The rattlesnakes are pretty harmless too, unless you step on them."

"All right," my uncle said. "You walk ahead and watch where   150 you're going. If you see a rattlesnake, don't step on it. I don't want you to die at the age of eleven."

"Yes, sir," I said, "I'll watch carefully."

We turned around and walked back to the Ford. I didn't see any rattlesnakes on the way back. We got into the car and my uncle lighted a cigarette.

"I'm going to make a garden of this awful desolation," he said.

"Yes, sir," I said.

---

[24] **conservatively**—estimating carefully.

"I know what my problems are," my uncle said, "and I know how to solve them." 160

"How?" I said.

"Do you mean the horny toads or the rattlesnakes?" my uncle said.

"I mean the problems," I said.

"Well," my uncle said, "the first thing I'm going to do is hire some Mexicans[25] and put them to work."

"Doing what?" I said.

"Clearing the land," my uncle said. "Then I'm going to have them dig for water."

"Dig where?" I said.

"Straight down," my uncle said. "After we get water, I'm going 170 to have them plow the land and then I'm going to plant."

"What are you going to plant?" I said. "Wheat?"

"Wheat?" my uncle shouted. "What do I want with wheat? Bread is five cents a loaf. I'm going to plant pomegranate trees."

"How much are pomegranates?" I said.

"Pomegranates," my uncle said, "are practically unknown in this country."

"Is that all you're going to plant?" I said.

"I have in mind," my uncle said, "planting several other kinds of trees." 180

"Peach trees?" I said.

"About ten acres," my uncle said.

"How about apricots?" I said.

"By all means," my uncle said. "The apricot is a lovely fruit. Lovely in shape, with a glorious flavor and a most delightful pit.[26] I shall plant about twenty acres of apricot trees."

"I hope the Mexicans don't have any trouble finding water," I said. "Is there any water under this land?"

"Of course," my uncle said. "The important thing is to get started. I shall instruct the men to watch out for rattlesnakes." "Pomegran- 190 ates," he said. "Peaches. Apricots. What else?"

"Figs?" I said.

"Thirty acres of figs," my uncle said.

"How about mulberries?" I said. The mulberry tree is a very nice-looking tree."

"Mulberries," my uncle said. He moved his tongue around in his

25 **Mexicans**—workers from Mexico, many of whom were hired as farm laborers in this area.   26 **pit**—hard center, much like a stone.

mouth. "A nice tree," he said. "A tree I knew well in the old country. How many acres would you suggest?"

"About ten," I said.

"All right," he said. "What else?"   200

"Olive trees are nice," I said.

"Yes, they are," my uncle said. "One of the nicest. About ten acres of olive trees. What else?"

"Well," I said, "I don't suppose apple trees would grow on this kind of land."

"I suppose not," my uncle said. "I don't like apples anyway."

He started the car and we drove off the dry land on to the dry road. The car bounced about slowly[27] until we reached the road and then we began to travel at a higher rate of speed.

"One thing," my uncle said. "When we get home I would rather   210 you didn't mention this *farm* to the folks."[28]

"Yes, sir," I said. (*"Farm?"* I thought. *"What farm?"*)

"I want to surprise them," my uncle said. "You know how your grandmother is. I'll go ahead with my plans and when everything is in order I'll take the whole family out to the farm and surprise them."

"Yes, sir," I said.

"Not a word to a living soul," my uncle said.

"Yes, sir," I said.

Well, the Mexicans went to work and cleared the land. They cleared about ten acres of it in about two months. There were seven   220 of them. They worked with shovels and hoes. They didn't understand anything about anything. It all seemed very strange, but they never complained. They were being paid and that was the thing that counted. They were two brothers and their sons. One day the older brother, Diego, very politely asked my uncle what it was they were supposed to be doing.

"Señor," he said, "please forgive me. Why are we cutting down the cactus?"

"I'm going to farm this land," my uncle said.

The other Mexicans asked Diego in Mexican[29] what my uncle had   230 said and Diego told them.

They didn't believe it was worth the trouble to tell my uncle he couldn't do it. They just went on cutting down the cactus.

The cactus, however, stayed down only for a short while. The land

---

[27] **bounced about slowly**—moved up and down slowly like a bouncing ball.   [28] **folks** (colloquial)—family.   [29] **in Mexican**—in Spanish or Mexican Spanish (similar to "He speaks American"—meaning American English).

which had been first cleared was already rich again with fresh cactus and brush. My uncle made this observation with considerable amazement.[30]

"It takes deep plowing to get rid of cactus," I said. "You've got to plow it out."

My uncle talked the matter over with Ryan, who had a farm-imple- 240 ment business.[31] Ryan told him not to fool with horses.[32] The modern thing to do was to turn a good tractor loose[33] on the land and do a year's work in a day.

So my uncle bought a John Deere tractor. It was beautiful. A mechanic from Ryan's taught Diego how to operate the tractor, and the next day when my uncle and I reached the land we could see the tractor away out in the desolation and we could hear it booming[34] in the awful emptiness of the desert. It sounded pretty awful. It *was* awful. My uncle thought it was wonderful.

"Progress," he said. "There's the modern age for you. Ten thou- 250 sand years ago," he said, "it would have taken a hundred men a week to do what the tractor's done today."

"Ten thousand years ago?" I said. "You mean yesterday."

"Anyway," my uncle said, "there's nothing like these modern conveniences."[35]

"The tractor isn't a convenience," I said.

"What is it, then?" my uncle said. "Doesn't the driver sit?"

"He couldn't very well stand," I said.

"Any time they let you sit," my uncle said, "it's a convenience. Can you whistle?" 260

"Yes, sir," I said. "What sort of song would you like to hear?"

"Song?" my uncle said. "I don't want to hear any song. I want you to whistle at that Mexican on the tractor."

"What for?" I said.

"Never mind what for," my uncle said. "Just whistle. I want him to know we are here and that we are pleased with his work. He's probably plowed twenty acres."

"Yes, sir," I said.

I put the second and third fingers of each hand into my mouth and blew with all my might. It was good and loud. Nevertheless, it 270

---

[30] considerable amazement—rather great surprise or wonder. [31] implement business —tool business. [32] not to fool with horses—not to bother with or try to raise horses. [33] to turn a good tractor loose—to put a tractor to work. [34] booming—making a noise similar to the sound of high waves crashing against the shore; also, similar to the sound of thunder from a distance. [35] modern conveniences—new devices or gadgets to make life easier or more comfortable.

didn't seem as if Diego had heard me. He was pretty far away. We were walking toward him anyway, so I couldn't figure out why my uncle wanted me to whistle at him.

"Once again," he said.

I whistled once again, but Diego didn't hear.

"Louder," my uncle said.

This time I gave all I had,[36] and my uncle put his hands over his ears. My face got very red, too. The Mexican on the tractor heard the whistle this time. He slowed the tractor down, turned it around, and began plowing straight across the field toward us.   280

"Do you want him to do that?" I said.

"It doesn't matter," my uncle said.

In less than a minute and a half the tractor and the Mexican arrived. The Mexican seemed very delighted. He wiped dirt and perspiration off his face and got down from the tractor.

"Señor," he said, "this is wonderful."

"I'm glad you like it," my uncle said.

"Would you like a ride?" the Mexican asked my uncle.

My uncle didn't know for sure. He looked at me.

"Go ahead," he said. "Hop on. Have a little ride."   290

Diego got on the tractor and helped me on. He sat on the metal seat and I stood behind him, holding him. The tractor began to shake, then jumped, and then began to move. It moved swiftly and made a good deal of noise. The Mexican drove around in a big circle and brought the tractor back to my uncle. I jumped off.

"All right," my uncle said to the Mexican. "Go back to your work."

The Mexican drove the tractor back to where he was plowing.

My uncle didn't get water out of the land until many months later. He had wells dug all over the place, but no water came out of the   300 wells. Of course he had motor pumps too, but even then no water came out. A water specialist named Roy came out from Texas with his two younger brothers and they began investigating the land. They told my uncle they'd get water for him. It took them three months and the water was muddy and there wasn't much of it. There was a trickle[37] of muddy water. The specialist told my uncle matters would improve with time and went back to Texas.

Now half the land was cleared and plowed and there was water, so the time had come to plant.

[36] **gave it all I had**—whistled as long and as loud as possible until my breath gave out; put all my energy into it.   [37] **trickle**—a very small stream.

We planted pomegranate trees. They were of the finest quality and 310
very expensive. We planted about seven hundred of them. I myself
planted a hundred. My uncle planted quite a few. We had a twenty-
acre orchard of pomegranate trees away over to hell and gone in the
strangest desolation anybody ever saw. It was the loveliest-looking absurdity[38] imaginable and my uncle was crazy about it. The only
trouble was, his money was giving out. Instead of going ahead and trying to make a garden of the whole six hundred and eighty acres, he
decided to devote[39] all his time and energy and money to the pomegranate trees.

"Only for the time being," he said. "Until we begin to market the 320
pomegranates and get our money back."

"Yes, sir," I said.

I didn't know for sure, but I figured we wouldn't be getting any
pomegranates to speak of[40] off those little trees for two or three years
at least, but I didn't say anything. My uncle got rid of the Mexican
workers and he and I took over the farm. We had the tractor and a
lot of land, so every now and then we drove out to the farm and drove
the tractor around, plowing up cactus and turning over the soil between the pomegranate trees. This went on for three years.

"One of these days," my uncle said, "you'll see the loveliest garden 330
in the world in this desert."

The water situation didn't improve with time, either. Every once
in a while there would be a sudden generous spurt[41] of water containing only a few pebbles and my uncle would be greatly pleased, but
the next day it would be muddy again and there would be only a little
trickle. The pomegranate trees fought bravely for life, but they never
did get enough water to come out with any fruit.

There were blossoms after the fourth year. This was a great triumph
for my uncle. He went out of his head with joy when he saw them.

Nothing ever came of the blossoms,[42] though. They were very beau- 340
tiful, but that was about all. Purple and lonely.

That year my uncle harvested three small pomegranates.

I ate one, he ate one, and we kept the other one up in his office.

The following year I was fifteen. A lot of wonderful things had happened to me. I mean, I had read a number of good writers and I'd
grown as tall as my uncle. The farm was still our secret. It had cost
my uncle a lot of money, but he was always under the impression that

---

[38] absurdity—ridiculous thing. [39] to devote—to give. [40] any pomegranates to speak
of—any pomegranates worth mentioning or counting on (that is, very few—if any—
pomegranates). [41] spurt—sudden gush or outpouring. [42] nothing ever came of the
blossoms—the blossoms didn't develop into fruit.

very soon he was going to start marketing his pomegranates and get his money back and go on with his plan to make a garden in the desert. 350

The trees didn't fare very well.[43] They grew a little, but it was hardly noticeable. Quite a few of them withered[44] and died.

"That's average," my uncle said. "Twenty trees to an acre is only average. We won't plant new trees just now. We'll do that later."

He was still paying for the land, too.

The following year he harvested about two hundred pomegranates. He and I did the harvesting. They were pretty sad-looking pomegranates. We packed them in nice-looking boxes and my uncle shipped them to a wholesale produce house in Chicago. There were eleven boxes. 360

We didn't hear from the wholesale produce house[45] for a month, so one night my uncle made a long-distance phone call. The produce man, D'Agostino, told my uncle nobody wanted pomegranates.

"How much are you asking per box?" my uncle shouted over the phone.

"One dollar," D'Agostino shouted back.

"That's not enough," my uncle shouted. "I won't take a nickel less than five dollars a box."

"They don't want them at one dollar a box," D'Agostino shouted.

"Why not?" my uncle shouted. 370

"They don't know what they are," D'Agostino shouted.

"What kind of a business man are you anyway?" my uncle shouted. "They're pomegranates. I want five dollars a box."

"I can't sell them," the produce man shouted. "I ate one myself and I don't see anything so wonderful about them."

"You're crazy," my uncle shouted. "There is no other fruit in the world like the pomegranate. Five dollars a box isn't half enough."

"What shall I do with them?" D'Agostino shouted. "I can't sell them. I don't want them."

"I see," my uncle whispered. "Ship them back. Ship them back 380 express collect."[46]

The phone call cost my uncle about seventeen dollars.

So the eleven boxes came back.

My uncle and I ate most of the pomegranates.

[43] **didn't fare very well**—didn't make out or grow very well. [44] **withered**—dried up.
[45] **wholesale produce house**—place where produce (fruits and vegetables) purchased from the growers is sold and distributed to the retailers who sell directly to the public.
[46] **express collect**—by express (fast) shipment, the freight charge to be collected from the receiver rather than the sender.

The following year my uncle couldn't make any more payments on the land. He gave the papers back[47] to the man who had sold him the land. I was in the office at the time.

"Mr. Griffith," my uncle said, "I've got to give you back your property, but I would like to ask a little favor. I've planted twenty acres of pomegranate trees out there on that land and I'd appreciate it very much if you'd let me take care of[48] those trees."

390

"Take care of them?" Mr. Griffith said. "What in the world for?"

My uncle tried to explain, but couldn't. It was too much to try to explain to a man who wasn't sympathetic.

So my uncle lost the land, and the trees, too.

About three years later he and I drove out to the land and walked out to the pomegranate orchard. The trees were all dead. The soil was heavy[49] again with cactus and desert brush. Except for the small dead pomegranate trees the place was exactly the way it had been all the years of the world.

400

We walked around in the orchard for a while and then went back to the car.

We got into the car and drove back to town.

We didn't say anything because there was such an awful lot[50] to say, and no language to say it in.

47 **gave the papers back**—returned the documents concerning the sale of the land. 48 **take care of**—look after; tend. 49 **heavy**—covered. 50 **such an awful lot**—so very much.

ERNEST HEMINGWAY (1898 – 1961)

Ernest Hemingway was born in Oak Park, near Chicago. After leaving high school, he went to work on the Kansas City *Star;* he learned a great deal about exactness and style in reporting for this newspaper, which was known for its high standards. His experiences in World War I gave him material for many of his short stories and some of his novels, including the well-known *A Farewell to Arms* and *The Sun Also Rises.* He gained background for the novel *For Whom the Bell Tolls* when he went to Spain during the Spanish Civil War to write newspaper articles. He was awarded the 1954 Nobel Prize for Literature.[1]

As a boy, Hemingway spent much time hunting, fishing, and exploring in the wild country of northern Michigan. In later years, he was attracted to bullfighting in Spain and big-game hunting in Africa. His observations provided background for other works, in which he concerned himself with man's courage in facing strong physical forces. These books include *Death in the Afternoon,* on bullfighting, and *Green Hills of Africa,* on big-game hunting.

In the story here (from a collection of stories, *Winner Take Nothing,* published in 1933), Hemingway shows the feelings of a boy who, through a misunderstanding, thought he was facing death. The story is very short and might appear on first reading to be nothing more than a simple anecdote; the theme, nonetheless, is a serious one.

A Day's Wait

*H*E CAME INTO THE ROOM TO SHUT the windows while we were still in bed and I saw he looked ill. He was shivering,[2] his face was white,[3] and he walked slowly as though it ached[4] to move.

"What's the matter, Schatz?"[5]

---

[1] **Nobel Prizes**—created by a fund left by Alfred B. Nobel, Swedish scientist; awarded annually since 1902 to persons of any nationality for distinguished work in literature, as well as in the fields of chemistry, physics, and medicine, and in the cause of peace. [2] **shivering**—shaking as if cold. [3] **white**—pale; lacking in color. [4] **ached**—hurt or pained him. [5] **Schatz**—a German term of endearment roughly equivalent to "darling." (The use of this term indicates that the family in the story has some acquaintance with European customs and culture.)

60

"I've got a headache."

"You better go back to bed."

"No. I'm all right."

"You go to bed. I'll see you when I'm dressed."   10

But when I came downstairs he was dressed, sitting by the fire, looking a very sick and miserable boy of nine years. When I put my hand on his forehead[6] I knew he had a fever.[7]

"You go up to bed," I said, "you're sick."

"I'm all right," he said.

When the doctor came he took the boy's temperature.[8]

"What is it?" I asked him.

"One hundred and two."[9]

Downstairs, the doctor left three different medicines in different colored capsules[10] with instructions for giving them. One was to bring   20
down[11] the fever, another a purgative,[12] the third to overcome an acid condition.[13] The germs of influenza can only exist in an acid condition, he explained. He seemed to know all about influenza[14] and said there was nothing to worry about[15] if the fever did not go above one hundred and four degrees. This was a light epidemic of flu[16] and there was no danger if you avoided pneumonia.[17]

Back in the room I wrote the boy's temperature down and made a note of the time to give the various capsules.

"Do you want me to read to you?"

"All right. If you want to," said the boy. His face was very white   30
and there were dark areas under his eyes. He lay still in the bed and seemed very detached[18] from what was going on.[19]

I read aloud from Howard Pyle's Book of Pirates; but I could see he was not following what I was reading.

"How do you feel, Schatz?" I asked him.

"Just the same, so far," he said.

I sat at the foot of the bed[20] and read to myself while I waited for

[6] forehead—part of the face from the hairline to the eyebrows. [7] fever—degree of temperature over the normal of 98.6 Fahrenheit. [8] took the boy's temperature—put a thermometer in the boy's mouth to determine the degree of temperature. [9] one hundred and two—102 degrees Fahrenheit, almost 39 degrees Centigrade. [10] capsules—tiny cylindrical containers for medicine. [11] bring down—reduce. [12] purgative—laxative (a medicine to produce bowel movements). [13] acid condition—overabundance of acid in the stomach or digestive tract. [14] influenza—grippe, an acute epidemic disease, usually accompanied by upset stomach, fever, inflammation of the nose and throat. [15] nothing to worry about—nothing to be concerned or alarmed about. [16] this was a light epidemic of flu—influenza had spread to several people in the community but not to an alarming number. [17] pneumonia—inflammation of the lungs, a serious illness. [18] detached—removed; far away. [19] going on—taking place. [20] at the foot of the bed—at the bottom or end of the bed.

it to be time to give another capsule. It would have been natural for him to go to sleep, but when I looked up he was looking at the foot of the bed, looking very strangely.   40

"Why don't you try to sleep? I'll wake you up for the medicine."

"I'd rather stay awake."

After a while he said to me, "You don't have to stay in here with me, Papa, if it bothers you."[21]

"It doesn't bother me."

"No, I mean you don't have to stay if it's going to bother you."

I thought perhaps he was a little lightheaded[22] and after giving him the prescribed capsules[23] at eleven o'clock I went out for a while. It was a bright,[24] cold day, the ground covered with a sleet[25] that had frozen so that it seemed as if all the bare[26] trees, the bushes, the cut 50 brush and all the grass and the bare ground had been varnished[27] with ice. I took the young Irish setter[28] for a walk up the road and along a frozen creek,[29] but it was difficult to stand or walk on the glassy surface[30] and the red dog slipped and slithered[31] and I fell twice, hard, once dropping my gun and having it slide away over the ice.

We flushed a covey of quail[32] under a high clay bank with overhanging brush[33] and I killed two as they went out of sight over the top of the bank. Some of the covey lit[34] in trees, but most of them scattered[35] into brush piles[36] and it was necessary to jump on the ice-coated mounds of brush[37] several times before they would flush.[38] Coming 60 out while you were poised[39] unsteadily on the icy, springy[40] brush they[41] made difficult shooting and I killed two, missed five, and started back pleased to have found a covey close to the house and happy there were so many left to find on another day.

At the house they said the boy had refused to let any one come into the room.

"You can't come in," he said. "You mustn't get what I have."[42]

---

[21] bothers you—disturbs you; makes you uncomfortable. [22] lightheaded—dizzy and faint. [23] prescribed capsules—medicine ordered by the doctor. [24] bright—sunny and clear. [25] sleet—combination of rain and snow. [26] bare—leafless; without leaves. [27] varnished—covered as with a polish. [28] Irish setter—type of dog with a red hair; a hunting dog. [29] creek—small stream. [30] glassy surface—smooth, highly polished (like glass). [31] slithered—slid unsteadily. [32] flushed a covey of quail: a) flushed—drove or forced out; b) covey—group; c) quail—small birds (both singular and plural: a quail; three quail). [33] clay bank with overhanging brush: a) clay—a type of soil; b) bank with overhanging brush—a small cliff with bushes, weeds, and branches hanging over the edge. [34] lit—landed or settled. [35] scattered—went off in all directions. [36] brush piles—stacks or heaps of brush. [37] mounds of brush—piles or little hills of brush. [38] flush—come out. [39] poised—balanced. [40] springy—quality of flexibility (as a spring moving up and down). [41] they—the quail. [42] mustn't get what I have —mustn't catch the illness I have.

I went up to him and found him in exactly the position I had left him, white-faced, but with the tops of his cheeks flushed[43] by the fever, staring[44] still, as he had stared, at the foot of the bed.   70

I took his temperature.

"What is it?"

"Something like a hundred," I said. It was one hundred and two and four tenths.

"It was a hundred and two," he said.

"Who said so?"

"The doctor."

"Your temperature is all right," I said. "It's nothing to worry about."

"I don't worry," he said, "but I can't keep from thinking."   80

"Don't think," I said. "Just take it easy."

"I'm taking it easy," he said and looked straight ahead. He was evidently holding tight onto himself[45] about something.

"Take this with water."

"Do you think it will do any good?"

"Of course it will."

I sat down and opened the *Pirate* book and commenced to read, but I could see he was not following, so I stopped.

"About what time do you think I'm going to die?" he asked.

"What?"   90

"About how long will it be before I die?"

"You aren't going to die. What's the matter with you?"

"Oh, yes, I am. I heard him say a hundred and two."

"People don't die with a fever of one hundred and two. That's a silly[46] way to talk."

"I know they do. At school in France the boys told me you can't live with forty-four degrees. I've got a hundred and two."

He had been waiting to die all day, ever since nine o'clock in the morning.

"You poor Schatz," I said. "Poor old Schatz. It's like miles and   100 kilometers. You aren't going to die. That's a different thermometer. On that thermometer thirty-seven is normal. On this kind it's ninety-eight."

"Are you sure?"

---

[43] cheeks flushed: *a*) cheeks—sides of the face; *b*) flushed—rosy or reddened by flow of blood to the face.   [44] staring—looking steadily straight ahead; gazing fixedly.   [45] holding tight onto himself—keeping rigid control over himself.   [46] silly—stupid; ridiculous; foolish.

"Absolutely," I said. "It's like miles and kilometers. You know, like how many kilometers we make when we do seventy miles in the car?"

"Oh," he said.

But his gaze at the foot of the bed relaxed slowly. The hold[47] over himself relaxed too, finally, and the next day it was very slack[48] and he cried very easily at little things that were of no importance.   110

[47] hold—control.   [48] slack—loose; no longer tense; relaxed.

WILLIAM CARLOS WILLIAMS (1883 –)

William Carlos Williams is known primarily as a poet, but he has occasionally expressed himself in prose in the form of short stories, novels, and essays. He has also practiced medicine for forty years in his home town, Rutherford, New Jersey. In "The Use of Force," the main character is a doctor; in fact, the story is told in the first person, from the doctor's point of view. Dr. Williams undoubtedly drew upon his experiences as a physician in the telling of this story. But it is well to remember that it is a piece of fiction, not a case history. This brief story centers around the conflict that arises during the doctor's visit to a sick child. Out of this conflict emerges the theme of "the use of force." The story appears in *Make Light of It*, first published in 1933.

The Use of Force

*T*HEY WERE NEW PATIENTS TO ME, all I had was the name, Olson.[1] "Please come down as soon as you can, my daughter is very sick."

When I arrived I was met by the mother, a big startled[2] looking woman, very clean and apologetic who merely said, "Is this the doctor?" and let me in. "In the back," she added. "You must excuse us, doctor, we have her in the kitchen where it is warm. It is very damp[3] here sometimes."

The child was fully dressed and sitting on her father's lap near the   10
kitchen table. He tried to get up, but I motioned for him not to bother, took off my overcoat and started to look things over. I could see that they were all very nervous, eyeing me up and down distrustfully.[4] As often, in such cases, they weren't telling me more than

[1] **all I had was the name, Olson**—the only information I had was the name of the family, Olson. [2] **startled**—alarmed. [3] **damp**—somewhat wet or moist. [4] **distrustfully**—suspiciously.

they had to, it was up to me to tell them; that's why they were spending three dollars on me.[5]

The child was fairly eating me up[6] with her cold, steady eyes, and no expression to her face whatever. She did not move and seemed, inwardly, quiet;[7] an unusually attractive little thing, and as strong as a heifer[8] in appearance. But her face was flushed, she was breathing   20
rapidly, and I realized that she had a high fever. She had magnificent blonde hair, in profusion.[9] One of those picture children[10] often reproduced in advertising leaflets and the photogravure sections of the Sunday papers.[11]

"She's had a fever for three days," began the father, "and we don't know what it comes from. My wife has given her things,[12] you know, like people do, but it don't do no good.[13] And there's been a lot of sickness around. So we tho't[14] you'd better look her over[15] and tell us what is the matter."

As doctors often do I took a trial shot at it as a point of departure.[16]   30
"Had she had a sore throat?"[17]

Both parents answered me together, "No . . . No, she says her throat don't[18] hurt her."

"Does your throat hurt you?" added the mother to the child. But the little girl's expression didn't change nor did she move her eyes from my face.

"Have you looked?"

"I tried to," said the mother, "but I couldn't see."

As it happens we had been having a number of cases of diphtheria[19] in the school to which this child went during that month and we   40
were all, quite apparently, thinking of that, though no one had as yet spoken of the thing.[20]

[5] **spending three dollars on me**—paying my three-dollar fee. [6] **fairly eating me up:** a) **fairly**—clearly, or really; b) **eating me up**—devouring me, or taking me all in. [7] **inwardly quiet**—calm inside. [8] **heifer**—a young female cow. [9] **profusion**—abundance; a large amount. [10] **picture children**—appealing children who photograph very well. [11] **photogravure section of the Sunday papers**—a special part of some Sunday newspapers that includes photographs reproduced by a process known as *photogravure* or *gravure* (the pages usually have a brownish or greenish tint). [12] **has given her things**—has given her various types of medicine. [13] **it don't do no good**—it doesn't do any good. ("It don't do no good" is substandard speech. You will notice other appearances of *don't* for *doesn't* in this story. Note that the Olsons use this form, but that the doctor doesn't.) [14] **tho't** (a variant spelling of *thought*)—thought. [15] **look her over** —examine her. [16] **took a trial shot at it as a point of departure:** a) **took a trial shot**—made a guess; b) **as a point of departure**—as a starting place. [17] **sore throat**— an inflamed, usually reddened, condition in the throat. [18] **don't**—(See *fn.* 13.). [19] **cases of diphtheria**—a) **cases**—occurrences; b) **diphtheria**—a contagious disease, characterized by the formation of a false membrane in the throat, produced by a specific bacillus. [20] **no one had yet spoken of the thing**—no one had mentioned the possibility that the child might have diphtheria.

"Well," I said, "suppose we take a look at the throat first." I smiled in my best professional manner and asking for the child's first name I said, "Come on, Mathilda, open your mouth and let's take a look at your throat."

Nothing doing.[21]

"Aw, come on," I coaxed,[22] "just open your mouth wide and let me take a look. Look," I said opening both hands wide,[23] "I haven't anything in my hands. Just open up and let me see."

"Such a nice man," put in the mother. "Look how kind he is to you. Come on, do what he tells you to. He won't hurt you."

At that I ground my teeth in disgust.[24] If only they wouldn't use the word "hurt" I might be able to get somewhere.[25] But I did not allow myself to be hurried or disturbed but speaking quietly and slowly I approached the child again.

As I moved my chair a little nearer suddenly with one catlike movement both her hands clawed[26] instinctively for my eyes and she almost reached them too. In fact she knocked my glasses flying and they fell, though unbroken, several feet away from me on the kitchen floor.

Both the mother and father almost turned themselves inside out in embarrassment and apology.[27] "You bad girl," said the mother, taking her and shaking her by one arm. "Look what you've done. The nice man . . ."

"For heaven's sake," I broke in.[28] "Don't call me a nice man to her. I'm here to look at her throat on the chance that she might have diphtheria and possibly die of it. But that's nothing to her.[29] Look here," I said to the child, "we're going to look at your throat. You're old enough to understand what I'm saying. Will you open it now by yourself or shall we have to open it for you?"

Not a move. Even her expression hadn't changed. Her breaths however were coming faster and faster. Then the battle began. I had to do it. I had to have a throat culture[30] for her own protection. But first I told the parents that it was entirely up to them. I explained the danger but said that I would not insist on a throat examination so long as they would take the responsibility.

[21] **nothing doing**—there was no response by either word or action. [22] **coaxed**—attempted to persuade her (with the words, "Aw, come on"). [23] **opening both hands wide**—opening both hands with palms up (so that the child could see that there was nothing in them). [24] **ground my teeth in disgust:** *a*) **ground my teeth**—rubbed my upper and lower teeth together; *b*) **in disgust**—showing dislike and annoyance. [25] **to get somewhere**—to make some progress. [26] **clawed**—scratched or reached (in the manner of an animal or bird). [27] **turned themselves inside out in embarrassment and apology**—outdid themselves, or surpassed themselves, in being embarrassed and in apologizing. [28] **broke in**—interrupted. [29] **that's nothing to her**—that doesn't mean anything to her. [30] **throat culture**—a specimen of bacteria from the throat area.

"If you don't do what the doctor says you'll have to go to the hospital," the mother admonished[31] her severely.

Oh yeah? I had to smile to myself. After all, I had already fallen in love with the savage brat,[32] the parents were contemptible[33] to me. In the ensuing struggle they grew more and more abject,[34] crushed, exhausted while she surely rose to magnificent heights of insane fury of effort bred of[35] her terror of me.   80

The father tried his best, and he was a big man but the fact that she was his daughter, his shame at her behavior and his dread[36] of hurting her made him release her just at the critical moment several times when I had almost achieved success, till I wanted to kill him. But his dread also that she might have diphtheria made him tell me to go on,[37] go on though he himself was almost fainting, while the mother moved back and forth behind us raising and lowering her   90
hands in an agony of apprehension.[38]

"Put her in front of you on your lap," I ordered, "and hold both her wrists."

But as soon as he did the child let out a scream. "Don't, you're hurting me. Let go of my hands. Let them go I tell you." Then she shrieked[39] terrifyingly, hysterically. "Stop it! Stop it! You're killing me!"

"Do you think she can stand it, doctor!" said the mother.

"You get out," said the husband to his wife. "Do you want her to die of diphtheria?"   100

"Come on now, hold her," I said.

Then I grasped[40] the child's head with my left hand and tried to get the wooden tongue depressor[41] between her teeth. She fought, with clenched teeth,[42] desperately![43] But now I also had grown furious —at a child. I tried to hold myself down[44] but I couldn't. I know how to expose a throat for inspection. And I did my best. When finally I got the wooden spatula behind the last teeth and just the point of it into the mouth cavity, she opened up for an instant but before I

---

[31] **admonished**—reprimanded; warned; cautioned. [32] **savage brat**—wild, untamed child. ("Brat" generally refers to an unruly child. The term is used either jokingly or scornfully; it is not a synonym for "young child.") [33] **contemptible**—deserving of scorn or extreme dislike; despicable. [34] **abject**—degraded; lacking in spirit; wretched; miserable. [35] **bred of**—produced by. [36] **dread**—fear. [37] **to go on**—to continue. [38] **agony of apprehension:** *a*) **agony of**—strong emotion of; *b*) **apprehension**—fear; dread; foreboding. ("Agony" also means "great physical or mental pain or distress.") [39] **shrieked**—screamed loudly and piercingly. [40] **grasped**—seized. [41] **wooden tongue depressor**—a narrow, flat instrument, shaped like a spatula, used for pressing down the tongue in order to examine the throat. [42] **with clenched teeth**—with teeth held tightly together. [43] **desperately**—violently (as a result of her despair and fear that she would lose the struggle). [44] **hold myself down**—control myself.

could see anything she came down again and gripping the wooden
blade between her molars she reduced it to splinters[45] before I could   110
get it out again.

"Aren't you ashamed," the mother yelled at her. "Aren't you
ashamed to act like that in front of the doctor?"

"Get me a smooth-handled spoon of some sort," I told the mother.
"We're going through with this."[46] The child's mouth was already
bleeding. Her tongue was cut and she was screaming in wild hysterical
shrieks. Perhaps I should have desisted[47] and come back in an hour
or more. No doubt it would have been better. But I have seen at
least two children lying dead in bed of neglect in such cases, and
feeling that I must get a diagnosis now or never I went at it again.   120
But the worst of it was that I too had got beyond reason.[48] I could
have torn the child apart in my own fury and enjoyed it. It was a
pleasure to attack her. My face was burning with it.

The damned little brat must be protected against her own idiocy,
one says to one's self at such times. Others must be protected against
her. It is a social necessity. And all these things are true. But a blind
fury, a feeling of adult shame, bred of a longing for muscular release
are the operatives.[49] One goes on to the end.

In a final unreasoning assault[50] I overpowered the child's neck and
jaws. I forced the heavy silver spoon back of her teeth and down her   130
throat till she gagged.[51] And there it was—both tonsils covered with
membrane.[52] She had fought valiantly[53] to keep me from knowing her
secret. She had been hiding that sore throat for three days at least
and lying to her parents in order to escape just such an outcome as
this.[54]

Now truly she *was* furious. She had been on the defensive before
but now she attacked. Tried to get off her father's lap and fly at me
while tears of defeat blinded her eyes.

[45] reduced it to splinters—broke the wooden spatula into many small pieces.   [46] going
through with this—going to finish this (the examination).   [47] desisted—stopped;
ceased.   [48] had got beyond reason—had lost control of myself.   [49] operatives—forces
(forces that drive one on).   [50] assault—attack.   [51] gagged—choked.   [52] covered
with membrane—had the sure sign of diphtheria.   [53] valiantly—bravely; courageously.
[54] to escape just such an outcome as this—to avoid having her secret discovered.

CARL SANDBURG (1878 –   )

Carl Sandburg's parents came to the United States from Sweden and settled in the Middle West. Sandburg, known as the "Chicago Poet," was born in Illinois and has spent most of his life there. As a young man, he worked at a variety of jobs, including truck driver, farm-hand, newspaper reporter, and secretary to a mayor. These early experiences gave him a feeling for and a faith in the working people which are reflected in his poetry. His works include *Chicago Poems*, published in 1916, which made him a controversial literary figure, mainly because of his realistic, unrestrained ideas, colloquial style, and free verse; *The People, Yes*, which reaffirmed his vigorous beliefs in ordinary people; *Potato Face*, a book of stories and poems for children; and *The American Songbag*, a collection of folk songs.

Perhaps his greatest literary labor was the impressive biography of Abraham Lincoln; he worked about thirty years preparing the six-volume work, the first two of which were published in 1926, the last four in 1939. These volumes, based on careful research into the life and meaning of Lincoln, won wide acclaim for Sandburg; for the 1939 volumes, he was awarded the Pulitzer Prize.[1] In the chapter quoted here, Sandburg's glimpse into Lincoln's early life may give some insight into the character of this great historical personage.

Abraham Lincoln Grows Up

*W*HEN HE WAS ELEVEN YEARS OLD, Abe Lincoln's young body began to change. The juices[2] and glands began to make a long, tall boy out of him. As the months and years went by, he noticed his lean[3] wrists getting longer, his legs too, and he was now looking over the heads of other boys. Men said, "Land o' Goshen, that boy air a-growin'!"[4]

[1] See *fn.* 1, p. 48.   [2] **juices**—body fluids, which control growth of the body.   [3] **lean** —thin; without an extra ounce of fat.   [4] **"Land o' Goshen, that boy air a-growin'!"**— Land of Goshen, that boy is growing ("Land of Goshen" is an expression like "Heavens!" or "My goodness!").

As he took on more length, they said he was shooting up into the air like green corn in the summer of a good corn-year. So he grew. When he reached seventeen years of age, and they measured him, he was six feet, nearly four inches, high, from the bottoms of his moccasins[5] to the top of his skull.

These were years he was handling the ax. Except in spring plowing-time and the fall fodder-pulling,[6] he was handling the ax nearly all the time. The insides of his hands took on callus[7] thick as leather. He cleared openings in the timber, cut logs and puncheons,[8] split fire-wood, built pig-pens.

He learned how to measure with his eye the half-circle swing of the ax so as to nick out[9] the deepest possible chip[10] from off a tree-trunk. The trick of swaying his body easily on the hips so as to throw the heaviest possible weight into the blow of the ax—he learned that.

On winter mornings he wiped the frost from the ax-handle, sniffed sparkles of air[11] into his lungs, and beat a steady cleaving[12] of blows into a big tree—till it fell—and he sat on the main log and ate his noon dinner of corn bread and fried salt pork—and joked with the gray squirrels that frisked[13] and peeped[14] at him from high forks of near-by walnut trees.

He learned how to make his ax flash[15] and bite into a sugar-maple or a sycamore.[16] The outside and the inside look of black walnut and black oak, hickory and jack oak, elm and white oak, sassafras, dog-wood, grapevines, sumac—he came on their secrets. He could guess close to the time of the year, to the week of the month, by the way the leaves and branches of trees looked. He sniffed[17] the seasons.

Often he worked alone in the timbers,[18] all day long with only the sound of his own ax, or his own voice speaking to himself, or the crackling and swaying[19] of branches in the wind, and the cries and whirs[20] of animals of brown and silver-gray squirrels,[21] of partridges, hawks, crows, turkeys, sparrows,[22] and the occasional wildcats.[23]

---

5 **moccasins**—type of shoes, usually made out of soft leather. 6 **fodder-pulling**—picking stalks of corn and grains used to feed farm animals. 7 **callus**—layers of hardened skin. 8 **puncheons**—pieces of timber. 9 **nick out**—cut out; notch out. 10 **chip**—piece (usually small and thin; in this case, wood). 11 **sniffed sparkles of air:** *a*) **sniffed**—inhaled in short breaths; *b*) **sparkles of air**—invigorating particles of air. 12 **cleaving**—cutting. 13 **frisked**—danced and leaped in play. 14 **peeped**—looked shyly or stealthily, not openly. 15 **flash**—move quickly. 16 **a sugar-maple or a syca-more**—varieties of trees (as are the names in the next sentence). 17 **sniffed**—detected (literally, smelled). 18 **timbers**—woods filled with trees suitable for building purposes. 19 **crackling and swaying**—the sound from movement and the gentle movement back and forth. 20 **whirs**—buzzing sounds (as from the moving wings of birds). 21 **squirrels**—small animals. 22 **partridges . . . sparrows**—types of birds. 23 **wildcats**—wild animals of the cat family.

The tricks and whimsies[24] of the sky, how to read clear skies and cloudy weather, the creeping vines of ivy and wild grape, the recurrence[25] of dogwood blossoms in spring, the ways of snow, rain, drizzle,[26] sleet,[27] the visitors of sky and weather coming and going hour by hour—he tried to read their secrets, he tried to be friendly with their mystery.

So he grew, to become hard, tough, wiry.[28] The muscle on his bones and the cords, tendons, cross-weaves of fiber,[29] and nerve centers, these became instruments to obey his wishes. He found with other men he could lift his own end of a log—and more too. One of the neighbors said he was strong as three men. Another said, "He can sink an ax deeper into wood than any man I ever saw." And another, "If you heard him fellin'[30] trees in a clearin',[31] you would say there was three men at work by the way the trees fell."

He was more than a tough, long rawboned[32] boy. He amazed men with his man's lifting power.[33] He put shoulders under a new-built corncrib[34] one day and walked away with it to where the farmer wanted it. Four men, ready with poles to put under it and carry it, didn't need their poles. He played the same trick with a chicken house; at the new, growing town of Gentryville near by, they said the chicken house weighed six hundred pounds, and only a big boy with a hard backbone could get under it and walk away with it.

A blacksmith shop, a grocery, and a store had started up on the crossroads of the Gentry farm. And one night after Abe had been helping thresh wheat on Dave Turnham's place, he went with Dennis Hanks, John Johnston, and some other boys to Gentryville where the farm-hands[35] sat around with John Baldwin, the blacksmith, and Jones, the storekeeper, passed the whisky jug, told stories, and talked politics and religion and gossip. Going home late that night, they saw something in a mud puddle alongside the road. They stepped over to see whether it was a man or a hog. It was a man—drunk—snoring—sleeping off his drunk—on a frosty night outdoors in a cold wind.

They shook him by the shoulders, doubled his knees to his stomach, but he went on sleeping, snoring. The cold wind was getting colder. The other boys said they were going home, and they went

[24] whimsies—fanciful notions; caprices. [25] recurrence—coming again; reappearance; return. [26] drizzle—very light rain. [27] sleet—combination of rain and snow. [28] wiry —lean and energetic; wirelike. [29] cords, tendons, and cross-weaves of fiber—connective tissue in the body. [30] fellin'—felling; cutting down. [31] clearin'—clearing; cleared spot in a forest. [32] rawboned—lean; gaunt. [33] lifting power—power or ability to lift heavy objects. [34] corncrib—corn bin; storage place for corn. [35] farm-hands—farm workers.

away leaving Abe alone with the snoring sleeper in the mud puddle. Abe stepped into the mud, reached arms around the man, slung[36] him over his shoulders, carried him to Dennis Hanks's cabin, built a fire, rubbed him warm and left him sleeping off the whisky.

And the man afterward said Abe saved his life. He told John Hanks, "It was mighty clever of Abe to tote[37] me to a warm fire that night." 80

So he grew, living in that Pigeon Creek cabin for a home, sleeping in the loft,[38] climbing up at night to a bed just under the roof, where sometimes the snow and the rain drove through the cracks, eating sometimes at a table where the family had only one thing to eat— potatoes. Once at the table, when there were only potatoes, his father spoke a blessing to the Lord for potatoes; the boy murmured, "Those are mighty poor blessings." And Abe made jokes once when company came and Sally Bush Lincoln brought out raw potatoes, gave the visitors a knife apiece, and they all peeled raw potatoes, and talked about the crops, politics, religion, gossip. 90

Days when they had only potatoes to eat didn't come often. Other days in the year they had "yaller[39]-legged chicken" with gravy, and corn dodgers[40] with shortening, and berries and honey. They tasted of bear meat, deer, coon,[41] quail, grouse, prairie turkey,[42] catfish, bass, perch.[43]

Abe knew the sleep that comes after long hours of work outdoors, the feeling of simple food changing into blood and muscle as he worked in those young years clearing timberland for pasture and corn crops, cutting loose the brush, piling it and burning it, splitting rails, pulling the crosscut saw and the whipsaw, driving the shovel-plow, 100 harrowing,[44] planting, hoeing, pulling fodder, milking cows, churning butter, helping neighbors at house-raisings, log-rollings, corn-husk-ings.[45]

He found he was fast, strong, and keen[46] when he went against other boys in sports. On farms where he worked, he held his own at scuffling,[47] knocking off hats, wrestling. The time came when around Gentryville and Spencer County he was known as the best "rassler"[48] of all, the champion. In jumping, foot-racing, throwing the maul,[49]

36 slung—threw. 37 tote (colloquial)—carry. 38 loft—attic; room immediately below the roof of a house. 39 "yaller"—yellow ("yaller" reflects the pronunciation of a particular dialect). 40 corn dodgers—cakes made with corn meal. 41 bear meat, deer, coon—animal meat (game). 42 quail, grouse, prairie turkey—bird meat (fowl). 43 catfish, bass, perch—types of fish. 44 harrowing—driving a harrow, a farm tool with spikes (like long teeth), used to break up plowed ground. 45 house-raisings, log-rollings, corn-huskings—work parties to build houses, roll logs, or husk corn (remove the dry coverings on ears of corn). 46 keen—sharp; quick-witted. 47 scuffling—fighting or pushing others about. 48 "rassler"—wrestler ("rassler" reflects the pronunciation of a particular dialect). 49 maul—type of hammer.

pitching the crowbar,[50] he carried away the decisions against the lads of his own age always, and usually won against those older than himself.   **110**

He earned his board, clothes, and lodgings, sometimes working for a neighbor farmer. He watched his father, while helping make cabinets, coffins, cupboards, window frames, doors. Hammers, saws, pegs,[51] cleats,[52] he understood first-hand, also the scythe and the cradle[53] for cutting hay and grain, the corn-cutter's knife, the leather piece to protect the hand while shucking corn,[54] and the horse, the dog, the cow, the ox, the hog. He could skin and cure the hides of coon and deer. He lifted the slippery two-hundred-pound hog carcass,[55] head down, holding the hind hocks[56] up for others of the gang[57]   **120** to hook, and swung the animal clear of the ground. He learned where to stick a hog in the under side of the neck so as to bleed it to death, how to split it in two, and carve out the chops, the parts for sausage grinding, for hams, for "cracklings."[58]

Farmers called him to butcher for them at thirty-one cents a day, this when he was sixteen and seventeen years old. He could "knock a beef in the head," swing a maul and hit a cow between the eyes, skin the hide, halve and quarter it, carve out the tallow,[59] the steaks, kidneys, liver.

And the hiding-places of fresh spring water under the earth crust   **130** had to be in his thoughts; he helped at well-digging; the wells Tom Lincoln dug went dry one year after another; neighbors said Tom was always digging a well and had his land "honey-combed";[60] and the boy, Abe, ran the errands and held the tools for the well-digging.

When he was eighteen years old, he could take an ax at the end of the handle and hold it out in a straight horizontal line, easy and steady—he had strong shoulder muscles and steady wrists early in life. He walked thirty-four miles in one day, just on an errand, to please himself, to hear a lawyer make a speech. He could tell his body to do almost impossible things, and the body obeyed.   **140**

Growing from boy to man, he was alone a good deal of the time. Days came often when he was by himself all the time except at break-

---

[50] **crowbar**—long, slender tool of iron or steel (ordinarily used for prying apart nailed objects). [51] **pegs**—wood or metal pins. [52] **cleats**—pieces of wood or metal, usually fastened to something to give strength. [53] **the scythe and the cradle:** a) scythe— tool for cutting hay and grain; b) cradle—frame attached to the scythe to catch the cut grain. [54] **shucking corn**—removing the corn husks (outer covering). [55] **carcass**— body. [56] **hind hocks**—joints on back legs of animals (equivalent to human ankles). [57] **gang**—group. [58] **"cracklings"**—browned, crisp skin or rind of pork. [59] **tallow**— hard fat used primarily to make soap and candles. [60] **"honey-combed"**—pitted with holes or marks like the comb where bees store honey.

fast and supper hours in the cabin home. In some years more of his time was spent in loneliness than in the company of other people. It happened, too, that this loneliness he knew was not like that of people in cities who can look from a window on streets where faces pass and repass. It was the wilderness loneliness[61] he became acquainted with, solved, filtered through[62] body, eye, and brain, held communion[63] within his ears, in the temples of his forehead, in the works of his beating heart.   150

He lived with trees, with the bush wet with shining raindrops, with the burning bush[64] of autumn, with the lone wild duck riding a north wind and crying down on a line north to south, the faces of open sky and weather, the ax which is an individual one-man instrument, these he had for companions, books, friends, talkers, chums of his endless changing soliloquies.[65]

His moccasin feet in the winter-time knew the white spaces of snowdrifts piled in whimsical[66] shapes against timber slopes or blown in levels across the fields of last year's cut corn stalks; in the summer-time his bare feet toughened in the gravel[67] of green streams while he   160 laughed back to the chatter of bluejays in the red-haw trees or while he kept his eyes ready in the slough[68] quack-grass for the cow-snake, the rattler, the copperhead.[69]

He rested between spells[70] of work in the springtime when the upward push of the coming out of the new grass can be heard, and in autumn weeks when the rustle of a single falling leaf[71] lets go a whisper that a listening ear can catch.

He found his life thrown in ways where there was a certain chance for a certain growth. And so he grew. Silence found him; he met silence. In the making of him as he was, the element[72] of silence was   170 immense.

[61] wilderness loneliness—solitude of an uninhabited region. [62] filtered through—passed slowly through; went through. [63] communion—an intimate conversation. [64] burning bush—bush with red and yellow leaves. [65] soliloquies—conversations with himself. [66] whimsical—fantastic. [67] gravel—coarse mixture of very small stones and rock fragments. [68] slough—swamp. [69] the cow-snake, the rattler, the copperhead —types of poisonous snakes. [70] spells—periods. [71] rustle of a single falling leaf—soft sound of a leaf rubbing against other leaves as it falls. [72] element—factor, or basic characteristic.

THOMAS WOLFE *(1900 – 1939)*

Thomas Wolfe was born in Asheville, North Carolina; he lived in the South until his graduation from the University of North Carolina in 1920, when he went to Harvard University and obtained a Master's degree. After that, he traveled abroad and for a time taught English at New York University. He was considered one of the most promising writers of his generation upon publication in 1929 of his first novel, *Look Homeward, Angel.* The rest of his short life, less than ten years after the appearance of his first book, was devoted to writing. Despite poor health and tortured emotions, he wrote three major novels as well as numerous short stories.

Much of Wolfe's writing is characterized by autobiographical self-examination. His lengthy novels have been criticized for their unrestrained, unformed style, but they have been praised for passages containing heights of intense feeling and flowing descriptions of persons, places, and moods. Some of the most vivid, powerful, and poetic passages from his books have been collected in *The Face of a Nation* (1953), including the two selections here, which originally appeared in the novel *Of Time and the River,* published in 1935: "Man's Youth," which reveals the searching and longing soul of the author, and "Hunger to Devour the Earth," which describes the frustrations of a man who wanted to discover everything—to know everyone in the world and to read every book—but who could not achieve this impossible ambition.

Man's Youth

*M*AN'S YOUTH IS A WONDERFUL thing: it is so full of anguish[1] and of magic[2] and he never comes to know it as it is,[3] until it has gone from him forever. It is the thing he cannot bear to lose,[4] it is the thing whose passing he watches with infinite sorrow and regret,[5] it is the thing whose loss he must lament

---

[1] anguish—pain; suffering; sorrow; frustration. [2] magic—joy; wonder; newness. [3] never comes to know it as it is—never fully understands or realizes what being young really is. [4] bear to lose—stand to part with. [5] infinite sorrow and regret—great sadness and disappointment.

forever,[6] and it is the thing whose loss he really welcomes with a sad and secret joy, the thing he would never willingly re-live again, could it be restored[7] to him by any magic.

Why is this? The reason is that the strange and bitter miracle of   10
life is nowhere else so evident[8] as in our youth. And what is the essence[9] of that strange and bitter miracle of life which we feel so poignantly,[10] so unutterably,[11] with such a bitter pain and joy, when we are young? It is this: that being rich, we are so poor; that being mighty, we can yet have nothing; that seeing, breathing, smelling, tasting all around us the impossible wealth and glory of this earth, feeling with an intolerable certitude[12] that the whole structure of the enchanted life—the most fortunate, wealthy, good, and happy life that any man has ever known—is ours—is ours at once, immediately and forever, the moment that we choose to take a step, or stretch a   20
hand, or say a word—we yet know that we can really keep, hold, take, and possess forever—nothing. All passes; nothing lasts: the moment that we put our hand upon it it melts away like smoke, is gone forever, and the snake is eating at our heart[13] again; we see then what we are and what our lives must come to.[14]

A young man is so strong, so mad,[15] so certain, and so lost.[16] He has everything and he is able to use nothing. He hurls the great shoulder of his strength[17] forever against phantasmal barriers,[18] he is a wave whose power explodes[19] in lost mid-oceans under timeless skies,[20] he reaches out to grip a fume of painted smoke;[21] he wants all,   30
feels the thirst and power for everything, and finally gets nothing. In the end, he is destroyed by his own strength, devoured by his own hunger,[22] impoverished by his own wealth.[23] Thoughtless of money[24] or the accumulation of[25] material possessions, he is none the less de-

6 lament forever—grieve for the rest of life.   7 restored—given back.   8 nowhere else so evident: a) nowhere else—at no other time or period; b) so evident—so apparent or obvious.   9 essence—true inner nature.   10 poignantly—sharply and deeply; keenly. 11 unutterably—unspeakably.   12 intolerable certitude: a) intolerable—unbearable; unjustifiable; b) certitude—certainty; sureness.   13 the snake is eating at our heart—a feeling of greed or of guilt is torturing us.   14 what our lives must come to—what the final result of our lives will be (that is, growing old and dying).   15 mad—blindly enthusiastic.   16 so strong, so mad, so certain, and so lost—so filled with contradictions. 17 hurls the great shoulder of his strength—spends great energy.   18 phantasmal barriers: a) phantasmal—imaginary; b) barriers—obstacles; difficulties.   19 explodes—bursts suddenly; breaks.   20 a wave whose power explodes in lost mid-oceans under timeless skies—like a great wave that breaks, not on the shore, but out in the middle of the ocean where strength is lost, where time is of no importance.   21 grip a fume of painted smoke—catch hold of a wisp of colored smoke (the word painted indicates that the smoke is attractive).   22 devoured by his own hunger—eaten up by his own desires.   23 impoverished by his own wealth—made poor by all that he possesses (strength, health, courage).   24 thoughtless of money—not thinking of money.   25 accumulation of—acquiring of; piling up of; collecting together of.

feated in the end by his own greed[26]—a greed that makes the avarice[27] of King Midas[28] seem paltry[29] by comparison.[30]

And that is the reason why, when youth is gone, every man will look back upon[31] that period of his life with infinite sorrow and regret. It is the bitter sorrow and regret of a man who knows that once he had a great talent and wasted it, of a man who knows that once he had a great treasure and got nothing from it, of a man who knows that he had strength enough for everything and never used it.

40

[26] **greed**—excessive desire for more than one has.   [27] **avarice**—great desire to possess and hold on to riches of some kind.   [28] **King Midas**—a legendary king who, at his request, was granted the power to turn into gold whatever he touched, but who wanted to be relieved of his power when he found that even his food turned to gold.   [29] **paltry** —insignificant.   [30] **by comparison**—when compared to youth's selfish desire to have everything, do everything, see everything.   [31] **look back upon**—remember; recall.

Hunger to Devour the Earth

*H*E NEVER KNEW; BUT NOW MAD fury[1] gripped[2] his life, and he was haunted[3] by the dream of time. Ten years must come and go without a moment's rest from fury, ten years of fury, hunger, all of the wandering in a young man's life. And for what? For what?

What is the fury which this youth will feel, which will lash him on against the great earth forever? It is the brain that maddens with its own excess, the heart that breaks from the anguish of its own frustration.[4] It is the hunger that grows from everything it feeds upon, the thirst that gulps down[5] rivers and remains insatiate.[6] It is to see a million men, a million faces and to be a stranger and an alien to them always. It is to prowl[7] the stacks of an enormous library at night, to tear the books out of a thousand shelves, to read in them with the mad hunger of the youth of man.

It is to have the old unquiet mind, the famished[8] heart, the restless soul; it is to lose hope, heart, and all joy utterly,[9] and then to have them wake again, to have the old feeling return with overwhelming[10] force that he is about to find the thing for which his life obscurely and desperately is groping[11]—for which all men on this earth have sought—one face out of the million faces, a wall, a door, a place of certitude and peace and wandering no more. For what is it that we Americans are seeking always on this earth? Why is it we have crossed the stormy seas so many times alone, lain in a thousand alien rooms at night hearing the sounds of time, dark time, and thought until heart, brain, flesh and spirit were sick and weary with the thought of it; "Where shall I go now? What shall I do?"

He did not know the moment that it came, but it came instantly, at once. And from that moment on mad fury seized him, from that moment on, his life, more than the life of any one that he would ever know, was to be spent in solitude[12] and wandering. Why this

10

20

30

1 **mad fury:** *a*) **mad**—unreasoning; insane; *b*) **fury**—uncontrollable craving or obsession. 2 **gripped**—seized; took hold of. 3 **haunted**—obsessed; troubled in the mind. 4 **of its own frustration**—of being unable to gratify its own desires. 5 **gulps down**—swallows quickly. 6 **insatiate**—never satisfied. 7 **prowl**—roam; wander about. 8 **famished**—starved. 9 **utterly**—completely. 10 **overwhelming**—overpowering. 11 **groping**—searching blindly or uncertainly. 12 **solitude**—isolation.

was true, or how it happened, he would never know; yet it was so. From this time on—save for two intervals in his life—he was to live about as solitary[13] a life as a modern man can have. And it is meant by this that the number of hours, days, months, and years—the actual time he spent alone—would be immense and extraordinary.

And this fact was all the more astonishing because he never seemed to seek out solitude, nor did he shrink from life, or seek to build himself into a wall away from all the fury and the turmoil[14] of the earth. Rather, he loved life so dearly that he was driven mad by   **40** the thirst and hunger which he felt for it. Of this fury, which was to lash and drive him on for fifteen years, the thousandth part could not be told, and what is told may seem unbelievable, but it is true. He was driven by a hunger so literal,[15] cruel and physical that it wanted to devour the earth and all the things and people in it, and when it failed in this attempt, his spirit would drown in an ocean of horror and desolation, smothered[16] below the overwhelming tides of this great earth, sickened and made sterile,[17] hopeless, dead, by the stupe-fying[18] weight of men and objects in the world, the everlasting flock and flooding of the crowd.   **50**

Now he would prowl the stacks of the library at night, pulling books out of a thousand shelves and reading in them like a madman. The thought of these vast stacks of books would drive him mad: the more he read, the less he seemed to know—the greater the number of the books he read, the greater the immense uncountable number of those which he could never read would seem to be. Within a period of ten years he read at least 20,000 volumes—deliberately the number is set low—and opened the pages and looked through many times that number. This may seem unbelievable, but it happened. Dryden said this about Ben Jonson: "Other men read books but he read li-   **60** braries"—and so now was it with this boy. Yet this terrific orgy of the books brought him no comfort, peace, or wisdom of the mind and heart. Instead, his fury and despair increased from what they fed upon, his hunger mounted[19] with the food it ate.

He read insanely, by the hundreds, the thousands, the ten thousands, yet he had no desire to be bookish; no one could describe this mad assault upon print as scholarly: a ravening[20] appetite in him demanded that he read everything that had ever been written about human experience. . . .

This fury which drove him on to read so many books had nothing   **70**

---

13 **solitary**—alone. 14 **turmoil**—confusion; uproar; great disturbance. 15 **literal**—actual; real. 16 **smothered**—suffocated. 17 **sterile**—unproductive. 18 **stupefying**—amazing; astounding. 19 **mounted**—increased. 20 **ravening**—insanely greedy.

to do with scholarship, nothing to do with academic honors, nothing
to do with formal learning. He was not in any way a scholar and did
not want to be one. He simply wanted to know about everything on
earth; he wanted to devour the earth, and it drove him mad when he
saw he could not do this. And it was the same with everything he did.
In the midst of a furious burst of reading in the enormous library, the
thought of the streets outside and the great city all around him would
drive through his body like a sword. It would now seem to him that
every second that he passed among the books was being wasted—that
at this moment something priceless, irrecoverable was happening in
the streets, and that if only he could get to it in time and see it, he
would somehow get the knowledge of the whole thing in him—the
source, the well, the spring from which all men and words and actions, and every design upon this earth proceeds.

And he would rush out in the streets to find it, be hurled through
the tunnel into Boston and then spend hours in driving himself
savagely[21] through a hundred streets, looking into the faces of a million people, trying to get an instant and conclusive[22] picture of all they
did and said and were, of all their million destinies, and of the great
city and the everlasting earth, and the immense and lonely skies that
bent above them. And he would search the furious streets until bone
and brain and blood could stand no more—until every sinew[23] of his
life and spirit was wrung, trembling and exhausted, and his heart
sank down beneath its weight of desolation and despair.

Yet a furious hope, a wild extravagant belief,[24] was burning in him
all the time. He would write down enormous charts and plans and
projects of all that he proposed to do in life—a program of work and
living which would have exhausted the energies of 10,000 men. He
would get up in the middle of the night to scrawl[25] down insane catalogs of all that he had seen and done:—the number of books he had
read, the number of miles he had travelled, the number of people he
had known, . . . the number of meals he had eaten, the number of
towns he had visited, the number of states he had been in.

And at one moment he would gloat and chuckle[26] over these stupendous[27] lists like a miser[28] gloating over his hoard,[29] only to groan
bitterly with despair the next moment, and to beat his head against

---

21 **savagely**—fiercely. 22 **conclusive**—decisive;   firm;   definite. 23 **sinew**—strength;
force.   24 **extravagant belief**—belief beyond the limits of reason. 25 **to scrawl**—to
write hastily (usually rapidly and without forming the letters carefully).   26 **gloat and
chuckle**—gaze and laugh with great satisfaction.   27 **stupendous**—amazingly large; overwhelming.   28 **miser**—person who stores or keeps money without making use of it.
29 **hoard**—store of money (or any other object of value).

the wall, as he remembered the overwhelming amount of all he had
not seen or done, or known. Then he would begin another list filled
with enormous catalogs of all the books he had not read, all the food
he had not eaten, . . . all the states he had not been in, all the towns   110
he had not visited. Then he would write down plans and programs
whereby all these things must be accomplished, how many years it
would take to do it all, and how old he would be when he had finished. An enormous wave of hope and joy would surge up in him, because it now looked easy, and he had no doubt at all that he could
do it.

He never asked himself in any practical way how he was going to
live while this was going on, where he was going to get the money for
this gigantic adventure, and what he was going to do to make it possible. If he thought about it, it seemed to have no importance or   120
reality whatever—he just dismissed it impatiently, or with a conviction
that some old man would die and leave him a fortune, that he was
going to pick up a purse containing hundreds of thousands of dollars
while walking in the Fenway, and that the reward would be enough
to keep him going, or that a beautiful and rich young widow, true-
hearted, tender, loving, and voluptuous, who had carrot-colored hair,
little freckles on her face, a snub nose[30] and luminous[31] gray-green
eyes with something wicked yet loving and faithful in them, and one
gold filling in her solid little teeth, was going to fall in love with him,
marry him, and be forever true and faithful to him while he went   130
reading, eating, drinking, . . . and devouring his way around the
world; or finally that he would write a book or play every year or so,
which would be a great success, and yield[32] him fifteen or twenty
thousand dollars at a crack.[33] Thus, he went storming away at the
whole earth about him, sometimes mad with despair, weariness, and
bewilderment; and sometimes wild with a jubilant and exultant[34] joy
and certitude as the conviction[35] came to him that everything would
happen as he wished. Then at night he would hear the vast sounds
and silence of the earth and of the city, he would begin to think of
the dark sleeping earth and of the continent of night, until it seemed   140
to him it all was spread before him like a map—rivers, plains, and
mountains and 10,000 sleeping towns; it seemed to him that he saw
everything at once.

[30] **snub nose**—short, turned-up nose.   [31] **luminous**—clear; bright.   [32] **yield**—give.
[33] **at a crack**—at a time.   [34] **jubilant and exultant**—elated (or joyful) and triumphant
(jubilant and exultant are synonymous).   [35] **conviction**—strong belief.

LINCOLN BARNETT (1909 –   )

Lincoln Barnett, a native of New York, began his career as a journalist after receiving a master's degree from the Columbia School of Journalism. From 1931 to 1937 he was a reporter on the *New York Herald Tribune*. Next he served on *Life* magazine as a writer and associate editor. In 1946 he left the magazine to devote his time to free-lance writing, which has included such important articles for *Life* as the text for "The World's Great Religions" and "The World We Live In." Of special reward to him has been the success of *The Universe and Dr. Einstein*, the first chapter of which is reprinted here. This book was first published in 1949 and won a National Book Award[1] special citation; it has since been published in several other countries, including England, Italy, and Japan. The book tells of the eminent scientist's search for essential truth about the universe. Although it is written for the intelligent layman, the author has not falsified the complexities of the subject. Dr. Einstein himself gave credit to the author in the Foreword to the first edition of the book: "Lincoln Barnett's book represents a valuable contribution to popular scientific writing."

Today Mr. Barnett lives with his family in upper New York on Lake Champlain within sight of the Adirondack Mountains—a spot he has described as "conducive to brooding about space and time."

The Universe and Dr. Einstein

*C*ARVED[2] IN THE WHITE WALLS OF the Riverside Church in New York, the figures of six hundred great men of the ages—saints, philosophers, kings—stand in limestone immortality, surveying space and time with blank[3] imperishable[4] eyes. One panel[5] enshrines the geniuses of science, fourteen of them,

---

[1] **National Book Awards**—awards given each year since 1950 for outstanding books of poetry, fiction, and nonfiction. The awards have been made possible by the American Book Publishers Council, the American Booksellers Association, and the Book Manufacturers' Institute.   [2] **carved**—sculptured.   [3] **blank**—empty; vacant.   [4] **imperishable**—indestructible; endurable.   [5] **panel**—section or strip on the wall.

spanning[6] the centuries from Hippocrates, who died around 370 B.C., to Albert Einstein, who died in 1955. In this whole sculptured gallery of the illustrious[7] dead, Einstein is the only one who shook the world[8] within the memory of most living men.　　　　　　　　　　10

It is equally noteworthy that of the thousands of people who worship weekly at Manhattan's most spectacular Protestant church, probably 99 per cent would be hard pressed[9] to explain why Einstein's image is there. It is there because a generation ago, when the iconography[10] of the church was being planned, Dr. Harry Emerson Fosdick[11] wrote letters to a group of the nation's leading scientists asking them to submit lists of the fourteen greatest names in scientific history. Their ballots varied. Most of them included Archimedes, Euclid, Galileo, and Newton. But on every list appeared the name of Albert Einstein.　　　　　　　　　　20

The vast gap[12] that has persisted[13] for more than fifty years—since 1905, when the Theory of Special Relativity was first published—between Einstein's scientific eminence[14] and public understanding of it is the measure of a gap in American education. Today most newspaper readers know vaguely that Einstein had something to do with the atomic bomb; beyond that his name is simply a synonym for the abstruse.[15] While his theories form part of the body of modern science, many of them are not yet part of the modern curriculum. It is not surprising therefore that many a college graduate still thinks of Einstein as a kind of mathematical surrealist[16] rather than as the　30 discoverer of certain cosmic laws of immense importance in man's slow struggle to understand physical reality. He may not realize that Relativity, over and above its scientific import,[17] comprises[18] a major philosophical system which augments[19] and illumines the reflections of the great epistemologists—[20] Locke, Berkeley, and Hume. Consequently he has very little notion of the vast, arcane,[21] and mysteriously ordered universe in which he dwells.

*　　*　　*

[6] spanning—extending over; reaching across; bridging.　[7] illustrious—distinguished. [8] who shook the world—who caused a revolution in thinking around the world; whose work created an impact felt around the world.　[9] would be hard pressed—would find it difficult.　[10] iconography—representation (in this case, the representation of great men by statues).　[11] Dr. Harry Emerson Fosdick—American clergyman; pastor of the Riverside Church, 1930–1946.　[12] vast gap: a) vast—extensive; large; b) gap—blank space.　[13] persisted—lasted; continued without change.　[14] eminence—prominence; greatness; distinction.　[15] the abstruse—the difficult to understand.　[16] surrealist—follower of movement in literature and art that seeks to express activities of the subconscious mind, characterized by irrational arrangement of material.　[17] import—implication; meaning; importance.　[18] comprises—includes; covers.　[19] augments—increases; enlarges.　[20] epistemologists—philosophers who investigate the origin, nature, and methods of how we come to know.　[21] arcane—secret.

Dr. Einstein, long professor emeritus[22] at the Institute for Advanced Study in Princeton, spent the last years of his life working on a problem which had baffled[23] him for more than a quarter of a century. This was his Unified Field Theory, which attempted to set forth in one series of mutually consistent equations the physical laws governing two of the fundamental forces of the universe, gravitation and electromagnetism. The significance of this task can be appreciated only when one realizes that most of the phenomena of our external world seem to be produced by these two primordial[24] forces. Until a hundred years ago electricity and magnetism—while known and studied since early Greek times—were regarded as separate quantities. But the experiments of Oersted and Faraday in the nineteenth century showed that a current of electricity is always surrounded by a magnetic field, and conversely[25] that under certain conditions magnetic forces can induce[26] electrical currents. From these experiments came the discovery of the electromagnetic field through which light waves, radio waves, and all other electromagnetic disturbances are propagated[27] in space.

Thus electricity and magnetism may be considered as aspects of a single force. Save for gravitation and the newly discovered, little understood meson[28] forces which appear to hold the various parts of the atomic nucleus together, nearly all other forces in the material universe—frictional forces, chemical forces which hold atoms together in molecules, cohesive forces which bind larger particles of matter, elastic forces which cause bodies to maintain their shape—are of electromagnetic origin; for all of these involve the interplay of matter, and all matter is composed of atoms which in turn are composed of electrical particles. Yet the similarities between gravitational and electromagnetic phenomena are very striking.[29] The planets spin in the gravitational field of the sun; electrons swirl[30] in the electromagnetic field of the atomic nucleus. The earth, moreover, is a big magnet—a peculiar fact which is apparent to anyone who has ever used a compass. The sun also has a magnetic field. And so have all the stars.

Although many attempts have been made to identify gravitational attraction as an electromagnetic effect, all have failed. Einstein thought he had succeeded in 1929 and published a unified field theory

---

[22] **professor emeritus**—professor retired honorably from teaching because of age. [23] **baffled**—puzzled.   [24] **primordial**—elementary; originating.   [25] **conversely**—in reverse order; the other way around.   [26] **induce**—cause; produce.   [27] **propagated**—transmitted.   [28] **meson**—elementary particle (located between the mass of the electron and the mass of the proton).   [29] **striking**—noticeable; remarkable; extraordinary.   [30] **swirl** —move in large circles.

which he later rejected as inadequate. His new theory, completed in the final days of 1949, was far more ambitious; for it promulgated[31] a set of universal laws designed to encompass[32] not only the boundless gravitational and electromagnetic fields of interstellar space but also the tiny, terrible field inside the atom. Whether the whole grand objective of a Unified Field Theory will be realized only many more months or years of mathematical and experimental work can determine. But in its vast cosmic picture, when fully revealed, the abyss[33] between macrocosmos and microcosmos—the very big and the very little—will surely be bridged, and the whole complex of the universe will resolve into a homogeneous fabric[34] in which matter and energy are indistinguishable and all forms of motion from the slow wheeling of the galaxies to the wild flight of electrons become simply changes in the structure and concentration of the primordial field.

Since the aim of science is to describe and explain the world we live in, such a theory would, by thus defining the manifold of nature within the terms of a single harmonious theory, attain its loftiest goal. The meaning of the word "explain," however, suffers a contraction[35] with man's every step in quest of reality. Science cannot yet really "explain" electricity, magnetism, and gravitation; their effects can be measured and predicted, but of their ultimate nature no more is known to the modern scientist than to Thales of Miletus, who first speculated on the electrification of amber[36] around 585 B.C. Most contemporary physicists reject the notion that man can ever discover what these mysterious forces "really" are. Electricity, Bertrand Russell says, "is not a thing, like St. Paul's Cathedral; it is a way in which things behave. When we have told how things behave when they are electrified, and under what circumstances they are electrified, we have told all there is to tell." Until recently scientists would have scorned[37] such a thesis. Aristotle, whose natural science dominated Western thought for two thousand years, believed that man could arrive at an understanding of ultimate reality by reasoning from *self-evident principles*. It is, for example, a self-evident principle that everything in the universe has its proper place, hence one can deduce[38] that objects fall to the ground because that's where they belong, and smoke goes up because that's where *it* belongs. The goal of Aristotelian science was

[31] **promulgated**—set forth.   [32] **encompass**—encircle; cover; comprise.   [33] **abyss**—bottomless gulf or pit (in this case, a deep, immeasurable space, or a wide gap or gulf).   [34] **fabric**—cloth; material; structure.   [35] **suffers a contraction**—undergoes a delimitation (the meaning of the word "explain" is increasingly restricted in scope).   [36] **amber**—a yellowish or reddish fossil resin (capable of gaining a negative electrical charge by friction).   [37] **scorned**—felt contempt for.   [38] **deduce**—arrive at a conclusion.

to explain *why* things happen. Modern science was born when Gali-   110
leo began trying to explain *how* things happen and thus originated the
method of controlled experiment which now forms the basis of scientific investigation.

Out of Galileo's discoveries and those of Newton in the next
generation there evolved[39] a mechanical universe of forces, pressures,
tensions, oscillations,[40] and waves. There seemed to be no process of
nature which could not be described in terms of ordinary experience,
illustrated by a concrete model or predicted by Newton's amazingly
accurate laws of mechanics. But before the turn of the past century
certain deviations[41] from these laws became apparent; and though   120
these deviations were slight, they were of such a fundamental nature
that the whole edifice[42] of Newton's machine-like universe began to
topple.[43] The certainty that science can explain *how* things happen
began to dim[44] about twenty years ago. And right now it is a question
whether scientific man is in touch with "reality" at all—or can ever
hope to be.

[39] **evolved**—gradually developed.   [40] **oscillations**—regular movements.   [41] **deviations**—
departures from the standard or normal course.   [42] **edifice**—structure.   [43] **topple**—
fall over.   [44] **dim**—fade; grow less bright.

JOHN STEINBECK (1902 –   )

John Steinbeck grew up in California and attended Stanford University, where he studied marine biology. He worked at various jobs before he rose to fame in the 1930's with his novels about the difficulties of farm workers during the Depression. His point of view was realistic but sympathetic toward his poverty-stricken characters. Perhaps best known is *The Grapes of Wrath*. His later writing included *The Moon Is Down*, an anti-Nazi novel, *Cannery Row*, a novel about some lovable idlers and a biologist who listened to their tales, and *The Sea of Cortez*, the account of an expedition to the Gulf of California.

The following selection is taken from "The Log" from *The Sea of Cortez* (1941), a day-by-day narration of the trip made on a small ship by Steinbeck, his good friend Edward F. Ricketts, a marine biologist, and their crew, including Tony, Sparky, and Tiny, who are mentioned in this selection. The objective of this trip was partly marine research and partly speculation and adventure, or, in Steinbeck's words, "This little trip of ours was . . . a dual thing, with collecting and eating and sleeping merging with the thinking-speculating activity." The log entry dated March 17, given here, tells of their approach to the Port of San Lucas, where they anchor to await the visit of Mexican port officials. It gives a good idea of the nature and spirit of the trip, for it includes descriptions of sea life and of collecting in the tide pools, wonderings about place names, and thoughts about Darwin.

The Log: March 17

*A*T TWO A.M. WE PASSED POINT LA-zaro,[1] one of the reputedly dangerous places[2] of the world, like Cedros Passage, or like Cape Horn, where the weather is always bad even when it is good elsewhere. There is a sense of relief when one is safely past these half-mythical places, for they are not only stormy but

---

[1] **Point Lazaro** (NOTE: In this selection, place names mentioned are for the most part located in Lower California. It is suggested that those interested in the exact location of these places should refer to a map of the Gulf of California.)   [2] **reputedly dangerous places**—places known to be dangerous.

treacherous,[3] and again the atavistic[4] fear arises—the Scylla-Charybdis[5] fear that made our ancestors people such places with monsters and enter them only after prayer and propitiation.[6] It was only reasonably rough when we passed, and immediately south the water was very   10 calm. About five in the morning we came upon an even denser concentration of the little red *Pleuroncodes*,[7] and we stopped again and took a great many of them. While we netted the *langustina*, a skipjack struck the line and we brought him in and had him for breakfast. During the meal we said the fish was *Katsuwonus pelamis*, and Sparky said it was a skipjack because he was eating it and he was quite sure he would not eat *Katsuwonus pelamis* ever. A few hours later we caught two small dolphins, startlingly beautiful fish of pure gold, pulsing and fading and changing colors. These fish are very widely distributed.   20

We were coming now toward the end of our day-and-night running; the engine had never paused since we left San Diego except for idling[8] the little time while we took the *langustina*. The coastline of the Peninsula slid along, brown and desolate and dry with strange flat mountains and rocks torn by dryness, and the heat shimmer hung over the land even in March. Tony had kept us well offshore, and only now we approached closer to land, for we would arrive at Cape San Lucas in the night, and from then on we planned to run only in the daytime. Some collecting stations we had projected, like Pulmo Reef and La Paz and Angeles Bay, but except for those, we planned to stop   30 wherever the shore looked interesting. Even this little trip of ninety hours, though, had grown long, and we were glad to be getting to the end of it. The dry hills were red gold that afternoon and in the night no one left the top of the deckhouse. The Southern Cross was well above the horizon, and the air was warm and pleasant. Tony spent a long time in the galley[9] going over the charts. He had been to Cape San Lucas once before. Around ten o'clock we saw the lighthouse on the false cape. The night was extremely dark when we

[3] **treacherous**—dangerous; not to be depended on.   [4] **atavistic fear**—primitive type of fear.   [5] **Scylla-Charybdis**—A dangerous rock (Scylla) on the Italian side of the Strait of Messina and a whirlpool (Charybdis) that faces it. (In Greek mythology the rock and the whirlpool were personified as female monsters and were thought of as two evils or dangers—one of which could be avoided only by taking the risks of the other.) [6] **propitiation**—act to win good will or to appease; appeasement.   [7] **Pleuroncodes**—technical term used in marine biology. (NOTE: Technical terms, occurring frequently in this selection, are not defined. Also, names of sea plants and animals, such as *sand verbena* and *dolphin*, are not usually defined. The assumption is that such definitions are not essential for a general understanding of the selection. Those interested in more specific information should consult a reliable dictionary.)   [8] **idling**—running slowly with the motor barely turning over.   [9] **galley**—ship's kitchen.

rounded the end; the great tall rocks called "The Friars" were blackly
visible. The *Coast Pilot*[10] spoke of a light on the end of the San Lucas   40
pier, but we could see no light. Tony edged[11] the boat slowly into the
dark harbor. Once a flashlight showed for a moment on the shore and
then went out. It was after midnight, and of course there would be no
light in a Mexican house at such a time. The searchlight on our deckhouse seemed to be sucked up[12] by the darkness. Sparky on the bow
with the leadline found deep water, and we moved slowly in, stopping
and drifting and sounding.[13] And then suddenly there was the beach,
thirty feet away, with little waves breaking on it, and still we had eight
fathoms on the lead.[14] We backed away a little and dropped the
anchor and waited until it took a firm grip. Then the engine stopped,   50
and we sat for a long time on the deckhouse. The sweet smell of the
land blew out to us on a warm wind, a smell of sand verbena and grass
and mangrove. It is so quickly forgotten, this land smell. We know
it so well on shore that the nose forgets it, but after a few days at sea
the odor memory pattern is lost so that the first land smell strikes a
powerful emotional nostalgia,[15] very sharp and strangely dear.

In the morning the black mystery of the night was gone and the
little harbor was shining and warm. The tuna cannery against the gathering rocks of the point and a few houses along the edge of the
beach were the only habitations visible. And with the day came the   60
answer to the lightlessness of the night before. The *Coast Pilot* had
not been wrong. There is indeed a light on the end of the cannery
pier, but since the electricity is generated by the cannery engine, and
since the cannery engine runs only in the daytime, so the light burns
only in the daytime. With the arrived day, this light came on and
burned bravely until dusk, when it went off again. But the *Coast Pilot*
was absolved, it had not lied. Even Tony, who had been a little bitter
the night before, was forced to revise his first fierceness.[16] And perhaps it was a lesson to Tony in exact thinking, like those carefully
worded puzzles in joke books; the *Pilot* said a light burned—it only   70
neglected to say when, and we ourselves supplied the fallacy.[17]

The great rocks on the end of the Peninsula are almost literary.
They are a fitting Land's End, standing against the sea, the end of a
thousand miles of peninsula and mountain. Good Hope is this way
too, and perhaps we take some of our deep feelings of termination

---

[10] **Coast Pilot**—book used as a navigational guide to the area.   [11] **edged**—cautiously
moved.   [12] **sucked up**—absorbed; pulled up.   [13] **sounding**—taking depth measure-
ments.   [14] **lead**—line to measure depth.   [15] **nostalgia**—the remembering of things in
the past with longing.   [16] **fierceness**—wild anger; savageness.   [17] **fallacy**—misleading
notion; unsound reasoning.

from these things, and they make our symbols. The Friars stood high and protective against an interminable[18] sea.

Clavigero, a Jesuit monk, came to the Point and the Peninsula over two hundred years ago. We quote from the Lake and Gray translation of his history of Lower California, page fifteen: "This Cape is its southern terminus, the Red River [Colorado] is the eastern limit, and the harbor of San Diego, situated at 33 degrees north latitude and about 156 degrees longitude, can be called its western limit. To the north and the northeast it borders on the countries of barbarous nations little known on the coasts and not at all in the interior. To the west it has the Pacific Sea and on the east the Gulf of California, already called the Red Sea because of its similarity to the Red Sea, and the Sea of Cortés, named in honor of the famous conqueror of Mexico who had it discovered and who navigated it. The length of the Peninsula is about 10 degrees, but its width varies from 30 to 70 miles and more.

"The name, California," Clavigero goes on, "was applied to a single port in the beginning, but later it was extended[19] to mean all the Peninsula. Some geographers have even taken the liberty of comprising under this denomination[20] New Mexico, the country of the Apaches,[21] and other regions very remote from the true California and which have nothing to do with it."

Clavigero says of its naming, "The origin of this name is not known, but it is believed that the conqueror, Cortés, who pretended to have some knowledge of Latin, named the harbor, where he put in, 'Callida fornax' because of the great heat which he felt there; and that either he himself or some one of the many persons who accompanied him formed the name California from these two words. If this conjecture[22] be not true, it is at least credible."[23]

We like Clavigero for these last words. He was a careful man. The observations set down in his history of Baja California are surprisingly correct, and if not all true, they are at least all credible. He always gives one his choice. Perhaps his Jesuit training is never more evident than in this. "If you believe this," he says in effect, "perhaps you are not right, but at least you are not a fool."

Lake and Gray include an interesting footnote in their translation. "The famous corsair,[24] Drake, called California 'New Albion' in honor of his native land. Father Scherer, a German Jesuit, and M. de

---

18 **interminable**—endless. 19 **extended**—broadened or enlarged in scope or meaning. 20 **denomination**—name given to something belonging to a certain class or category (in this case, California). 21 **Apaches**—Apache Indians. 22 **conjecture**—idea or theory; calculated guess. 23 **credible**—believable; possible. 24 **corsair**—pirate.

Fer, a French geographer, used the name 'Carolina Island' to designate California, which name began to be used in the time of Charles II, King of Spain, when that Peninsula was considered an island, but these and other names were soon forgotten and that given it by the conqueror, Cortés, prevailed."

And in a second footnote, Lake and Gray continue, "We shall add the opinion of the learned ex-Jesuit, Don José Campoi, on the etymology[25] of the name, 'California,' or 'Californias' as others say. This Father believes that the said name is composed of the Spanish word '*Cala*' which means a small cove of the sea, and the latin word '*fornix*' which means an arch; because there is a small cove at the cape of San Lucas on the western side of which there overhangs a rock pierced in such a way that in the upper part of that great opening is seen an arch formed so perfectly that it appears made by human skill. Therefore Cortés, noticing the cove and arch, and understanding Latin, probably gave to that port the name 'California' or *Cala-y-fornix*, speaking half Spanish and half Latin.

"To these conjectures we could add a third one, composed of both, by saying that the name is derived from *Cala*, as Campoi thinks, and *fornax*, as the author believes, because of the cove, and the heat which Cortés felt there, and that the latter might have called that place *Cala, y fornax*." This ends the footnote.

Our feeling about this, and all the erudite[26] discussion of the origin of this and other names, is that none of these is true. Names attach themselves to places and stick or fall away. When men finally go to live in Antarctica it is unlikely that they will ever speak of the Rockefeller Mountains or use the name designated by breakfast food companies. More likely a name emerges almost automatically from a place as well as from a man and the relationship between name and thing is very close. In the naming of places in the West this has seemed apparent. In this connection there are two examples: in the Sierras there are two little mountains which were called by the early settlers "Maggie's Bubs." This name was satisfactory and descriptive, but it seemed vulgar to later and more delicate[27] lovers of nature, who tried to change the name a number of times and failing, in usage at least, finally surrendered and called them "The Maggies," explaining that it was an Indian name. In the same way Dog————Point (and I am delicate only for those same nature lovers) has had finally to be called in print "The Dog." It does not look like a dog, but it does look like

[25] **etymology**—origin and development (of a word).   [26] **erudite**—learned; scholarly.
[27] **delicate**—over-nice; modest.

that part of a dog which first suggested its name. However, anyone seeing this point immediately reverts to the designation which was anatomically accurate and strangely satisfying to the name-giving faculty. And this name-giving faculty is very highly developed and deeply rooted in our atavistic magics. To name a thing has always been to make it familiar and therefore a little less dangerous to us. "Tree" the abstract may harbor some evil until it has a name, but once having a name one can cope with it.[28] A tree is not dangerous, but the forest is. Among primitives sometimes evil is escaped by never mentioning the name, as in Malaysia, where one never mentions a tiger by name for fear of calling him. Among others, as even among ourselves, the giving of a name establishes familiarity which renders the thing impotent. It is interesting to see how some scientists and philosophers, who are an emotional and fearful group, are able to protect themselves against fear. In a modern scene, when the horizons stretch out and your philosopher is likely to fall off the world like a Dark Ages mariner, he can save himself by establishing a taboo-box which he may call "mysticism" or "supernaturalism" or "radicalism." Into this box he can throw all those thoughts which frighten him and thus be safe from them. But in geographic naming it seems almost as though the place contributed something to its own name. As Tony says, "The point draws the waves"—we say, "The place draws the name." It doesn't matter what California means; what does matter is that with all the names bestowed upon this place, "California" has seemed right to those who have seen it. And the meaningless word "California" has completely routed[29] all the "New Albions" and "Carolinas" from the scene.

The strangest case of nicknaming[30] we know concerns a man whose first name is Copeland. In three different parts of the country where he has gone, not knowing anyone, he has been called first "Copenhagen" and then "Hagen." This has happened automatically. He is Hagen. We don't know what quality of Hagen-ness he has, but there must be some. Why not "Copen" or "Cope"? It is never that. He is invariably Hagen. This, we realize, has become mystical, and anyone who wishes may now toss the whole thing into his taboo-box and slam the lid down on it.

The tip of the Cape at San Lucas, with the huge gray Friars standing up on the end, has behind the rocks a little beach which is a small

160

170

180

190

[28] cope with it—deal with it on equal terms. [29] routed—uprooted or driven out; forced out. [30] nicknaming—giving a name, usually short, in addition to or instead of the real name (for example, a boy named John Smith, who has bright red hair, might be called "Red" instead of "John").

boy's dream of pirates. It seems the perfect place to hide and from which to dart out[31] in a pinnace[32] on the shipping of the world; a place to which to bring the gold bars and jewels and beautiful ladies, all of which are invariably carried by the shipping of the world. And this little beach must so have appealed to earlier men, for the names of pirates are still in the rock, and the pirate ships did dart out of here and did come back. But now in back of the Friars on the beach there is a great pile of decaying hammer-head sharks, the livers torn out and the fish left to rot. Some day, and that soon, the more mature piracy which has abandoned the pinnace for the coast gun will stud[33] this   200
point with gray monsters and will send against the shipping of the Gulf, not little bands of ragged men, but projectiles filled with TNT. And from that piracy no jewels or beautiful ladies will come back to the beach behind the rocks.

On that first morning we cleaned ourselves well and shaved while we waited for the Mexican officials to come out and give us the right to land. They were late in coming, for they had to find their official uniforms, and they had to shave. Few boats put in here. It would not be well to waste the occasion of the visit of even a fishing boat like ours. It was noon before the well-dressed men in their sun helmets   210
came down to the beach and were rowed out to us. They were armed with the .45-caliber automatics which everywhere in Mexico designate officials. And they were armed also with the courtesy which is unique in official Mexico. No matter what they do to you, they are nice about it. We soon learned the routine in other ports as well as here. Everyone who has or can borrow a uniform comes aboard—the collector of customs in a washed and shiny uniform; the business agent in a business suit having about him what Tiny calls "a double-breasted look";[34] then soldiers if there are any; and finally the Indians, who row the boat and rarely have uniforms. They come over the side like ambassadors.   220
We shake hands all around. The galley has been prepared: coffee is ready and perhaps a drop of rum. Cigarettes are presented and then comes the ceremonial of the match. In Mexico cigarettes are cheap, but matches are not. If a man wishes to honor you, he lights your cigarette, and if you have given him a cigarette, he must so honor you. But having lighted your cigarette and his, the match is still burning and not being used. Anyone may now make use of this match. On a

[31] dart out—come out suddenly. [32] pinnace—a small sailing boat. [33] stud—strew; scatter. [34] double-breasted—pertaining to a coat or jacket that overlaps so that there are two thicknesses of the width of the breast, usually with buttons on each half of the front, in contrast to the single-buttoned or single-breasted style.

street, strangers who have been wishing for a light come up quickly and light from your match, bow,[35] and pass on.

We were impatient for the officials, and this time we did not have   230 to wait long. It developed that the Governor of the southern district had very recently been to Cape San Lucas and just before that a yacht[36] had put in. This simplified matters, for, having recently used them, the officials knew exactly where to find their uniforms, and, having found them, they did not, as sometimes happens, have to send them to be laundered before they could come aboard. About noon they trooped to the beach, scattering the pigs and Mexican vultures which browsed[37] happily there. They filled the rowboat until the gunwales[38] just missed dipping, and majestically they came along-side. We conducted the ceremony of clearing with some dignity, for   240 if we spoke to them in very bad Spanish, they in turn honored us with very bad English. They cleared us, drank coffee, smoked, and finally left, promising to come back. Much as we had enjoyed them, we were impatient, for the tide was dropping and the exposed rocks looked very rich with animal life.

All the time we were indulging in courtliness[39] there had been light gunfire on the cliffs, where several men were shooting at black cor-morants;[40] and it developed that everyone in Cape San Lucas hates cormorants. They are the flies in a perfect ecological ointment.[41] The cannery cans tuna; the entrails and cuttings of the tuna are thrown   250 into the water from the end of the pier. This refuse[42] brings in schools of small fish which are netted[43] and used for bait to catch tuna. This closed and tight circle is interfered with by the cormorants, who try to get at the bait-fish. They dive and catch fish, but also they drive the schools away from the pier out of easy reach of the baitmen. Thus they are considered interlopers, radicals, subversive forces against the perfect and God-set balance on Cape San Lucas. And they are rightly slaughtered, as all radicals should be. As one of our number remarked, "Why, pretty soon they'll want to vote."

Finally we could go. We unpacked the Hansen Sea-Cow[44] and   260 fastened it on the back of the skiff.[45] This was our first use of the Sea-

---

[35] bow (rhymes with "cow")—bend the body, usually from the waist, as a sign of respect. [36] yacht—type of boat.   [37] browsed—moved aimlessly, or without definite purpose; grazed.   [38] gunwales—the upper edge of the side of a ship or boat.   [39] indulging in courtliness—behaving according to manners or courtesies of the court.   [40] cormorants —type of birds.   [41] flies in a perfect ecological ointment: a) flies in the ointment— the bad thing that spoils what otherwise might be perfect; b) ecological—pertaining to study of relations between organisms and environment; c) ointment—a type of salve, a cream-like medication.   [42] refuse—discarded materials; garbage.   [43] netted—caught in a net.   [44] Hansen Sea-Cow—a type of motor to propel the boat.   [45] skiff—a type of small boat.

Cow. The shore was very close and we were able just by pulling on the starter rope to spin the propeller enough to get us to shore. The Sea-Cow did not run that day but it seemed to enjoy having its fly-wheel spun.

The shore-collecting equipment usually consisted of a number of small wrecking bars;[46] wooden fish-kits with handles; quart jars with screw caps; and many glass tubes. These tubes are invaluable for small and delicate animals: the chance of bringing them back uninjured is greatly increased if each individual, or at least only a few of like species, are kept in separate containers. We filled our pockets with these tubes. The soft animals must never be put in the same container with any of the livelier crabs, for these, when restrained or inhibited in any way, go into paroxysms of rage[47] and pinch[48] everything at random, even each other; sometimes even themselves.

The exposed rocks had looked rich with life under the lowering tide, but they were more than that: they were ferocious[49] with life. There was an exuberant[50] fierceness in the littoral[51] here, a vital competition for existence. Everything seemed speeded-up; starfish and urchins were more strongly attached than in other places, and many of the univalves were so tightly fixed that the shells broke before the animals would let go their hold. Perhaps the force of the great surf which beats on this shore has much to do with the tenacity[52] of the animals here. It is noteworthy that the animals, rather than deserting such beaten shores for the safe cove and protected pools, simply increase their toughness and fight back at the sea with a kind of joyful survival. This ferocious survival quotient excites us and makes us feel good, and from the crawling, fighting, resisting qualities of the animals, it almost seems that they are excited too.

We collected down the littoral as the water went down. We didn't seem to have time enough. We took samples of everything that came to hand. The uppermost rocks swarmed[53] with Sally Lightfoots, those beautiful and fast and sensitive crabs. With them were white periwinkle snails. Below that, barnacles and Purpura snails; more crabs and many limpets. Below that many serpulids—attached worms in calcareous[54] tubes with beautiful purple floriate heads. Below that, the multi-rayed starfish, *Heliaster kubiniji* of Xanthus. With *Heliaster* were a few urchins, but not many, and they were so placed in

---

[46] **wrecking bars**—pipes used to wreck or take things apart. [47] **paroxysms of rage**—sudden violent outbursts of anger. [48] **pinch**—squeeze painfully (with their claws). [49] **ferocious**—wildly savage; fierce. [50] **exuberant**—superabundant; overflowing. [51] **littoral**—shore region. [52] **tenacity**—persistence; refusal to let go or to give up. [53] **swarmed**—were covered. [54] **calcareous**—chalky.

crevices[55] as to be hard to dislodge.[56] Several resisted the steel bar to the extent of breaking—the mouth remaining tight to the rock while 300 the shell fell away. Lower still there were to be seen swaying in the water under the reefs the dark gorgonians, or sea-fans. In the lowest surf-levels there was a brilliant gathering of the moss animals known as bryozoa; flatworms; flat crabs; the large sea-cucumber; some anemones; many sponges of two types, a smooth, encrusting[57] purple one, the other erect, white, and calcareous. There were great colonies of tunicates, clusters of tiny individuals joined by a common tunic and looking so like the sponges that even a trained worker must await the specialist's determination to know whether his find is sponge or tunicate. This is annoying, for the sponge being one step above the 310 protozoa, at the bottom of the evolutionary ladder, and the tunicate near the top, bordering the vertebrates, your trained worker is likely to feel that a dirty trick has been played upon him by an entirely too democratic Providence.

We took many snails, including cones and murexes; a small red tectibranch (of a group to which the sea-hares belong); hydroids; many annelid worms; and a red pentagonal starfish. There were the usual hordes[58] of hermit crabs, but oddly enough we saw no chitons (sea-cradles), although the region seemed ideally suited to them.

We collected in haste. As the tide went down we kept a little ahead 320 of it, wading in rubber boots, and as it came up again it drove us back. The time seemed very short. The incredible beauty of the tide pools, the brilliant colors, the swarming species ate up the time. And when at last the afternoon surf began to beat on the littoral and covered it over again, we seemed barely to have started. But the buckets and jars and tubes were full, and when we stopped we discovered that we were very tired.

Our collecting ends were different from those ordinarily entertained. In most cases at the present time, collecting is done by men who specialize in one or more groups. Thus, one man interested in hy- 330 droids will move out on a reef, and if his interest is sharp enough, he will not even see other life forms about him. For him, the sponge is something in the way of his hydroids. Collecting large numbers of animals presents an entirely different aspect and makes one see an entirely different picture. Being more interested in distribution than in individuals, we saw dominant species and changing sizes, groups which thrive[59] and those which recede under varying conditions. In a

[55] **crevices**—cracks or openings in rocks.   [56] **dislodge**—shake loose; pull out.   [57] **encrusting**—hard-coated; crusty.   [58] **hordes**—great numbers; large groups.   [59] **thrive**—grow healthy and numerous.

way, ours is the older method, somewhat like that of Darwin on the *Beagle*. He was called a "naturalist." He wanted to see everything, rocks and flora and fauna;[60] marine and terrestrial. We came to envy 340 this Darwin on his sailing ship. He had so much room and so much time. He could capture his animals and keep them alive and watch them. He had years instead of weeks, and he saw so many things. Often we envied the inadequate transportation of his time—the *Beagle* couldn't get about rapidly. She moved slowly along under sail. And we can imagine that young Darwin, probably in a bos'n's chair[61] hung over the side, with a dip-net in his hands, scooping up jellyfish. When he went inland, he rode a horse or walked. This is the proper pace for a naturalist. Faced with all things he cannot hurry. We must have time to think and to look and to consider. And the modern process— 350 that of looking quickly at the whole field and then diving down to a particular—was reversed by Darwin. Out of long long consideration of the parts he emerged with a sense of the whole. Where we wished for a month at a collecting station and took two days, Darwin stayed three months. Of course he could see and tabulate. It was the pace that made the difference. And in the writing of Darwin, as in his thinking, there is the slow heave[62] of a sailing ship, and the patience of waiting for a tide. The results are bound up with the pace. We *could* not do this even if we could. We have thought in this connection that the speed and tempo and tone of modern writing might be 360 built on the nervous clacking[63] of a typewriter; that the brittle jerky thinking of the present might rest on the brittle jerky curricula of our schools with their urge to "turn them out."[64] To turn them out. They use the phrase in speeches; turn them out to what? And the young biologists tearing off pieces of their subject, tatters of the life forms, like sharks tearing out hunks of a dead horse, looking at them, tossing them away. This is neither a good nor a bad method; it is simply the one of our time. We can look with longing back to Charles Darwin, staring into the water over the side of the sailing ship, but for us to attempt to imitate that procedure would be romantic and silly. To 370 take a sailing boat, to fight tide and wind, to move four hundred miles on a horse when we could take a plane, would be not only ridiculous but ineffective. For we first, before our work, are products of our time. We might produce a philosophical costume piece, but it would be

---

[60] **flora and fauna**—plant and animal life of a particular region. [61] **bos'n's** (pronounced *bo'-sun's*, means *"boatswain's"*) **chair**—a strip of wood slung by a rope through a hole at each end, and used to sit on while at work aloft. [62] **heave**—wavelike movement. [63] **clacking**—sound of typewriter keys being struck. [64] **turn them out**—graduate students in an assembly-line fashion.

completely artificial. However, we can and do look on the measured, slow-paced accumulation of sight and thought of the Darwins with a nostalgic longing.

Even our boat hurried us, and while the Sea-Cow would not run, it had nevertheless infected us[65] with the idea of its running. Six weeks we had, and no more. Was it a wonder that we collected furiously; spent every low-tide moment on the rocks, even at night? And in the times between low tides we kept the bottom nets down and the lines and dip-nets working. When the charter was up, we would be through. How different it had been when John Xantus was stationed in this very place, Cape San Lucas, in the sixties. Sent down by the United States Government as a tidal observer, but having lots of time, he collected animals for our National Museum. The first fine collections of Gulf forms came from Xantus. And we do not feel that we are injuring his reputation, but rather broadening it, by repeating a story about him. Speaking to the manager of the cannery at the Cape, we remarked on what a great man Xantus had been. Where another would have kept his tide charts and brooded[66] and wished for the Willard Hotel, Xantus had collected animals widely and carefully. The manager said, "Oh, he was even better than that." Pointing to three little Indian children he said, "Those are Xantus's great-grand-children," and he continued, "In the town there is a large family of Xantuses, and a few miles back in the hills you'll find a whole tribe of them." There were giants in the earth in those days.

We wonder what modern biologist, worried about titles and pre-ferment[67] and the gossip of the Faculty Club, would have the warmth and breadth, or even the fecundity[68] for that matter, to leave a "whole tribe of Xantuses." We honor this man for all his activities. He at least was one who literally did proliferate[69] in all directions.

Many people have spoken at length of the Sally Lightfoots. In fact, everyone who has seen them has been delighted with them. The very name they are called by reflects the delight of the name. These little crabs, with brilliant cloisonné carapaces,[70] walk on their tiptoes. They have remarkable eyes and an extremely fast reaction time. In spite of the fact that they swarm on the rocks at the Cape, and to a less degree inside the Gulf, they are exceedingly hard to catch. They seem to be able to run in any one of four directions; but more than this, perhaps

---

[65] **infected us**—affected so as to influence us. [66] **brooded**—thought about continually and somewhat gloomily. [67] **preferment**—promotion; advancement. [68] **fecundity**—fruitfulness; fertility. [69] **proliferate**—grow or produce (by multiplication of parts). [70] **cloisonné carapaces:** a) **cloisonné**—a type of enamel work; b) **carapaces**—shell coverings.

because of their rapid reaction time, they appear to read the mind of their hunter. They escape the long-handled net, anticipating from what direction it is coming. If you walk slowly, they move slowly ahead of you in droves. If you hurry, they hurry. When you plunge at them, they seem to disappear in little puffs of blue smoke—at any rate, they disappear. It is impossible to creep up on them. They are very beautiful, with clear brilliant colors, reds and blues and warm browns. We tried for a long time to catch them. Finally, seeing fifty or sixty in a big canyon of rock, we thought to outwit them. Surely we were more   420
intelligent, if slower, than they. Accordingly, we pitted[71] our obviously superior intelligence against the equally obvious physical superiority of Sally Lightfoot. Near the top of the crevice a boulder protruded.[72] One of our party, taking a secret and circuitous[73] route, hid himself behind this boulder, net in hand. He was completely concealed even from the stalk eyes of the crabs. Certainly they had not seen him go there. The herd of Sallys drowsed on the rocks in the lower end of the crevice. Two more of us strolled in from the seaward side, noncha-lance[74] in our postures and ingenuousness[75] on our faces. One might have thought that we merely strolled along in a contemplation which   430
severely excluded Sally Lightfoots. In time the herd moved ahead of us, matching our nonchalance. We did not hurry, they did not hurry. When they passed the boulder, helpless and unsuspecting, a large net was to fall over them and imprison them. But they did not know that. They moved along until they were four feet from the boulder, and then as one crab they turned to the right, climbed up over the edge of the crevice and down to the sea again.

Man reacts peculiarly but consistently in his relationship with Sally Lightfoot. His tendency eventually is to scream curses,[76] to hurl himself at them, and to come up foaming with rage[77] and bruised all   440
over his chest. Thus, Tiny, leaping forward, slipped and fell and hurt his arm. He never forgot nor forgave his enemy. From then on he at-tacked Lightfoots by every foul[78] means he could contrive[79] (and a training in Monterey street fighting had equipped him well for this kind of battle). He hurled rocks at them; he smashed at them with boards; and he even considered poisoning them. Eventually we did catch a few Sallys, but we think they were the halt[80] and the blind,

---

[71] pitted—matched. [72] boulder protruded: *a*) boulder—huge rock; *b*) protruded—stuck out; extended. [73] circuitous—indirect. [74] nonchalance—casualness. [75] ingenu-ousness—openness; innocence. [76] curses—profane expressions. [77] foaming with rage—violent with anger or fury (as if foaming at the mouth like a mad dog). [78] foul—unfair. [79] contrive—devise; invent. [80] halt—crippled; lame.

the simpletons of their species. With reasonably well-balanced and non-neurotic Lightfoots we stood no chance.

We came back to the boat loaded with specimens, and immediately **450** prepared to preserve them. The square, enameled pans were laid out on the hatch,[81] the trays and bowls and watch-glasses (so called because at one time actual watch-crystals were used). The pans and glasses were filled with fresh sea water, and into them we distributed the animals by families—all the crabs in one, anemones in another, snails in another, and delicate things like flatworms and hydroids in others. From this distribution it was easier to separate them finally by species.

[81] hatch—cover over the opening in the deck that leads to the space where cargo is stored.

RACHEL CARSON (1907 –   )

Rachel Carson was born in Pennsylvania. As a child, she loved to observe the animals, plants, rocks, and streams around her—an attraction that grew into a devoted pursuit in later years. She studied biology at the Pennsylvania College for Women and went on for graduate study at The Johns Hopkins University and the Marine Biological Laboratory at Woods Hole, Massachusetts. Eventually her interest centered on ocean studies, and her fortunate combination of gifts—scholarly fascination and literary talent—led her to the position of Editor-in-Chief of the United States Fish and Wildlife Service. Over the years she has written many articles on her observations of the natural world for magazines like the *Atlantic Monthly*; her books have received wide acclaim because of their combination of scientific knowledge with charm and beauty of style. In 1951, she was awarded the National Book Award[1] for nonfiction for *The Sea Around Us*; in that same year, she also received a Guggenheim Fellowship[2] to continue her ocean studies. "Wealth of the Salt Seas" is a chapter from *The Sea Around Us*; it describes the riches to be found in the depths of the ocean.

Wealth from the Salt Seas

A *sea change into something rich and strange.*
SHAKESPEARE

*J*HE OCEAN IS THE EARTH'S GREATest storehouse of minerals. In a single cubic mile of sea water there are, on the average, 166 million tons of dissolved salts, and in all the ocean waters of the earth there are about 50 quadrillion tons. And it is in the nature of things for this quantity to be gradually increasing

[1] See *fn.* 1, page 83. [2] **Guggenheim Fellowships**—created in 1925 by the John Simon Guggenheim Memorial Foundation (Guggenheim was a wealthy industrialist and United States Senator). The awards—usually 40 or 50—are given annually for creative work in the arts or research in any branch of knowledge.

over the millennia,[3] for although the earth is constantly shifting her component[4] materials from place to place, the heaviest movements are forever seaward.

It has been assumed that the first seas were only faintly saline[5] and that their saltiness has been growing over the eons[6] of time. For the primary source of the ocean's salt is the rocky mantle[7] of the continents. When those first rains came—the centuries-long rains that fell from the heavy clouds enveloping the young earth—they began the processes of wearing away the rocks and carrying their contained minerals to the sea. The annual flow of water seaward is believed to be about 6500 cubic miles, this inflow of river water adding to the ocean several billion tons of salts.

It is a curious[8] fact that there is little similarity between the chemical composition of river water and that of sea water. The various elements are present in entirely different proportions. The rivers bring in four times as much calcium[9] as chloride, for example, yet in the ocean the proportions are strongly reversed—46 times as much chloride as calcium. An important reason for the difference is that immense amounts of calcium salts are constantly being withdrawn from the sea water by marine animals and are used for building shells[10] and skeletons[11]—for the microscopic shells that house the foraminifera,[12] for the massive structures of the coral reefs, and for the shells of oysters and clams and other mollusks.[13] Another reason is the precipitation[14] of calcium from sea water. There is a striking difference, too, in the silicon[15] content of river and sea water—about 500 per cent greater in rivers than in the sea. The silica is required by diatoms[16] to make their shells, and so the immense quantities brought in by rivers are largely utilized by these ubiquitous[17] plants of the sea. Often there are exceptionally heavy growths of diatoms off the mouths of rivers.

[3] millennia—great periods of time (a millennium is a period of one thousand years). [4] component—constituent. [5] saline—salty. [6] the eons—the largest dimensions of geologic time; two or more eras; indefinitely long time. [7] mantle—layer of decomposed rock fragments. [8] curious—unusual; strange. [9] calcium—a chemical element. (NOTE: Names pertaining to minerals and elements are not usually defined in these notes. The same is true for names of certain plants and animals found in the sea. The assumption is that such definitions are not essential for a general understanding of the article. Those interested in or requiring more specific information should consult a reliable dictionary.) [10] shells—hard outer coverings (in this case, of mollusks, or sea animals). [11] skeletons—bones of animal bodies. [12] foraminifera—order of marine snails, squids, etc., having porous shells. [13] mollusks—sea animals with shells (such as oysters and clams). [14] precipitation—in chemistry, the act of separating out a solid from a solution. [15] silicon—nonmetallic element. (It occurs in combination with minerals and rocks and makes up more than a fourth of the earth's crust.) [16] diatoms—marine algae that are microscopic and unicellular. [17] ubiquitous—everywhere present; omnipresent.

Because of the enormous total chemical requirements of all the fauna and flora of the sea, only a small part of the salts annually brought in by rivers goes to increasing the quantity of dissolved minerals in the water. The inequalities of chemical make-up are further reduced by reactions that are set in motion immediately the fresh water is dis- **40** charged[18] into the sea, and by the enormous disparities[19] of volume between the incoming fresh water and the ocean.

There are other agencies by which minerals are added to the sea—from obscure[20] sources buried deep within the earth. From every volcano chlorine and other gases escape into the atmosphere and are carried down in rain onto the surface of land and sea. Volcanic ash and rock bring up other materials. And all the submarine volcanoes, discharging through unseen craters[21] directly into the sea, pour in boron, chlorine, sulphur, and iodine.

All this is a one-way flow of minerals to the sea. Only to a very **50** limited extent is there any return of salts to the land. We attempt to recover some of them directly by chemical extraction[22] and mining, and indirectly by harvesting the sea's plants and animals. There is another way, in the long, recurring cycles[23] of the earth, by which the sea itself gives back to the land what it has received. This happens when the ocean waters rise over the lands, deposit their sediments,[24] and at last withdraw, leaving over the continent another layer of sedimentary rocks. These contain some of the water and salts of the sea. But it is only a temporary loan of minerals to the land and the return payment begins at once by way of the old, familiar channels— **60** rain, erosion,[25] run-off to the rivers, transport to the sea.

There are other curious little exchanges of materials between sea and land. While the process of evaporation, which raises water vapor into the air, leaves most of the salts behind, a surprising amount of salt does intrude[26] itself into the atmosphere and rides long distances on the wind. The so-called 'cyclic salt' is picked up by the winds from the spray[27] of a rough, cresting sea or breaking surf and is blown inland, then brought down in rain and returned by rivers to the ocean. These tiny, invisible particles of sea salt drifting in the atmosphere are, in fact, one of the many forms of atmospheric nuclei around which **70** raindrops form. Areas nearest the sea, in general, receive the most salt.

---

[18] **discharged**—unloaded.   [19] **disparities**—inequalities; dissimilarities.   [20] **obscure**—hidden.   [21] **craters**—cup-shaped depressions or cavities at the mouth of volcanoes.   [22] **by chemical extraction**—removal by chemical process.   [23] **cycles**—periods of time in which a series of operations is completed (as in the seasons of a year).   [24] **sediments**—matter deposited by water; minerals or organic matter.   [25] **erosion**—act of wearing away of the earth's surface by the water.   [26] **intrude**—thrust; force.   [27] **spray** —a stream of tiny particles of water blown through the air.

Published figures have listed 24 to 36 pounds per acre per year for England and more than 100 pounds for British Guiana. But the most astounding example of long-distance, large-scale transport of cyclic salts is furnished by Sambhar Salt Lake in northern India. It receives 3000 tons of salt a year, carried to it on the hot dry monsoons[28] of summer from the sea, 400 miles way.

The plants and animals of the sea are very much better chemists than men, and so far our own efforts to extract the mineral wealth of the sea have been feeble compared with those of lower forms of life. They have been able to find and to utilize elements present in such minute traces[29] that human chemists could not detect their presence until, very recently, highly refined methods of spectroscopic analysis[30] were developed.

We did not know, for example, that vanadium[31] occurred in the sea until it was discovered in the blood of certain sluggish and sedentary[32] sea creatures, the holothurians[33] (of which sea cucumbers[34] are an example) and the ascidians.[35] Relatively huge quantities of cobalt[36] are extracted by lobsters and mussels, and nickel[37] is utilized by various mollusks, yet it is only within recent years that we have been able to recover even traces of these elements. Copper is recoverable only as about a hundredth part in a million of sea water, yet it helps to constitute the life blood of lobsters, entering into their respiratory pigments[38] as iron does into human blood.

In contrast to the accomplishments of invertebrate[39] chemists, we have so far had only limited success in extracting sea salts in quantities we can use for commercial purposes, despite their prodigious[40] quantity and considerable variety. We have recovered about fifty of the known elements by chemical analysis, and shall perhaps find that all the others are there, when we can develop proper methods to discover them. Five salts predominate[41] and are present in fixed proportions. As we would expect, sodium chloride is by far the most abundant, making up 77.8 per cent of the total salts; magnesium chloride follows,

[28] monsoons—seasonal winds of the Indian Ocean and southern Asia. (The winds blow from the southwest in the summer and usually bring heavy rains.)   [29] traces—evidences.   [30] spectroscopic analysis—analysis with the spectroscope, an optical instrument for producing and examining the spectrum of light or radiation from any source.   [31] vanadium—a rare element occurring in certain minerals, used as ingredient in steel production.   [32] sluggish and sedentary: a) sluggish—slow-moving; b) sedentary—inactive.   [33] holothurians—genus name.   [34] sea cucumbers—a type of creeping plant.   [35] ascidians—a group of water animals, usually shaped like sacks.   [36] cobalt—a steel-gray metallic element found in various areas; its compounds are used in making ink and paint.   [37] nickel—a hard silver-white metallic element allied to iron and cobalt.   [38] pigments—substances that produce color in the tissues or cells of animals.   [39] invertebrate—animals without a backbone or spine.   [40] prodigious—extraordinarily large.   [41] predominate—are the leading elements.

with 10.9 per cent; then magnesium sulphate, 4.7 per cent; calcium sulphate, 3.6 per cent; and potassium sulphate, 2.5 per cent. All others combined make up the remaining .5 per cent.

Of all the elements present in the sea, probably none has stirred men's dreams[42] more than gold. It is there—in all the waters covering the greater part of the earth's surface—enough in total quantity to make every person in the world a millionaire. But how can the sea be made to yield it? The most determined attempt to wrest[43] a substantial quantity of gold from ocean waters—and also the most complete study of the gold in sea water—was made by the German chemist Fritz Haber[44] after the First World War. Haber conceived the idea of extracting enough gold from the sea to pay the German war debt and his dream resulted in the German South Atlantic Expedition of the *Meteor*. The *Meteor* was equipped with a laboratory and filtration plant, and between the years 1924 and 1928 the vessel crossed and recrossed the Atlantic, sampling[45] the water. But the quantity found was less than had been expected, and the cost of extraction far greater than the value of the gold recovered. The practical economics of the matter are about as follows: in a cubic mile of sea water there is about $93,000,000 in gold and $8,500,000 in silver. But to treat this volume of water in a year would require the twice-daily filling and emptying of 200 tanks of water, each 500 feet square and 5 feet deep. Probably this is no greater feat,[46] relatively, than is accomplished regularly by corals, sponges, and oysters, but by human standards it is not economically feasible.[47]

Most mysterious, perhaps, of all substances in the sea is iodine. In sea water it is one of the scarcest of the nonmetals, difficult to detect[48] and resisting exact analysis. Yet it is found in almost every marine plant and animal. Sponges, corals, and certain seaweeds accumulate vast quantities of it. Apparently the iodine in the sea is in a constant state of chemical change, sometimes being oxidized, sometimes reduced, again entering into organic combinations. There seem to be constant interchanges between air and sea, the iodine in some form perhaps being carried into the air in spray, for the air at sea level contains detectable quantities, which decrease with altitude. From the time living things first made iodine a part of the chemistry of their tissues, they seem to have become increasingly dependent on it; now we ourselves could not exist without it as a regulator of the basal

110

120

130

140

[42] **stirred men's dreams**—fired men's imaginations. [43] **wrest**—take away by force. [44] **Fritz Haber**—a German chemist, who was awarded the 1918 Nobel Prize. [45] **sampling**—taking tests of; testing. [46] **feat**—extraordinary act or accomplishment. [47] **feasible**—capable of being done; practicable. [48] **detect**—discover.

metabolism[49] of our bodies, through the thyroid gland[50] which accumulates it.

All commercial iodine was formerly obtained from seaweeds; then the deposits of crude nitrate of soda from the high deserts of North Chile were discovered. Probably the original source of this raw material—called 'caliche'—was some prehistoric sea filled with marine vegetation, but that is a subject of controversy. Iodine is obtained also from brine[51] deposits and from the subterranean[52] waters of oil-bearing rocks—all indirectly of marine origin.

A monopoly on the world's bromine is held by the ocean, where 99 per cent of it is now concentrated. The tiny fraction present in rocks was originally deposited there by the sea. First we obtained it from the brines left in subterranean pools by prehistoric oceans; now there are large plants on the seacoasts—especially in the United States—which use ocean water as their raw material and extract the bromine directly. Thanks to modern methods of commercial production of bromine we have high-test gasoline for our cars. There is a long list of other uses, including the manufacture of sedatives,[53] fire extinguishers, photographic chemicals, dyestuffs, and chemical warfare materials.

One of the oldest bromine derivatives[54] known to man was Tyrian purple, which the Phoenicians made in their dyehouses from the purple snail,[55] Murex. This snail may be linked in a curious and wonderful way with the prodigious and seemingly unreasonable quantities of bromine found today in the Dead Sea, which contains, it is estimated, some 850 million tons of the chemical. The concentration of bromine in Dead Sea water is 100 times that in the ocean. Apparently the supply is constantly renewed by underground hot springs, which discharge into the bottom of the Sea of Galilee, which in turn sends its waters to the Dead Sea by way of the River Jordan. Some authorities believe that the source of the bromine in the hot springs is a deposit of billions of ancient snails, laid down by the sea of a bygone age in a stratum long since buried.

Magnesium is another mineral we now obtain by collecting huge volumes of ocean water and treating it with chemicals, although originally it was derived only from brines or from the treatment of such magnesium-containing rocks as dolomite, of which whole mountain ranges are composed. In a cubic mile of sea water there are about

---

49 basal metabolism—basic energy of the body when tested at a low level of activity.
50 thyroid gland—the gland with a secretion that controls the rate of metabolism.
51 brine—water heavily saturated with salt solution.   52 subterranean—underground.
53 sedatives—drugs that produce sleep or that have a calming effect.   54 bromine derivatives—substances originating from bromine.   55 snail—a mollusk.

4 million tons of magnesium. Since the direct extraction method was developed about 1941, production has increased enormously. It was 180 magnesium from the sea that made possible the wartime growth of the aviation industry, for every airplane made in the United States (and in most other countries as well) contains about half a ton of magnesium metal. And it has innumerable[56] uses in other industries where a light-weight metal is desired, besides its long-standing utility as an insulating material,[57] and its use in printing inks, medicines, and toothpastes, and in such war implements as incendiary bombs, star shells, and tracer ammunition.

Wherever climate has permitted it, men have evaporated salt from sea water for many centuries. Under the burning sun of the tropics 190 the ancient Greeks, Romans, and Egyptians harvested the salt men and animals everywhere must have in order to live. Even today in parts of the world that are hot and dry and where drying winds blow, solar evaporation of salt is practiced—on the shores of the Persian Gulf, in China, India, and Japan, in the Philippines, and on the coast of California and the alkali flats of Utah.

Here and there are natural basins where the action of sun and wind and sea combine to carry on evaporation of salt on a scale far greater than human industry could accomplish. Such a natural basin is the Rann of Cutch on the west coast of India. The Rann is a flat plain, 200 some 60 by 185 miles, separated from the sea by the island of Cutch. When the southwest monsoons blow, sea water is carried in by way of a channel to cover the plain. But in summer, in the season when the hot northeast monsoon blows from the desert, no more water enters, and that which is collected in pools over the plain evaporates into a salt crust, in some places several feet thick.

Where the sea has come in over the land, laid down its deposits, and then withdrawn, there have been created reservoirs of chemicals, upon which we can draw with comparatively little trouble. Hidden deep under the surface of our earth are pools of 'fossil salt water,' 210 the brine of ancient seas; 'fossil deserts,' the salt of old seas that evaporated away under conditions of extreme heat and dryness; and layers of sedimentary rock in which are contained the organic sediments and the dissolved salts of the sea that deposited them.

During the Permian period, which was a time of great heat and dryness and widespread deserts, a vast inland sea formed over much of Europe, covering parts of the present Britain, France, Germany, and

[56] innumerable—very numerous; countless. [57] insulating material—material that prevents passage of heat, sound, or electicity.

Poland. Rains came seldom and the rate of evaporation was high. The sea became exceedingly salty, and it began to deposit layers of salts. For a period covering thousands of years, only gypsum[58] was de- 220 posited, perhaps representing a time when water fresh from the ocean occasionally entered the inland sea to mix with its strong brine. Alternating with the gypsum were thicker beds of salt. Later, as its area shrank and the sea grew still more concentrated, deposits of potassium and magnesium sulphates were formed (this stage representing perhaps 500 years); still later, and perhaps for another 500 years, there were laid down mixed potassium and magnesium chlorides or carnallite. After the sea had completely evaporated, desert conditions prevailed, and soon the salt deposits were buried under sand. The richest beds form the famous deposits of Stassfurt and Alsace; toward 230 the outskirts of the original area of the old sea (as, for example, in England) there are only beds of salt. The Stassfurt beds are about 2500 feet thick; their springs of brine have been known since the thirteenth cenutry, and the salts have been mined since the seventeenth century.

At an even earlier geological period—the Silurian—a great salt basin was deposited in the northern part of the United States, extending from central New York State across Michigan, including northern Pennsylvania and Ohio and part of southern Ontario. Because of the hot, dry climate of that time, the inland sea lying over this place grew 240 so salty that beds of salt and gypsum were deposited over a great area covering about 100,000 square miles. There are 7 distinct beds of salt at Ithaca, New York, the uppermost lying at a depth of about half a mile. In southern Michigan some of the individual salt beds are more than 500 feet thick, and the aggregate[59] thickness of salt in the center of the Michigan Basin is approximately 2000 feet. In some places rock salt is mined; in others wells are dug, water is forced down, and the resulting brine is pumped to the surface and evaporated to recover the salt.

One of the greatest stock piles of minerals in the world came from 250 the evaporation of a great inland sea in the western United States. This is Searles Lake in the Mohave Desert of California. An arm of the sea that overlay this region was cut off from the ocean by the thrusting up of a range of mountains; as the lake evaporated away, the water that remained became ever more salty through the inwash of minerals from all the surrounding land. Perhaps Searles Lake be-

[58] gypsum—hydrated sulfate of calcium, used in making of plaster of Paris. [59] aggregate—total, or whole combination of particulars.

gan its slow transformation from a landlocked sea to a 'frozen' lake—
a lake of solid minerals—only a few thousand years ago; now its surface is a hard crust of salts 50 to 70 feet deep. Below that is mud.
Engineers have recently discovered a second layer of salts and brine,   260
probably at least as thick as the upper layer, underlying the mud.
Searles Lake was first worked in the 1870's for borax; then teams of
20 mules each carried the borax across desert and mountains to the
railroads. In the 1930's the recovery of other substances from the
lake began—bromine, lithium,[60] and salts of potassium and sodium.
Now Searles Lake yields 40 per cent of the production of potassium
chloride in the United States and half of all the borax and lithium
salts produced in the world.

In some future era the Dead Sea will probably repeat the history of
Searles Lake, as the centuries pass and evaporation continues. The   270
Dead Sea as we know it is all that remains of a much larger inland sea
that once filled the entire Jordan Valley and was about 190 miles
long; now it has shrunk to about a fourth of this length and a fourth
of its former volume. And with the shrinkage and the evaporation in
the hot dry climate has come the concentration of salts that makes
the Dead Sea a great reservoir of minerals. No animal life can exist in
its brine; such luckless fish as are brought down by the River Jordan
die and provide food for the sea birds. It is 1300 feet below the Mediterranean, lying farther below sea level than any other body of water
in the world. It occupies the lowest part of the rift valley of the Jor-   280
dan, which was created by a down-slipping of a block of the earth's
crust. The water of the Dead Sea is warmer than the air, a condition
favoring evaporation, and clouds of its vapor float, nebulous and half
formed, above it, while its brine grows more bitter and the salts accumulate.

Of all legacies[61] of the ancient seas the most valuable is petroleum.
Exactly what geologic processes have created the precious pools of
liquid deep within the earth no one knows with enough certainty to
describe the whole sequence of events. But this much seems to be
true: Petroleum is a result of fundamental earth processes that have   290
been operating ever since an abundant and varied life was developed
in the sea—at least since the beginning of Paleozoic time, probably
longer. Exceptional and catastrophic[62] occurrences may now and
then aid its formation but they are not essential; the mechanism that
regularly generates petroleum consists of the normal processes of

[60] lithium—a soft silver-white metallic element; lightest of all metals.   [61] legacies—
gifts; things handed down.   [62] catastrophic—violently destructive.

earth and sea—the living and dying of creatures, the deposit of sediments, the advance and retreat of the seas over the continents, the upward and downward foldings of the earth's crust.

The old inorganic theory that linked petroleum formation with volcanic action has been abandoned[63] by most geologists. The origin of petroleum is most likely to be found in the bodies of plants and animals buried under the fine-grained sediments of former seas and there subjected to slow decomposition.[64]

Perhaps the essence[65] of conditions favoring petroleum production is represented by the stagnant[66] waters of the Black Sea or of certain Norwegian fiords. The surprisingly abundant life of the Black Sea is confined[67] to the upper layers; the deeper and especially the bottom waters are devoid[68] of oxygen and are often permeated with[69] hydrogen sulphide. In these poisoned waters there can be no bottom scavengers to devour the bodies of marine animals that drift down from above, so they are entombed in the fine sediments. In many Norwegian fiords the deep layers are foul[70] and oxygenless because the mouth of the fiord is cut off from the circulation of the open sea by a shallow sill.[71] The bottom layers of such fiords are poisoned by the hydrogen sulphide from decomposing organic matter. Sometimes storms drive in unusual quantities of oceanic water and through turbulence[72] of waves stir deeply the waters of these lethal[73] pools; the mixing of the water layers that follows brings death to hordes of fishes and invertebrates living near the surface. Such a catastrophe leads to the deposit of a rich layer of organic material on the bottom.

Wherever great oil fields are found, they are related to past or present seas. This is true of the inland fields as well as of those near the present seacoast. The great quantities of oil that have been obtained from the Oklahoma fields, for example, were trapped in spaces within sedimentary rocks laid down under seas that invaded[74] this part of North America in Paleozoic time.

The search for petroleum has also led geologists repeatedly to those 'unstable belts, covered much of the time by shallow seas, which lie around the margins of the main continental platforms, between them and the great oceanic deeps.'

An example of such a depressed[75] segment of crust lying between

300

310

320

330

63 abandoned—given up. 64 decomposition—decaying. 65 essence—central feature. 66 stagnant—still; not running or flowing; foul from standing still; sluggish. 67 confined to—limited to; restricted to. 68 devoid—empty; void; destitute. 69 permeated with—penetrated by. 70 foul—filthy; bad smelling. 71 shallow sill: a) shallow—not deep; b) sill—ledge (as a window sill). 72 turbulence—disorder; commotion. 73 lethal—deadly. 74 invaded—ran over. 75 depressed—forced down.

continental masses is the one between Europe and the Near East, occupied in part by the Persian Gulf, the Red, Black, and Caspian seas, and the Mediterranean Sea. The Gulf of Mexico and the Caribbean Sea lie in another basin or shallow sea between the Americas. A shallow, island-studded sea[76] lies between the continents of Asia and Australia. Lastly, there is the nearly landlocked sea[77] of the Arctic. In past ages all of these areas have been alternately raised and depressed, belonging at one time to the land, at another to the encroaching[78] sea. During their periods of submersion[79] they have re-   340
ceived thick deposits of sediments, and in their waters a rich marine fauna has lived, died, and drifted down into the soft sediment carpet.

There are vast oil deposits in all these areas. In the Near East are the great fields of Saudi Arabia, Iran, and Iraq. The shallow depression between Asia and Australia yields the oil of Java, Sumatra, Borneo, and New Guinea. The American mediterranean is the center of oil production in the Western Hemisphere—half the proved resources of the United States come from the northern shore of the Gulf of Mexico, and Colombia, Venezuela, and Mexico have rich oil fields along the western and southern margins of the Gulf. The   350
Arctic is one of the unproved frontiers of the petroleum industry, but oil seepages[80] in northern Alaska, on islands north of the Canadian mainland, and along the Arctic coast of Siberia hint[81] that this land recently raised from the sea may be one of the great oil fields of the future.

In recent years, the speculations of petroleum geologists have been focused in a new direction—under sea. By no means all of the land resources of petroleum have been discovered, but probably the richest and most easily worked fields are being tapped,[82] and their possible production is known. The ancient seas gave us the oil that is   360
now being drawn out of the earth. Can the ocean today be induced[83] to give up some of the oil that must be trapped in sedimentary rocks under its floor, covered by water scores or hundreds of fathoms[84] deep?

Oil is already being produced from offshore wells, on the continental shelf. Off California, Texas, and Louisiana, oil companies have drilled into the sediments of the shelf and are obtaining oil. In

---

[76] island-studded sea—sea containing many islands.   [77] nearly landlocked sea—sea nearly surrounded by land.   [78] encroaching—advancing; forward-creeping.   [79] periods of submersion—periods under water.   [80] seepages—leakages (as oil that leaks or seeps out).   [81] hint—suggest; imply.   [82] are being tapped—have been opened to draw off oil. [83] induced—persuaded.   [84] fathoms—units of measurement of depth. (A fathom is six feet.)

the United States the most active exploration has been centered in the Gulf of Mexico. Judging from its geologic history, this area has rich promise. For eons of time it was either dry land or a very shallow sea basin, receiving the sediments that washed into it from high lands to the north. Finally, about the middle of the Cretaceous period, the floor of the Gulf began to sink under the load of sediments and in time it acquired its present deep central basin.

By geophysical exploration, we can see that the layers of sedimentary rock underlying the coastal plain tilt steeply[85] downward and pass under the broad continental shelf of the Gulf. Down in the layers deposited in the Jurassic period is a thick salt bed of enormous extent, probably formed when this part of the earth was hot and dry, a place of shrinking[86] seas and encroaching deserts. In Louisiana and Texas, and also, it now appears, out in the Gulf itself, extraordinary features known as salt domes[87] are associated with this deposit. These are fingerlike plugs of salt,[88] usually less than a mile across, pushing up from the deep layer toward the earth's surface. They have been described by geologists as 'driven up through 5,000 to 15,000 feet of sediments by earth pressures, like nails through a board.' In the states bordering the Gulf such structures have often been associated with oil. It seems probable that on the continental shelf, also, the salt domes may mark large oil deposits.

In exploring the Gulf for oil, therefore, geologists search for the salt domes where the larger oil fields are likely to lie. They use an instrument known as a magnetometer, which measures the variations in magnetic intensity brought about by the salt domes. Gravity meters also help locate the domes by measuring the variation in gravity near them, the specific gravity of salt being less than that of the surrounding sediments. The actual location and outline of the dome are discovered by seismographic exploration, which traces the inclination[89] of the rock strata by recording the reflection of sound waves produced by dynamite explosions. These methods of exploration have been used on land for some years, but only since about 1945 have they been adapted to use in offshore Gulf waters. The magnetometer has been so improved that it will map continuously while being towed[90] behind a boat or carried in or suspended from a plane. A gravity meter can now be lowered rapidly to the bottom and readings made by remote control. (Once an operator had to descend with it in a

370
380
390
400

---

[85] tilt steeply: a) tilt—incline, slant, lean; b) steeply—very sharply; almost perpendicularly. [86] shrinking—contracting. [87] domes—curved mounds or piles. [88] fingerlike plugs of salt—rocks of salt, shaped like fingers. [89] inclination—degree of slope or slant. [90] towed—pulled along.

diving bell.) Seismic crews now shoot off their dynamite charges and make continuous recordings while their boats are under way.

Despite all these improvements which allow exploration to proceed rapidly, it is no simple matter to obtain oil from undersea fields. Prospecting must be followed by the leasing of potential oil-produc- 410 ing areas, and then by drilling to see whether oil is actually there. Offshore drilling platforms rest on piles that must be driven as far as 250 feet into the floor of the Gulf to withstand the force of waves, especially during the season for hurricanes. Winds, storm waves, fogs, the corrosive gnawing[91] of sea water upon metal structures—all these are hazards[92] that must be faced and overcome. Yet the technical difficulties of far more extensive offshore operations than any now attempted do not discourage specialists in petroleum engineering.

So our search for mineral wealth often leads us back to the seas of ancient times—to the oil pressed from the bodies of fishes, seaweeds, 420 and other forms of plant and animal life and then stored away in ancient rocks; to the rich brines hidden in subterranean pools where the fossil water of old seas still remains; to the layers of salts that are the mineral substance of those old seas laid down as a covering mantle over the continents. Perhaps in time, as we learn the chemical secrets of the corals and sponges and diatoms, we shall depend less on the stored wealth of prehistoric seas and shall go more and more directly to the ocean and the rocks now forming under its shallow waters.

[91] **corrosive gnawing:** *a)* **corrosive**—destructive; *b)* **gnawing**—eating away. [92] **hazards** —risks; dangers.

KATHERINE ANNE PORTER (1894–)

Texas-born Miss Porter grew up in a family atmosphere rooted in the deep South and in the frontier life of the Southwest. Although she has used a variety of places in the setting of her short stories and novels, she has come back time and again to the scenes of her early years. Many of her stories, including the one here, deal with the same group of characters—Cornelia, her Mother ("Granny" of this story) and other members of her family, and the family's Negro servants.

"The Jilting¹ of Granny Weatherall" (from *Flowering Judas and Other Stories*, published in 1930) is set in the South at about the turn of the century; it gives us a glimpse of a way of life that is gone. Granny, a woman of eighty, clings to it, not admitting that anything is "wrong with me" even as death nears. Granny's last words, "I'm not going, Cornelia. I'm taken by surprise. I can't go," suggest her unwillingness to let go in the knowledge that she has been jilted once. In death she fears that she will again fail of fulfillment. The story contains two carefully interwoven narratives—the story of the events of Granny's last days as seen through her eyes and ears, and the story of her past life, which springs from her memory.

The Jilting of Granny Weatherall

SHE FLICKED² HER WRIST NEATLY³ out of Doctor Harry's pudgy⁴ careful fingers and pulled the sheet up to her chin. The brat ought to be in knee breeches.⁵ Doctoring around the country with spectacles on his nose! "Get along now, take your schoolbooks and go. There's nothing wrong with me."

Doctor Harry spread a warm paw⁶ like a cushion on her forehead

---

¹ **jilting**—rejection. ² **flicked**—quickly removed. ³ **neatly**—skillfully. ⁴ **pudgy**—soft and fat. ⁵ **knee breeches**—short pants (knee-length pants worn by a small boy). ⁶ **paw** —hand.

where the forked green vein danced and made her eyelids twitch.[7]
"Now, now, be a good girl, and we'll have you up in no time."

"That's no way to speak to a woman nearly eighty years old just   10
because she's down. I'd have you respect your elders, young man."

"Well, Missy,[8] excuse me." Doctor Harry patted her cheek.[9] "But
I've got to warn you, haven't I? You're a marvel,[10] but you must be
careful or you're going to be good and sorry."[11]

"Don't tell me what I'm going to be. I'm on my feet now, morally
speaking.[12] It's Cornelia. I had to go to bed to get rid of her."

Her bones felt loose, and floated around in her skin, and Doctor
Harry floated like a balloon around the foot of the bed. He floated
and pulled down his waistcoat[13] and swung his glasses on a cord.[14]
"Well, stay where you are, it certainly can't hurt you."   20

"Get along and doctor your sick," said Granny Weatherall. "Leave
a well woman alone. I'll call for you when I want you. . . . Where
were you forty years ago when I pulled through milk-leg and double
pneumonia?[15] You weren't even born. Don't let Cornelia lead you
on," she shouted, because Doctor Harry appeared to float up to the
ceiling and out. "I pay my own bills, and I don't throw my money
away on nonsense!"

She meant to wave good-by, but it was too much trouble. Her eyes
closed of themselves, it was like a dark curtain drawn around the bed.
The pillow rose and floated under her, pleasant as a hammock[16]   30
in a light wind. She listened to the leaves rustling outside the window. No, somebody was swishing newspapers:[17] no, Cornelia and
Doctor Harry were whispering together. She leaped broad awake,[18]
thinking they whispered in her ear.

"She was never like this, *never* like this!" "Well, what can we expect?" "Yes, eighty years old . . ."

Well, and what if she was? She still had ears. It was like Cornelia
to whisper around doors. She always kept things secret in such a public
way. She was always being tactful[19] and kind. Cornelia was dutiful;[20]

---

[7] **twitch**—move suddenly and with jerky movements.   [8] **Missy**—Miss.   [9] **patted her
cheek**—gently stroked her cheek several times.   [10] **a marvel**—a wonder; an amazing
person.   [11] **good and sorry**—very sorry; regretful.   [12] **morally speaking**—practically
speaking; virtually.   [13] **waistcoat**—vest (a short sleeveless jacket worn under a coat).
[14] **swung his glasses on a cord**—swung his glasses on the cord or heavy string to which
they were attached.   [15] **milk-leg and double pneumonia:** *a)* **milk-leg**—a condition,
usually following childbirth, characterized by a painful swelling of the legs; *b)* **double
pneumonia**—a serious disease of the lungs characterized by inflamed, hardened tissue.
[16] **hammock**—a length of canvas suspended from ropes at both ends, used as a bed
or couch.   [17] **swishing newspapers**—opening pages of a newspaper.   [18] **broad awake**
—wide awake.   [19] **tactful**—skillful in doing the right thing at the right moment in
order not to offend others.   [20] **dutiful**—obedient; respectful.

that was the trouble with her. Dutiful and good: "So good and duti-   40
ful," said Granny, "that I'd like to spank her." She saw herself spank-
ing Cornelia and making a fine job of it.

"What'd you say, Mother?"

Granny felt her face tying up in hard knots.

"Can't a body[21] think, I'd like to know?"

"I thought you might want something."

"I do. I want a lot of things. First off, go away and don't whisper."

She lay and drowsed, hoping in her sleep that the children would
keep out and let her rest a minute. It had been a long day. Not that
she was tired. It was always pleasant to snatch[22] a minute now and   50
then. There was always so much to be done, let me see: tomorrow.

Tomorrow was far away and there was nothing to trouble about.
Things were finished somehow when the time came; thank God there
was always a little margin over for peace: then a person could spread
out the plan of life and tuck in the edges orderly.[23] It was good to
have everything clean and folded away, with the hair brushes and
tonic bottles sitting straight on the white embroidered linen: the day
started without fuss[24] and the pantry shelves laid out with rows
of jelly glasses and brown jugs and white stone-china jars with blue
whirligigs[25] and words painted on them: coffee, tea, sugar, ginger,   60
cinnamon, allspice: and the bronze clock with the lion on top nicely
dusted off. The dust that lion could collect in twenty-four hours! The
box in the attic with all those letters tied up, well, she'd have to go
through that tomorrow. All those letters—George's letters and John's
letters and her letters to them both—lying around for the children
to find afterwards made her uneasy. Yes, that would be tomorrow's
business. No use to let them know how silly she had been once.

While she was rummaging[26] around she found death in her mind
and it felt clammy[27] and unfamiliar. She had spent so much time
preparing for death there was no need for bringing it up again. Let   70
it take care of itself now. When she was sixty she had felt very old,
finished, and went around making farewell trips to see her children
and grandchildren, with a secret in her mind: This is the very last of
your mother, children! Then she made her will and came down with
a long fever. That was all just a notion like a lot of other things, but
it was lucky too, for she had once for all got over the idea of dying for
a long time. Now she couldn't be worried. She hoped she had better

---

[21] **a body** (colloquial)—a person. [22] **snatch**—take; get; avail oneself of. [23] **tuck in the edges orderly**—turn down the edges in an orderly manner. [24] **fuss**—unnecessary bother or activity. [25] **whirligigs**—marks that seem to whirl and spin. [26] **rummaging**—searching busily and thoroughly. [27] **clammy**—moist and cold.

sense now. Her father had lived to be one hundred and two years old and had drunk a noggin[28] of strong hot toddy[29] on his last birthday. He told the reporters it was his daily habit, and he owed his long life   80 to that. He had made quite a scandal and was very pleased about it. She believed she'd just plague[30] Cornelia a little.

"Cornelia! Cornelia!" No footsteps, but a sudden hand on her cheek. "Bless you, where have you been?"

"Here, Mother."

"Well, Cornelia, I want a noggin of hot toddy."

"Are you cold, darling?"

"I'm chilly, Cornelia. Lying in bed stops the circulation. I must have told you that a thousand times."

Well, she could just hear Cornelia telling her husband that   90 Mother was getting a little childish and they'd have to humor her.[31] The thing that most annoyed her was that Cornelia thought she was deaf, dumb, and blind. Little hasty glances and tiny gestures tossed around her and over her head saying, "Don't cross[32] her, let her have her way, she's eighty years old," and she sitting there as if she lived in a thin glass cage. Sometimes Granny almost made up her mind to pack up and move back to her own house where nobody could remind her every minute that she was old. Wait, wait, Cornelia, till your own children whisper behind your back!

In her day she had kept a better house and had got more work   100 done. She wasn't too old yet for Lydia to be driving eighty miles for advice when one of the children jumped the track,[33] and Jimmy still dropped in and talked things over: "Now, Mammy, you've a good business head, I want to know what you think of this? . . ." Old. Cornelia couldn't change the furniture around without asking. Little things, little things! They had been so sweet when they were little. Granny wished the old days were back again with the children young and everything to be done over. It had been a hard pull, but not too much for her. When she thought of all the food she had cooked, and all the clothes she had cut and sewed, and all the gar-   110 dens she had made—well, the children showed it. There they were, made out of her, and they couldn't get away from that. Sometimes she wanted to see John again and point to them and say, Well, I didn't do so badly, did I? But that would have to wait. That was for tomorrow. She used to think of him as a man, but now all the chil-

---

[28] **noggin**—small cup or mug.   [29] **hot toddy**—a drink of brandy or whiskey mixed with hot water.   [30] **plague**—annoy.   [31] **to humor her**—to let her have her own way; to spoil her.   [32] **cross**—oppose; thwart.   [33] **jumped the track**—got out of control; got out of hand; became unmanageable.

dren were older than their father, and he would be a child beside her if she saw him now. It seemed strange and there was something wrong in the idea. Why, he couldn't possibly recognize her. She had fenced in[34] a hundred acres once, digging the post holes herself and clamping the wires with just a Negro boy to help. That changed a 120 woman. John would be looking for a young woman with the peaked Spanish comb[35] in her hair and the painted fan. Digging post holes changed a woman. Riding country roads in the winter when women had their babies was another thing: sitting up nights with sick horses and sick Negroes and sick children and hardly ever losing one. John, I hardly ever lost one of them! John would see that in a minute, that would be something he could understand, she wouldn't have to explain anything!

It made her feel like rolling up her sleeves and putting the whole place to rights again. No matter if Cornelia was determined to be 130 everywhere at once, there were a great many things left undone on this place. She would start tomorrow and do them. It was good to be strong enough for everything, even if all you made melted and changed and slipped under your hands, so that by the time you finished you almost forgot what you were working for. What was it I set out to do? she asked her self intently,[36] but she could not remember. A fog rose over the valley, she saw it marching across the creek swallowing the trees and moving up the hill like an army of ghosts. Soon it would be at the near edge of the orchard, and then it was time to go in and light the lamps. Come in, children, don't stay 140 out in the night air.

Lighting the lamps had been beautiful. The children huddled up to[37] her and breathed like little calves waiting at the bars in the twilight. Their eyes followed the match and watched the flame rise and settle in a blue curve, then they moved away from her. The lamp was lit, they didn't have to be scared and hang on to mother any more. Never, never, never more. God, for all my life I thank Thee. Without Thee, my God, I could never have done it. Hail, Mary, full of grace.

I want you to pick all the fruit this year and see that nothing is 150 wasted. There's always someone who can use it. Don't let good things rot for want of using. You waste life when you waste good food. Don't let things get lost. It's bitter to lose things. Now, don't

[34] **had fenced in**—had built a fence around. [35] **peaked Spanish comb**—tall, Spanish-type comb used to ornament the hair. [36] **intently**—earnestly; seriously. [37] **huddled up to**—crowded around.

let me get to thinking, not when I am tired and taking a little nap before supper. . . .

The pillow rose about her shoulders and pressed against her heart and the memory was being squeezed out of it: oh, push down the pillow, somebody: it would smother her if she tried to hold it. Such a fresh breeze blowing and such a green day with no threats in it. But he had not come, just the same. What does a woman do when 160 she has put on the white veil and set out the white cake for a man and he doesn't come? She tried to remember. No, I swear he never harmed me but in that. He never harmed me but in that . . . and what if he did? There was the day, the day, but a whirl of dark smoke rose and covered it, crept up and over into the bright field where everything was planted so carefully in orderly rows. That was hell, she knew hell when she saw it. For sixty years she had prayed against remembering him and against losing her soul in the deep pit of hell, and now the two things were mingled in one and the thought of him was a smoky cloud from hell that moved and crept 170 in her head when she had just got rid of Doctor Harry and was trying to rest a minute. Wounded vanity,[38] Ellen, said a sharp voice in the top of her mind. Don't let your wounded vanity get the upper hand of you.[39] Plenty of girls get jilted. You were jilted, weren't you? Then stand up to it. Her eyelids wavered[40] and let in streamers of blue-gray light like tissue paper over her eyes. She must get up and pull the shades down or she'd never sleep. She was in bed again and the shades were not down. How could that happen? Better turn over, hide from the light, sleeping in the light gave you nightmares. "Mother, how do you feel now?" and a stinging wetness on her fore- 180 head. But I don't like having my face washed in cold water!

Hapsy? George? Lydia? Jimmy? No, Cornelia, and her features were swollen[41] and full of little puddles. "They're coming, darling, they'll all be here soon." Go wash your face, child, you look funny.

Instead of obeying, Cornelia knelt down and put her head on the pillow. She seemed to be talking but there was no sound. "Well, are you tongue-tied? Whose birthday is it? Are you going to give a party?"

Cornelia's mouth moved urgently in strange shapes. "Don't do that, you bother me, daughter."

"Oh, no, Mother. Oh, no . . ." 190

Nonsense. It was strange about children. They disputed your every word.[42] "No what, Cornelia?"

---

[38] **wounded vanity**—hurt pride. [39] **the upper hand of you**—the better of you. [40] **wavered**—fluttered (moved quickly and irregularly). [41] **swollen** (variant, past participle of *swell*)—puffed up; puffy. [42] **disputed your every word**—opposed you or argued with you no matter what you said.

"Here's Doctor Harry."

"I won't see that boy again. He just left five minutes ago."

"That was this morning, Mother. It's night now. Here's the nurse."

"This is Doctor Harry, Mrs. Weatherall. I never saw you look so young and happy!"

"Ah, I'll never be young again—but I'd be happy if they'd let me lie in peace and get rested."

She thought she spoke up loudly, but no one answered. A warm 200
weight on her forehead,[43] a warm bracelet on her wrist,[44] and a breeze went on whispering, trying to tell her something. A shuffle of leaves in the everlasting hand of God, He blew on them and they danced and rattled. "Mother, don't mind, we're going to give you a little hypodermic."[45] "Look here, daughter, how do ants get in this bed? I saw sugar ants yesterday." Did you send for Hapsy too?

It was Hapsy she really wanted. She had to go a long way back through a great many rooms to find Hapsy standing with a baby on her arm. She seemed to herself to be Hapsy also, and the baby on Hapsy's arm was Hapsy and himself and herself, all at once, and 210
there was no surprise in the meeting. Then Hapsy melted from within and turned flimsy[46] as gray gauze[47] and the baby was a gauzy shadow, and Hapsy came up close and said, "I thought you'd never come," and looked at her very searchingly and said, "You haven't changed a bit!" They leaned forward to kiss, when Cornelia began whispering from a long way off, "Oh, is there anything you want to tell me? Is there anything I can do for you?"

Yes, she had changed her mind after sixty years and she would like to see George. I want you to find George. Find him and be sure to tell him I forgot him. I want him to know I had my husband just 220
the same and my children and my house like any other woman. A good house too and a good husband that I loved and fine children out of him. Better than I hoped for even. Tell him I was given back everything he took away and more. Oh, no, oh, God, no, there was something else besides the house and the man and the children. Oh, surely they were not all? What was it? Something not given back. . . .
Her breath crowded down under her ribs and grew into a monstrous[48] frightening shape with cutting edges; it bored up into her head, and the agony was unbelievable: Yes, John, get the doctor now, no more talk, my time has come. 230

[43] a warm weight on her forehead—a hand (the doctor's) on her forehead.   [44] a warm bracelet on her wrist—the doctor's fingers taking her pulse.   [45] hypodermic—injection (an injection of medicine or a drug under the skin).   [46] flimsy—fragile; thin; without substance.   [47] gauze—very light, thin, loosely woven material.   [48] monstrous—horrible; hideous.

When this one was born it should be the last. The last. It should have been born first, for it was the one she had truly wanted. Everything came in good time. Nothing left out, left over. She was strong, in three days she would be as well as ever. Better. A woman needed milk in her to have her full health.

"Mother, do you hear me?"

"I've been telling you—"

"Mother, Father Connolly's here."

"I went to Holy Communion only last week. Tell him I'm not so sinful as all that."   240

"Father just wants to speak to you."

He could speak as much as he pleased. It was like him to drop in and inquire about her soul as if it were a teething baby,[49] and then stay on for a cup of tea and a round[50] of cards and gossip. He always had a funny story of some sort, usually about an Irishman who made his little mistakes and confessed them, and the point lay in some absurd thing he would blurt out in the confessional showing his struggles between native piety and original sin. Granny felt easy about her soul. Cornelia, where are your manners? Give Father Connolly a chair. She had her secret comfortable understanding with a few   250 favorite saints who cleared a straight road to God for her. All as surely signed and sealed as the papers for the new Forty Acres. Forever . . . heirs and assigns forever.[51] Since the day the wedding cake was not cut, but thrown out and wasted. The whole bottom dropped out of the world, and there she was blind and sweating with nothing under her feet and the walls falling away. His hand had caught her under the breast, she had not fallen, there was the freshly polished floor with the green rug on it, just as before. He had cursed[52] like a sailor's parrot and said, "I'll kill him for you." Don't lay a hand on him, for my sake leave something to God. "Now,   260 Ellen, you must believe what I tell you. . . ."

So there was nothing, nothing to worry about any more, except sometimes in the night one of the children screamed in a nightmare, and they both hustled out[53] shaking and hunting for the matches and calling, "There, wait a minute, here we are!" John, get the doctor now, Hapsy's time has come. But there was Hapsy standing by the bed in a white cap. "Cornelia, tell Hapsy to take off her cap. I can't see her plain."[54]

[49] teething baby—baby getting his teeth.   [50] a round—a series (that ends more or less where it begins).   [51] heirs and assigns forever—legal terms pertaining to the deeding or willing of property.   [52] had cursed—had sworn; had used profane language.   [53] hustled out—hurried out.   [54] plain—plainly; clearly.

Her eyes opened very wide and the room stood out like a picture she had seen somewhere. Dark colors with the shadows rising toward the ceiling in long angles. The tall black dresser gleamed with nothing on it but John's picture, enlarged from a little one, with John's eyes very black when they should have been blue. You never saw him, so how do you know how he looked? But the man insisted the copy was perfect, it was very rich and handsome. For a picture, yes, but it's not my husband. The table by the bed had a linen cover and a candle and a crucifix. The light was blue from Cornelia's silk lampshades. No sort of light at all, just frippery.[55] You had to live forty years with kerosene lamps to appreciate honest electricity. She felt very strong and she saw Doctor Harry with a rosy nimbus[56] around him.

"You look like a saint, Doctor Harry, and I vow[57] that's as near as you'll ever come to it."

"She's saying something."

"I heard you, Cornelia. What's all this carrying-on?"

"Father Connolly's saying—"

Cornelia's voice staggered[58] and bumped[59] like a cart in a bad road. It rounded corners and turned back again and arrived nowhere. Granny stepped up in the cart very lightly and reached for the reins, but a man sat beside her and she knew him by his hands, driving the cart. She did not look in his face, for she knew without seeing, but looked instead down the road where the trees leaned over and bowed to each other and a thousand birds were singing a Mass. She felt like singing too, but she put her hand in the bosom of her dress and pulled out a rosary,[60] and Father Connolly murmured Latin in a very solemn voice and tickled her feet. My God, will you stop that nonsense? I'm a married woman. What if he did run away and leave me to face the priest by myself? I found another a whole world better. I wouldn't have exchanged my husband for anybody except Saint Michael himself, and you may tell him that for me with a thank you in the bargain.[61]

Light flashed on her closed eyelids, and a deep roaring shook her. Cornelia, is that lightning? I hear thunder. There's going to be a storm. Close all the windows. Call the children in. . . . "Mother, here we are, all of us." "Is that you, Hapsy?" "Oh, no, I'm Lydia. We drove as fast as we could." Their faces drifted above her, drifted

---

270

280

290

300

[55] **frippery**—showy display. [56] **nimbus**—halo (a bright cloud or disk surrounding the head of a divinity). [57] **vow**—say emphatically; promise. [58] **staggered**—moved unsteadily. [59] **bumped**—jolted; jerked; jarred. [60] **rosary**—in the Roman Catholic Church, a string of beads used to keep count in saying prayers. [61] **in the bargain**—for good measure; in addition.

away. The rosary fell out of her hands and Lydia put it back. Jimmy
tried to help, their hands fumbled[62] together, and Granny closed two
fingers around Jimmy's thumb. Beads wouldn't do, it must be something alive. She was so amazed her thoughts ran round and round.
So, my dear Lord, this is my death and I wasn't even thinking about it.   310
My children have come to see me die. But I can't, it's not time. Oh,
I always hated surprises. I wanted to give Cornelia the amethyst set
—Cornelia, you're to have the amethyst set,[63] but Hapsy's to wear
it when she wants, and, Doctor Harry, do shut up. Nobody sent for
you. Oh, my dear Lord, do wait a minute. I meant to do something
about the Forty Acres, Jimmy doesn't need it and Lydia will later on,
with that worthless husband of hers. I meant to finish the altar cloth
and send six bottles of wine to Sister Borgia for her dyspepsia.[64] I
want to send six bottles of wine to Sister Borgia, Father Connolly,
now don't let me forget.   320

Cornelia's voice made short turns and tilted over and crashed.
"Oh, Mother, oh, Mother, oh, Mother . . ."

"I'm not going, Cornelia. I'm taken by surprise. I can't go."

You'll see Hapsy again. What about her? "I thought you'd never
come." Granny made a long journey outward, looking for Hapsy.
What if I don't find her? What then? Her heart sank down and
down, there was no bottom to death, she couldn't come to the end
of it. The blue light from Cornelia's lampshade drew into a tiny point
in the center of her brain, it flickered[65] and winked an eye, quietly
it fluttered and dwindled.[66] Granny lay curled down within herself   330
amazed and watchful, staring at the point of light that was herself;
her body was now only a deeper mass of shadow in an endless darkness and this darkness would curl around the light and swallow it up.
God, give a sign!

For the second time there was no sign. Again no bridegroom and
the priest in the house. She could not remember any other sorrow
because this grief wiped them all away. Oh, no, there's nothing more
cruel than this—I'll never forgive it. She stretched herself with a deep
breath and blew out the light.

[62] **fumbled**—clumsily groped or searched.   [63] **amethyst set**—set of jewelry, probably
bracelet, ring, and necklace, made of a variety of purple or violet stones known as
amethysts.   [64] **dyspepsia**—indigestion.   [65] **flickered**—fluttered (moved and gleamed
like a burning candle).   [66] **dwindled**—grew less; decreased.

WILLIAM FAULKNER (1897 – 1962)

William Faulkner was born in Mississippi. Except for occasional periods of work on films in Hollywood or travel abroad, he has preferred to stay at home with his large family in Oxford, Mississippi, a university town. After serving in World War I, he attended the University of Mississippi and worked for a short time on a newspaper in New Orleans. He has written numerous novels and stories about characters of a few Southern families who live in the imaginary Yoknapatawpha County, which Faulkner has created. His literary style is usually complex—a style that seems to go with his intricate themes of good and evil, of the decay and the decline of the deep South. In 1949, he was awarded the Nobel Prize for Literature.[1]

The story here (from *These Thirteen*, published in 1930) presents a typical theme of Faulkner's: the decay of the "old order" in the South. He chooses as his symbol Miss Emily, the pitiable heroine of the story. With Miss Emily we see the final fading and deteriorization of a once-grand and noble Southern aristocracy; with her, we find the old order becoming like her house "an eyesore among eyesores" and "filled with dust and shadows," and like "Poor Emily" something to be pitied.

A Rose for Emily

WHEN MISS EMILY GRIERSON DIED, our whole town went to her funeral: the men through a sort of respectful affection for a fallen monument,[2] the women mostly out of curiosity to see the inside of her house, which no one save an old manservant—a combined gardener and cook—had seen in at least ten years.

It was a big, squarish frame house that had once been white,

[1] See *fn.* 1, page 60. [2] **monument**—a structure built to keep alive the memory of a person or an event (in this case, the word refers to the dead woman, indicating that her status was like a "fallen monument").

decorated with cupolas and spires[3] and scrolled balconies[4] in the heavily lightsome style of the seventies, set on what had once been our most select street. But garages and cotton gins had encroached and obliterated[5] even the august[6] names of that neighborhood; only Miss Emily's house was left, lifting its stubborn and coquettish[7] decay above the cotton wagons and the gasoline pumps—an eyesore[8] among eyesores. And now Miss Emily had gone to join the representatives of those august names where they lay in the cedar-bemused cemetery[9] among the ranked[10] and anonymous[11] graves of Union and Confederate soldiers who fell at the battle of Jefferson.

10

Alive, Miss Emily had been a tradition, a duty, and a care; a sort of hereditary obligation upon the town, dating from that day in 1894 when Colonel Sartoris, the mayor—he who fathered the edict[12] that no Negro woman should appear on the streets without an apron— remitted her taxes,[13] the dispensation[14] dating from the death of her father on into perpetuity.[15] Not that Miss Emily would have accepted charity. Colonel Sartoris invented an involved tale to the effect that Miss Emily's father had loaned money to the town, which the town, as a matter of business, preferred this way of repaying. Only a man of Colonel Sartoris' generation and thought could have invented it, and only a woman could have believed it.

20

When the next generation, with its more modern ideas, became mayors and aldermen,[16] this arrangement created some little dissatisfaction. On the first of the year they mailed her a tax notice. February came, and there was no reply. They wrote her a formal letter, asking her to call at the sheriff's office at her convenience. A week later the mayor wrote her himself, offering to call or to send his car for her, and received in reply a note on paper of an archaic[17] shape, in a thin, flowing calligraphy[18] in faded ink, to the effect that she no longer went out at all. The tax notice was also enclosed, without comment.

30

They called a special meeting of the Board of Aldermen. A deputation[19] waited upon her, knocked at the door through which no visitor had passed since she ceased giving china-painting lessons eight or ten years earlier. They were admitted by the old Negro into a dim hall from which a stairway mounted into still more shadow. It smelled of

40

[3] cupolas and spires—small domes and towers or steeples on the roof of a building. [4] scrolled balconies—balconies decorated with spiral designs. [5] obliterated—erased; blotted out. [6] august—imposing; high-ranking. [7] coquettish—flirtatious. [8] eyesore— an unpleasant sight. [9] cedar-bemused cemetery—cemetery (burial place) with many cedar trees. [10] ranked—arranged in lines. [11] anonymous—unmarked. [12] edict—or der; proclamation; decree. [13] remitted her taxes—exempted her from the payment of taxes. [14] dispensation—exemption. [15] perpetuity—eternity. [16] aldermen—town officials. [17] archaic—old-fashioned. [18] calligraphy—handwriting. [19] deputation—delegation (the members appointed for this mission).

dust and disuse—a close, dank[20] smell. The Negro led them into the
parlor. It was furnished in heavy, leather-covered furniture. When the
Negro opened the blinds of one window, they could see that the
leather was cracked; and when they sat down, a faint dust rose slug-
gishly about their thighs, spinning with slow motes[21] in the single
sun-ray. On a tarnished gilt easel[22] before the fireplace stood a crayon
portrait of Miss Emily's father.   50

They rose when she entered—a small, fat woman in black, with a
thin gold chain descending to her waist and vanishing into her belt,
leaning on an ebony cane with a tarnished gold head. Her skeleton
was small and spare;[23] perhaps that was why what would have been
merely plumpness in another was obesity[24] in her. She looked
bloated,[25] like a body long submerged in motionless water, and of
that pallid hue.[26] Her eyes, lost in the fatty ridges of her face, looked
like two small pieces of coal pressed into a lump of dough as they
moved from one face to another while the visitors stated their errand.

She did not ask them to sit. She just stood in the door and listened   60
quietly until the spokesman came to a stumbling halt. Then they
could hear the invisible watch ticking at the end of the gold chain.

Her voice was dry and cold. "I have no taxes in Jefferson. Colonel
Sartoris explained it to me. Perhaps one of you can gain access to the
city records and satisfy yourselves."

"But we have. We are the city authorities, Miss Emily. Didn't you
get a notice from the sheriff, signed by him?"

"I received a paper, yes," Miss Emily said. "Perhaps he considers
himself the sheriff . . . I have no taxes in Jefferson."

"But there is nothing on the books to show that, you see. We must   70
go by the—"

"See Colonel Sartoris. I have no taxes in Jefferson."

"But, Miss Emily—"

"See Colonel Sartoris." (Colonel Sartoris had been dead almost ten
years.) "I have no taxes in Jefferson. Tobe!" The Negro appeared.
"Show these gentlemen out."

II

So she vanquished them,[27] horse and foot,[28] just as she had vanquished their fathers thirty years before about the smell. That was

---

[20] dank—disagreeably damp. [21] motes—specks; small particles. [22] tarnished gilt
easel: a) tarnished—discolored by chemical action of the air; b) gilt—thin layer of
gold (or a substance like gold); c) easel—frame to hold canvas that an artist paints on.
[23] spare—small-boned (less in size than the ordinary woman of her build)   [24] obesity
—stoutness. [25] bloated—swollen. [26] pallid hue: a) pallid—very pale; b) hue—color;
shade. [27] vanquished them—defeated them; forced them into submission. [28] horse
and foot—horse soldiers and foot soldiers; that is, all of them.

two years after her father's death and a short time after her sweetheart—the one we believed would marry her—had deserted her. After   80
her father's death she went out very little; after her sweetheart went
away, people hardly saw her at all. A few of the ladies had the temerity[29] to call, but were not received, and the only sign of life about the
place was the Negro man—a young man then—going in and out with
a market basket.

"Just as if a man—any man—could keep a kitchen properly," the
ladies said; so they were not surprised when the smell developed. It
was another link between the gross, teeming world and the high and
mighty Griersons.

A neighbor, a woman, complained to the mayor, Judge Stevens,   90
eighty years old.

"But what will you have me do about it, madam?" he said.

"Why, send her word to stop it," the woman said. "Isn't there a
law?"

"I'm sure that won't be necessary," Judge Stevens said. "It's probably just a snake or a rat that nigger of hers killed in the yard. I'll
speak to him about it."

The next day he received two more complaints, one from a man
who came in diffident deprecation.[30] "We really must do something
about it, Judge. I'd be the last one in the world to bother Miss Emily,   100
but we've got to do something." That night the Board of Aldermen
met—three graybeards and one younger man, a member of the rising
generation.

"It's simple enough," he said. "Send her word to have her place
cleaned up. Give her a certain time to do it in, and if she don't. . . ."

"Dammit, sir," Judge Stevens said, "will you accuse a lady to her
face of smelling bad?"

So the next night, after midnight, four men crossed Miss Emily's
lawn and slunk[31] about the house like burglars, sniffing[32] along the base
of the brickwork and at the cellar openings while one of them per-   110
formed a regular sowing motion with his hand out of a sack slung[33]
from his shoulder. They broke open the cellar door and sprinkled
lime there, and in all the outbuildings. As they recrossed the lawn, a
window that had been dark was lighted and Miss Emily sat in it, the
light behind her, and her upright torso motionless as that of an idol.

[29] temerity—boldness; rashness. [30] diffident depreciation: a) diffident—shy; lacking in
confidence; b) deprecation—protest; disapproval; c) diffident deprecation—shy protest
(he was shy about his protest). [31] slunk—moved quietly; sneaked. [32] sniffing—
smelled (in an attempt to detect where the bad smell was coming from). [33] slung—
suspended.

They crept quietly across the lawn and into the shadow of the locusts that lined the street. After a week or two the smell went away.

That was when people had begun to feel really sorry for her. People in our town, remembering how old lady Wyatt, her great-aunt, had gone completely crazy at last, believed that the Griersons held themselves a little too high for what they really were. None of the young men were quite good enough for Miss Emily and such. We had long thought of them as a tableau,[34] Miss Emily a slender figure in white in the background, her father a spraddled silhouette[35] in the foreground, his back to her and clutching a horsewhip, the two of them framed by the back-flung front door. So when she got to be thirty and was still single, we were not pleased exactly, but vindicated;[36] even with insanity in the family she wouldn't have turned down all of her chances if they had really materialized.

When her father died, it got about that the house was all that was left to her; and in a way, people were glad. At last they could pity Miss Emily. Being left alone, and a pauper,[37] she had become humanized.[38] Now she too would know the old thrill and the old despair of a penny more or less.

The day after his death all the ladies prepared to call at the house and offer condolence[39] and aid, as is our custom. Miss Emily met them at the door, dressed as usual and with no trace of grief on her face. She told them that her father was not dead. She did that for three days, with the ministers calling on her, and the doctors, trying to persuade her to let them dispose of the body. Just as they were about to resort to law and force, she broke down, and they buried her father quickly.

We did not say she was crazy then. We believed she had to do that. We remembered all the young men her father had driven away, and we knew that with nothing left, she would have to cling to that which had robbed her, as people will.

III

She was sick for a long time. When we saw her again, her hair was cut short, making her look like a girl, with a vague resemblance to those angels in colored church windows—sort of tragic and serene.

[34] tableau—picture. [35] spraddled silhouette: a) spraddled—with legs spread apart; b) silhouette—a dark shape placed against a light background; c) spraddled silhouette—a dark shape with legs spread apart (against the background of Miss Emily in a white dress). [36] vindicated—justified (in our own belief that the Griersons held themselves too high). [37] pauper—very poor person; person who lives on charity. [38] humanized—human; like other people. [39] condolence—expression of sympathy.

The town had just let the contracts for paving the sidewalks, and 150
in the summer after her father's death they began the work. The construction company came with niggers and mules and machinery, and a
foreman named Homer Barron, a Yankee—a big, dark, ready man,
with a big voice and eyes lighter than his face. The little boys would
follow in groups to hear him cuss the niggers, and the niggers singing
in time to the rise and fall of picks. Pretty soon he knew everybody in
town. Whenever you heard a lot of laughing anywhere about the
square, Homer Barron would be in the center of the group. Presently
we began to see him and Miss Emily on Sunday afternoons driving in
the yellow-wheeled buggy and the matched team of bays from the 160
livery stable.

At first we were glad that Miss Emily would have an interest, because the ladies all said, "Of course a Grierson would not think seriously of a Northerner, a day laborer." But there were still others, older
people, who said that even grief could not cause a real lady to forget
noblesse oblige[40]—without calling it *noblesse oblige*. They just said,
"Poor Emily. Her kinsfolk should come to her." She had some kin in
Alabama; but years ago her father had fallen out with them over the
estate of old lady Wyatt, the crazy woman, and there was no communication between the two families. They had not even been repre- 170
sented at the funeral.

And as soon as the old people said, "Poor Emily," the whispering
began. "Do you suppose it's really so?" they said to one another. "Of
course it is. What else could . . ." This behind their hands; rustling
of craned[41] silk and satin behind jalousies[42] closed upon the sun of
Sunday afternoon as the thin, swift clop-clop-clop of the matched
team passed: "Poor Emily."

She carried her head high enough—even when we believed that she
was fallen. It was as if she demanded more than ever the recognition
of her dignity as the last Grierson; as if it had wanted[43] that touch 180
of earthiness to reaffirm her imperviousness.[44] Like when she bought
the rat poison, the arsenic. That was over a year after they had begun
to say "Poor Emily," and while the two female cousins were visiting
her.

"I want some poison," she said to the druggist. She was over thirty
then, still a slight woman, though thinner than usual, with cold,

---

[40] **noblesse oblige** (French)—the idea that people of high birth or position should behave nobly toward others. [41] **craned**—stretched. [42] **jalousies**—window shades of
horizontal slats. [43] **wanted**—needed. [44] **imperviousness**—impenetrable position (a
position that prevented anyone from getting close to her).

haughty[45] black eyes in a face the flesh of which was strained across the temples and about the eye-sockets as you imagine a lighthouse-keeper's face ought to look. "I want some poison," she said.

"Yes, Miss Emily. What kind? For rats and such? I'd recom—" 190

"I want the best you have. I don't care what kind."

The druggist named several. "They'll kill anything up to an elephant. But what you want is—"

"Arsenic," Miss Emily said. "Is that a good one?"

"Is . . . arsenic? Yes, ma'am. But what you want—"

"I want arsenic."

The druggist looked down at her. She looked back at him, erect, her face like a strained flag. "Why, of course," the druggist said. "If that's what you want. But the law requires you to tell what you are going to use it for." 200

Miss Emily just stared at him, her head tilted back in order to look him eye for eye, until he looked away and went and got the arsenic and wrapped it up. The Negro delivery boy brought her the package; the druggist didn't come back. When she opened the package at home there was written on the box, under the skull and bones: "For rats."

IV

So the next day we all said, "She will kill herself"; and we said it would be the best thing. When she had first begun to be seen with Homer Barron, we had said, "She will marry him." Then we said, "She will persuade him yet," because Homer himself had remarked— he liked men, and it was known that he drank with the younger men 210 in the Elks' Club—that he was not a marrying man. Later we said, "Poor Emily" behind the jalousies as they passed on Sunday afternoon in the glittering buggy. Miss Emily with her head high and Homer Barron with his hat cocked[46] and a cigar in his teeth, reins and whip in a yellow glove.

Then some of the ladies began to say that it was a disgrace to the town and a bad example to the young people. The men did not want to interfere, but at last the ladies forced the Baptist minister—Miss Emily's people were Episcopal—to call upon her. He would never divulge[47] what happened during the interview, but he refused to go 220 back again. The next Sunday they again drove about the streets, and the following day the minister's wife wrote to Miss Emily's relations in Alabama.

---

[45] haughty—proud; arrogant.   [46] cocked—set on one side.   [47] divulge—reveal; disclose.

So she had blood-kin under her roof again and we sat back to watch developments. At first nothing happened. Then we were sure that they were to be married. We learned that Miss Emily had been to the jeweler's and ordered a man's toilet set in silver, with the letters H. B. on each piece. Two days later we learned that she had bought a complete outfit of men's clothing, including a nightshirt, and we said, "They are married." We were really glad. We were glad because the two female cousins were even more Grierson than Miss Emily had ever been.

So we were not surprised when Homer Barron—the streets had been finished some time since—was gone. We were a little disappointed that there was not a public blowing-off, but we believed that he had gone on to prepare for Miss Emily's coming, or to give her a chance to get rid of the cousins. (By that time it was a cabal,[48] and we were all Miss Emily's allies to help circumvent[49] the cousins.) Sure enough, after another week they departed. And, as we had expected all along, within three days Homer Barron was back in town. A neighbor saw the Negro man admit him at the kitchen door at dusk one evening.

And that was the last we saw of Homer Barron. And of Miss Emily for some time. The Negro man went in and out with the market basket, but the front door remained closed. Now and then we would see her at a window for a moment, as the men did that night when they sprinkled the lime, but for almost six months she did not appear on the streets. Then we knew that this was to be expected too; as if that quality of her father which had thwarted[50] her woman's life so many times had been too virulent[51] and too furious to die.

When we next saw Miss Emily, she had grown fat and her hair was turning gray. During the next few years it grew grayer and grayer until it attained an even pepper-and-salt iron-gray, when it ceased turning. Up to the day of her death at seventy-four it was still that vigorous iron-gray, like the hair of an active man.

From that time on her front door remained closed, save for a period of six or seven years, when she was about forty, during which she gave lessons in china-painting. She fitted up a studio in one of the downstairs rooms, where the daughters and granddaughters of Colonel Sartoris' contemporaries were sent to her with the same regularity and in the same spirit that they were sent to church on Sundays with a twenty-five-cent piece for the collection plate. Meanwhile her taxes had been remitted.

[48] cabal—a small group joined together in a plot or scheme.   [49] circumvent—outwit.
[50] thwarted—hindered; obstructed.   [51] virulent—violently antagonistic; strongly opposed.

Then the newer generation became the backbone and the spirit of the town, and the painting pupils grew up and fell away and did not send their children to her with boxes of color and tedious brushes and pictures cut from the ladies' magazines. The front door closed upon the last one and remained closed for good. When the town got free postal delivery, Miss Emily alone refused to let them fasten the metal numbers above her door and attach a mailbox to it. She would not listen to them.

270

Daily, monthly, yearly we watched the Negro grow grayer and more stooped, going in and out with the market basket. Each December we sent her a tax notice, which would be returned by the post office a week later, unclaimed. Now and then we would see her in one of the downstairs windows—she had evidently shut up the top floor of the house—like the carven torso[52] of an idol in a niche,[53] looking or not looking at us, we could never tell which. Thus she passed from generation to generation—dear, inescapable, impervious, tranquil, and perverse.[54]

And so she died. Fell ill in the house filled with dust and shadows,   280 with only a doddering[55] Negro man to wait on her. We did not even know she was sick; we had long since given up trying to get any information from the Negro. He talked to no one, probably not even to her, for his voice had grown harsh and rusty, as if from disuse.

She died in one of the downstairs rooms, in a heavy walnut bed with a curtain, her gray head propped on a pillow yellow and moldy[56] with age and lack of sunlight.

V

The Negro met the first of the ladies at the front door and let them in, with their hushed, sibilant[57] voices and their quick, curious glances, and then he disappeared. He walked right through the house and out   290 the back and was not seen again.

The two female cousins came at once. They held the funeral on the second day, with the town coming to look at Miss Emily beneath a mass of bought flowers, with the crayon face of her father musing[58] profoundly above the bier[59] and the ladies sibilant and macabre;[60] and the very old men—some in their brushed Confederate uniforms—

[52] **carven torso:** *a)* **carven** (poetic)—carved; *b)* **torso**—body. [53] **niche**—a hollow place in a wall (where a statue might be placed); a particularly fitting place for an object. [54] **perverse**—contrary; difficult to get along with or put up with. [55] **doddering**—shaky (as from old age). [56] **moldy**—covered with mold (growth on the surface of organic matter—in this case, caused by decay). [57] **sibilant**—hissing. [58] **musing**—meditating. [59] **bier**—stand on which the coffin is placed. [60] **macabre**—grim; ghastly.

on the porch and the lawn, talking of Miss Emily as if she had been a contemporary of theirs, believing that they had danced with her and courted her perhaps, confusing time with its mathematical progression, as the old do, to whom all the past is not a diminishing road but, instead, a huge meadow which no winter ever quite touches, divided from them now by the narrow bottle-neck of the most recent decade of years.   300

Already we knew that there was one room in that region above stairs which no one had seen in forty years, and which would have to be forced. They waited until Miss Emily was decently in the ground before they opened it.

The violence of breaking down the door seemed to fill this room with pervading dust.[61] A thin, acrid pall[62] as of the tomb, seemed to lie everywhere upon this room decked and furnished as for a bridal: 310 upon the valance curtains[63] of faded rose color, upon the rose-shaded lights, upon the dressing table, upon the delicate array of crystal and the man's toilet things backed with tarnished silver, silver so tarnished that the monogram was obscured. Among them lay a collar and tie, as if they had just been removed, which, lifted, left upon the surface a pale crescent in the dust. Upon a chair hung the suit, carefully folded; beneath it the two mute shoes and the discarded socks.

The man himself lay in the bed.

For a long while we just stood there, looking down at the profound and fleshless grin. The body had apparently once lain in the attitude   320 of an embrace, but now the long sleep that outlasts love, that conquers even the grimace[64] of love, had cuckolded[65] him. What was left of him, rotted beneath what was left of the nightshirt, had become inextricable from the bed in which he lay; and upon him and upon the pillow beside him lay that even coating of the patient and biding dust.

Then we noticed that in the second pillow was the indentation of a head. One of us lifted something from it, and leaning forward, that faint and invisible dust dry and acrid in the nostrils, we saw a long strand of iron-gray hair.   330

[61] pervading dust—dust spread throughout. [62] acrid pall: a) acrid—sharp, bitter (to the taste or smell); b) pall—dark covering. [63] valance curtains—short curtains across the top of a window. [64] grimace—facial expression. [65] had cuckolded him— had made a cuckold of him (that is, a man whose wife has deceived him).

GEORGE SANTAYANA (1863 – 1952)

George Santayana was born in Spain. When he was nine years old, he was brought to the United States. He graduated from Harvard University and served as professor of philosophy there from 1889 to 1912. After leaving Harvard, he spent most of the time in Europe, first in England and France, later in Italy, where he died in 1952.

While a professor, he wrote many works that established him as one of the important philosophers of our time. He also became known as a poet and as perhaps the only philosopher to write a best-selling novel, *The Last Puritan.* Santayana once said of himself, "My period was 1890 and after that it has been a survival period." Still, his ideas survive him. In many ways, for example, *The Sense of Beauty* (first published in 1896), from which the selection here is taken, is still unequaled in its close analysis of elements and values related to the aesthetic sense. Here, he discusses the contrast between *work* and *play,* showing how these terms may be used in different ways.

Work and Play

*W*E HAVE HERE, THEN, AN IMPORTANT element of the distinction between aesthetic and moral values. It is the same that has been pointed to in the famous contrast between work and play. These terms may be used in different senses and their importance in moral classification differs with the meaning attached to them. We may call everything play which is useless activity, exercise that springs from the physiological impulse[1] to discharge the energy which the exigencies[2] of life have not called out. Work will then be all action that is necessary or useful for life. Evidently if work   10

---

[1] **impulse**—motivation; instinct.   [2] **exigencies**—urgent, important, and pressing needs.

and play are thus objectively distinguished as useful and useless action, work is a eulogistic term[3] and play a disparaging[4] one. It would be better for us that all our energy should be turned to account, that none of it should be wasted in aimless motion.[5] Play, in this sense, is a sign of imperfect adaptation. It is proper to childhood, when the body and mind are not yet fit[6] to cope with[7] the environment, but it is unseemly[8] in manhood and pitiable in old age, because it marks an atrophy[9] of human nature, and a failure to take hold of the opportunities of life.

Play is thus essentially frivolous.[10] Some persons, understanding the term in this sense, have felt an aversion,[11] which every liberal mind will share, to classing social pleasures, art, and religion under the head of play, and by that epithet[12] condemning them, as a certain school seems to do, to gradual extinction as the race approaches maturity. But if all the useless ornaments[13] of our life are to be cut off in the process of adaptation, evolution would impoverish[14] instead of enriching our nature. Perhaps that is the tendency[15] of evolution, and our barbarous[16] ancestors amid their toils[17] and wars, with their flaming passions and mythologies, lived better lives than are reserved to our well-adapted descendants.[18]   **30**

We may be allowed to hope, however, that some imagination may survive parasitically[19] even in the most serviceable brain. Whatever course history may take,—and we are not here concerned with prophecy,[20]—the question of what is desirable is not affected. To condemn spontaneous[21] and delightful occupations because they are useless for self-preservation shows an uncritical prizing[22] of life irrespective[23] of its content. For such a system the worthiest function of the universe should be to establish perpetual[24] motion. Uselessness is a fatal accusation to bring against any act which is done for its presumed utility, but those which are done for their own sake are their own justification.   **40**

At the same time there is an undeniable[25] propriety[26] in calling all

---

[3] **eulogistic term**—expression or word of praise.   [4] **disparaging**—discrediting; slighting. [5] **aimless motion**—purposeless activity.   [6] **are not yet fit**—are not yet developed.   [7] **to cope with**—to be a match for; to struggle equally with.   [8] **unseemly**—unattractive; unbecoming.   [9] **atrophy**—a failure to grow; a wasting away; a degeneration.   [10] **frivolous**—light, not serious.   [11] **aversion**—extreme dislike; loathing; a turning away from. [12] **epithet**—a descriptive name, title, or term.   [13] **ornaments**—decorations; not absolutely essential features.   [14] **impoverish**—make poor.   [15] **tendency**—inclination.   [16] **barbarous**—savage; wild; unrefined.   [17] **toils**—various kinds of work.   [18] **descendants**—those who come after us.   [19] **parasitically**—as a parasite, an organism that lives on another.   [20] **prophecy**—a prediction of the future.   [21] **spontaneous**—unpremeditated; unplanned; performed without planning.   [22] **prizing**—evaluation.   [23] **irrespective**—regardless; not taking into consideration; without reference to.   [24] **perpetual**—continual. [25] **undeniable**—not to be denied; indisputable; unquestionable.   [26] **propriety**—fitness; appropriateness; correctness.

the liberal and imaginative activities of man play, because they are spontaneous, and not carried on under pressure of external necessity or danger. Their utility for self-preservation may be very indirect and accidental, but they are not worthless for that reason. On the contrary, we may measure the degree of happiness and civilisation which any race has attained by the proportion of its energy which is devoted to free and generous pursuits,[27] to the adornment of life and the culture of the imagination. For it is in the spontaneous play of his faculties[28] that man finds himself and his happiness. Slavery is the most degrad-[29] ing condition of which he is capable, and he is as often a slave to the niggardliness[30] of the earth and the inclemency[31] of heaven, as to a master or an institution. He is a slave when all his energy is spent in avoiding suffering and death, when all his action is imposed[32] from without, and no breath or strength is left him for free enjoyment. 50

Work and play here take on a different meaning, and become equivalent to servitude and freedom. The change consists in the subjective point of view from which the distinction is now made. We no longer mean by work all that is done usefully, but only what is done unwillingly and by the spur[33] of necessity. By play we are designating,[34] no longer what is done fruitlessly,[35] but whatever is done spontaneously and for its own sake, whether it have or not[36] an ulterior utility.[37] Play, in this sense, may be our most useful occupation. So far would a gradual adaptation to the environment be from making this play obsolete,[38] that it would tend to abolish[39] work, and to make play universal. For with the elimination of[40] all the conflicts and errors of instinct,[41] the race would do spontaneously whatever conduced to[42] its welfare and we should live safely and prosperously without external stimulus or restraint.[43] 60

[27] pursuits—activities followed. [28] faculties—mental powers. [29] degrading—debasing; lowering. [30] niggardliness—meanness; stinginess. [31] inclemency—lack of mercy; harshness; severity. [32] imposed—placed upon. [33] by the spur—by the prompting, or the urging. [34] designating—indicating; specifying; describing. [35] fruitlessly—without purpose; aimlessly. [36] whether it have or not—if it has or if it doesn't have. (The "it" would ordinarily be followed by "has"; the author, in this instance, is using the subjunctive mood, indicating doubt or supposition. Other examples: "If it be true . . ." or "Whether or not she come . . ." The tendency today is to use the indicative mood in these structures unless one wants to be formal in style. The essay is formal in style, so the use of the structure seems appropriate.) [37] ulterior utility—a future utility; a subsequent use; a utility not seen or disclosed at the moment. [38] obsolete—outmoded; no longer in use. [39] abolish—do away with; put an end to. [40] elimination of—removing of. [41] instinct—an inborn, natural tendency to behave a certain way (in contrast to behavior dictated or guided by reason). [42] conduced to—added to; contributed to; led to. [43] restraint—holding back; control.

2

The Exercises

VOCABULARY QUIZ (I)

DIRECTIONS

Substitute the appropriate term from the list below for the boldface term in each sentence. Write in the space provided, using each term only once.

awkward	hating	undertaken
complicated	job	unfortunately
connected	mainly	uninteresting
constantly	perfectly	valuable
developed	sound	vocabulary
encouraged	stressed	weakness
essential	turned around	widely

1. The traditional methods of teaching languages to adults has almost completely **reversed** the process by which a child learns his mother tongue. _____

2. With adults, reading usually comes first, closely **linked** with writing. _____

3. What is the major **deficiency** of language teaching largely the result of? _____

4. Language learning is often a **boring** process. _____

5. Infrequent, **clumsy,** oral reading of sentences cannot be called learning to speak a language. _____

6. A student is often faced with many **intricate** rules before he has become acquainted with the flow of the language. _____

7. Many students end up **detesting** the language. _____

8. The student often does not have the opportunity to read **extensively.** _____

9. We have **tackled** the study of language from the wrong end. _____

10. The primary importance of listening is **emphasized.** _____

11. In Spanish, the system of spelling quite **consistently** represents the meaningful distinctions in sound. _____

12. It is a difficult **task** to learn Chinese symbols. _____

13. Auditory perception should be **cultivated** and improved. _____

14. Our training is **predominantly** one of sight. _____

15. We should do well to concentrate on this **vital** factor. _____

VOCABULARY QUIZ (II)

DIRECTIONS *Complete the sentences below with whichever meaning (a, b, c, d) best fits the situation from the standpoint of meaning.*

1. A valid procedure is a _____.
   a) worthwhile procedure
   b) sound procedure
   c) valuable procedure
   d) good procedure

2. A man says that his ability to speak Japanese is nil. He means that _____.
   a) he speaks Japanese with a foreign accent
   b) he can read Japanese better than he can write it
   c) he speaks Japanese very well
   d) he has no ability to carry on a conversation in Japanese

3. When one embarks on the study of Chinese symbols, he _____.
   a) begins the process of learning to read and write Chinese
   b) puts off learning to read and write Chinese for several months
   c) begins the study of Chinese customs and culture
   d) begins to learn Chinese symbols before he has learned to speak properly

4. If a person has considerable facility in understanding and speaking English, he _____.
   a) understands and speaks English like an American
   b) has considerable talent for learning to speak English
   c) has considerable difficulty in understanding and speaking English
   d) understands and speaks English with relative ease

5. People have different aptitudes for language learning. This means that _____.
   a) people have different special abilities for language learning
   b) people have different attitudes toward language learning
   c) people have different reasons for learning languages
   d) people have different methods of teaching languages

COMPREHENSION QUESTIONS

DIRECTIONS — *Answer the questions briefly according to your understanding of the author's intention, whether or not you agree with him.*

1. What does the scientifically valid procedure in language learning involve?

2. What is the order in which a child learns to speak his mother tongue?

3. What process has the traditional method of teaching language to adults followed?

4. What factors are largely responsible for the failure of many teachers to teach languages in the order that a child learns his native language?

5. What two factors make the learning of a language a boring and inefficient process?

6. According to the author, a student who is taught by traditional methods rarely learns to use a language? Why?

7. What comparison does the author use to illustrate his point that we have tackled the study of language from the wrong end?

8. What is learning to speak dependent upon?

9. The author says that if one is studying a language such as French or English it is a disadvantage at first to read traditionally spelled words. Why? What kind of an alphabet does he recommend at first?

10. Why do many linguists recommend putting off learning to read Chinese until one has pretty good conversational ability in everyday situations?

11. What processes besides the auditory process are used in learning a language? Do these processes have the same importance for all people in the memorization of materials? Explain.

12. What example does the author use to show that auditory memory can be developed to an astonishing degree?

QUESTIONS FOR DISCUSSION AND COMPOSITION

A. What method of language teaching does Nida recommend? Were you taught a foreign language by this method? Describe the methods that your teachers used.

B. In memorizing materials for a language class, do you find it most helpful to listen to expressions several times, to repeat them several times, to read them several times, or to write them several times? Do you think that you have good auditory memory? How can it be improved?

C. Does the writing system of your language consistently represent the sound system? Give examples to illustrate the points you wish to make. (*Example*: The writing system in English does not consistently represent the sound system. For example, the letter "a" is pronounced one way in "cat," another in "ate," another in "arm," and still another in "talk.")

VOCABULARY QUIZ (I)

DIRECTIONS — *Substitute the appropriate term from the list below for the boldface term in each sentence. Write in the space provided, using each term only once.*

carefreeness	efficient	hasty
checked	extreme	incorrect
commonplace	feeling of importance	irritation
complete	feeling of well-being	satisfied
concern	firm	threatening
control	great pleasure	unusual

1. Vocabulary was a **dire** and pressing need. _____

2. A chance to use his crayons always increased Mr. Kaplan's natural **euphoria**. _____

3. Mrs. Markowitz prepared her notebook with **stolid** solemnity. _____

4. Mr. Kaplan tackled his three words with **gusto**. _____

5. He replied with **consummate** simplicity. _____

6. Before replying, Mr. Kaplan gazed at the ceiling with great **insouciance**. _____

7. He couldn't bear the thought of humiliation at the **mundane** hands of Miss Mitnick. _____

8. His silence was **ominous**. _____

9. **Rebuffed**, Mr. Kaplan allowed Miss Mitnick to continue unchallenged. _____

10. Mr. Parkhill attempted to forestall a **rash** correction by Mr. Kaplan. _____

VOCABULARY QUIZ (II)

A.

DIRECTIONS

Arrange the following words in lists under the numbered blanks in the sentences below. If the word fits blank 1, it is a noun; if it fits blank 2, it is an adjective; if it fits blank 3, it is an adverb.

solemnity	conspicuously	tolerant
solemnly	conspicuous	tolerantly
solemn	conspicuousness	tolerance
niggardly	ecstatic	serenity
niggardliness	ecstatically	serenely
niggardly	ecstasy	serene
rashness	subtlety	reluctance
rash	subtle	reluctantly
rashly	subtly	reluctant

His ____(1)____ surprised us.   He was ____(2)____ .

a)	a)
b)	b)
c)	c)
d)	d)
e)	e)
f)	f)
g)	g)
h)	h)
i)	i)

He ____(3)____ took the money.

a)
b)
c)
d)
e)
f)
g)
h)
i)

B. Which of the nouns listed under 1 above would be most likely to occur, from the standpoint of meaning, in the following sentences? (It is possible that more than one word from the list will fit the blanks.)

    1. Mr. Parkhill's _____ to call on Mr. Kaplan was very notice-
able.

    2. Mr. Kaplan smiled with sweet _____, as if he were communi-
cating with one of the gods.

    3. His face was illuminated with _____ as he went to the black-
board to present his sentences.

C. Which of the adjectives listed under 2 above would be most likely to
occur, from the standpoint of meaning, in the following sentences?

    1. She looked _____ in her red hat.

    2. Mr. Parkhill spoke hurriedly to prevent Mr. Kaplan from making
a _____ correction.

    3. Mr. Kaplan had a _____ plan. By watching Mr. Parkhill's
face as he whispered possible answers, he hoped to discover the correct one.

D. Which of the adverbs listed under 3 above would be most likely to occur, from the standpoint of meaning, in the following sentences?

    1. The other students were excited as they began to prepare the as-
signment, but Mrs. Moskowitz _____ opened her notebook and
began to write her three sentences.

    2. Mr. Kaplan smiled _____ as Mr. Parkhill continued to ques-
tion him about the use of the word "pitcher."

    3. Mr. Parkhill looked about the room. Then he _____ called
on Mr. Kaplan.

COMPREHENSION QUESTIONS

DIRECTIONS   *Answer the questions briefly according to
your understanding of the author's inten-
tion, whether or not you agree with him.*

1. What kind of class did Mr. Kaplan attend? Who was the teacher?

2. What did the teacher think the students' greatest need was? Why?
Why was he reluctant to teach more pronunciation?

3. What kind of a student was Mr. Kaplan?

4. What kind of assignment did Mr. Parkhill give that night? How did
the students in the class react?

5. Describe the way Mr. Kaplan printed his name.

6. How did Mr. Kaplan attack his three words? What did he do? What
did he hope to achieve by whispering his answers loudly to himself?

7. Did the students who recited before Mr. Kaplan carry out the assignment successfully? Was Mr. Parkhill pleased with the way the lesson was going?

8. How did Mr. Kaplan attempt to get around the words *picture* and *pitcher?* What did Mr. Parkhill say? How did Mr. Kaplan answer him?

9. What was the mistake that Miss Mitnick pointed out? How did Mr. Kaplan take this correction? How did he behave during the next few recitations?

10. How did Mr. Kaplan attempt to get even with Miss Mitnick? Was he successful?

11. When Mr. Parkhill gave the students a hint as to the meaning of the word "dock," what did the class do? When the students could not give another meaning of the word "dock," Mr. Parkhill gave them a hint by saying, "Each of you, in coming to America, has had *direct experience with a dock.*" How did the class react?

12. What was Mr. Kaplan's final contribution to the vocabulary lesson? What was the reaction to his startling use of the word "dock"?

QUESTIONS FOR DISCUSSION AND COMPOSITION

A. Describe Mr. Kaplan. What is his attitude toward Mr. Parkhill? What is his attitude toward his fellow students?

B. Describe Mr. Parkhill. What is his attitude toward Mr. Kaplan? What is his general attitude toward his students?

C. Do you think that the author is sympathetic toward his two major characters, Mr. Kaplan and Mr. Parkhill? Why or why not? Discuss.

D. Discuss the importance of vocabulary study for students learning a language. Do you think that Mr. Parkhill's method of teaching vocabulary is effective? Why or why not?

E. Discuss the importance of mastering the sound system of the language one is learning. Mr. Parkhill seems to feel that accurate pronunciation is practically impossible for some of his students. Do you agree?

F. (1) Mr. Kaplan's pronunciation of "fish" is "feesh." In this word, he substitutes the vowel /iy/, as in *eat*, for the vowel /i/, as in *it*. What vowel substitution does Mr. Kaplan make in the following group of words?

cremps	cramps
heng	hang
fency	fancy
fescinate	fascinate

(2) Mr. Kaplan's pronunciation of "third" is "toid." In this word, he substitutes the consonant /t/, as in *t*in, for the consonant /th/, as in *th*in. What consonant substitutions does he make in the following groups of words?

a)

ve	we	*b*)	de	the	*c*)	usink	using
vall	wall		dis	this		commink	coming
vife	wife		anoder	another		givink	giving
vaves	waves		dey	they		havink	having

(3) What is the correct pronunciation of the following words? What sound substitutions does Mr. Kaplan make?

foist	first
void	word
toid	third
annivoisery	anniversary
univoisity	university
Clock	Clark
Pockheel	Parkhill
tvalft	twelfth
leetle	little
pipple	people
minninks	meanings
plizz	please
dock	duck

VOCABULARY QUIZ (I)

DIRECTIONS *Place a check mark (√) before the item (a, b, c) that is nearest in meaning to the bold-face word or phrase.*

1. The author says **bluntly** that marking up a book is an act of love.
_____*a*) in a straightforward manner
_____*b*) in an effective manner
_____*c*) in a courteous manner

2. Some people have a false **reverence** for paper, binding, and type.
_____*a*) respect
_____*b*) disregard
_____*c*) regret

3. Sometimes we may wish **to keep a book intact.**
_____*a*) to reserve a book for ourselves
_____*b*) to leave a book untouched
_____*c*) to own a book personally

4. The author believes that marking up a book is **indispensable** to reading
_____*a*) valuable but not necessary
_____*b*) usually necessary
_____*c*) absolutely necessary

5. Notes become an **integral** part of the book.
_____*a*) essential
_____*b*) unnecessary
_____*c*) interesting

6. The **deluded** individual who has all the standard sets and best sellers owns paper and ink, not books.
_____*a*) misled
_____*b*) foolish
_____*c*) unintelligent

7. Sheets used to take notes should not **protrude from** the book.
_____*a*) stick out of
_____*b*) fall out of
_____*c*) be taken out of

8. Another person may be **distracted** by your notes in a book.
_____*a*) amused
_____*b*) annoyed
_____*c*) side-tracked

9. Notes in the margin may be used to indicate where other points **relevant** to the point may be found.
_____*a*) similar
_____*b*) pertinent
_____*c*) opposite

150

10. Some people are **restrained from** marking books by a false respect for physical appearance.

_____*a*) made free from
_____*b*) held back from
_____*c*) removed from

VOCABULARY QUIZ (II)

DIRECTIONS *Complete the following sentences with the term that best fits the situation from the standpoint of meaning.*

acquaintance	mark	teach
container	put	understand
effortlessly	receptionist	unmarked
finish	resist	unused
good friend	resume	welcome
laboriously		

1. If a book is unblemished, it is _____.

2. If you have a good grasp of a subject, you _____ the subject well.

3. If you pick up where you left off, you _____ an activity at the point where you had stopped.

4. A receptacle is a _____.

5. A die-hard will _____ changing his opinions to the end.

6. To insert a page in a book means to _____ a page in a book.

7. One who reads without difficulty reads _____.

8. One who reads with a great deal of difficulty reads _____.

9. One who gets through several books manages to _____ reading several books.

10. A person whom you know only slightly is an _____.

COMPREHENSION QUESTIONS

DIRECTIONS   *Answer the questions briefly according to your understanding of the author's intention, whether or not you agree with him.*

1. What does the author mean when he says he wants to persuade you to "write between the lines"?

2. Should all books be marked? Explain.

3. Explain how one may own a book in two different ways.

4. Does owning a fine library necessarily prove that one has enriched his mind by the books? Explain.

5. What kinds of books does the author say he could not write notes in?

6. Why does Adler say that marking a book is absolutely necessary to reading?

7. Why does the physical act of writing give one a better understanding of the book he has read?

8. The author says that reading a book should be a conversation between the reader and the author. Explain.

9. What are some of the devices that the author suggests for marking a book?

10. What use does the author make of the front and back end papers of a book?

11. What procedure does the author suggest for the die-hard anti-book-marker?

12. What answer does the author give to the objection that marking a book slows up reading?

13. According to the author, is the important thing how many books one can manage to read? Explain.

14. Why doesn't the author believe in lending a marked book to a friend?

15. What does the author say one should tell a friend who wants to borrow a book that has been marked?

QUESTIONS FOR DISCUSSION AND COMPOSITION

A. What is the general purpose of the selection?

B. Do you find it useful to mark a book? If so, why? If not, why not? What books have you marked? Are you marking this one?

C. What points that the author makes do you agree with? What points do you question or challenge?

D. Using the third paragraph on page 15 of the selection as a model, compose a paragraph of your own. For example, you might begin: *There are three kinds of students.*

VOCABULARY QUIZ (I)

DIRECTIONS

Substitute the appropriate term from the list below for the boldface term in each sentence. Write in the space provided, using each term only once.

examined	painful cramp	removed
give up	periods	sick
headaches	physical examination	undergo
illnesses	start playing	uninteresting person
nervous	operation	very severe
nervous person		

1. Mr. A hates people who talk about their **ailments**. _____
2. Mr. A had a **splitting** headache. _____
3. He had one of his dizzy **spells**. _____
4. Mr. A defines a hypochondriac as a **bore**. _____
5. Mr. A was **jumpy**. _____
6. The doctor **took** Mr. A's appendix just in time. _____
7. He complained of a **crick** in his neck. _____
8. The doctor gave him a thorough **going-over**. _____
9. Mr. A didn't want his worst enemy to **go through** what he had experienced. _____
10. The doctor told him to **take up** golf. _____

VOCABULARY QUIZ (II)

DIRECTIONS

Read the statements in each group below. On the basis of the information in statements a, b, c, fill in the blank in d with Mr. A, B, or C.

Group 1
 a) Mr. A constantly complains about his state of health.
 b) Mr. B constantly talks about medicine.
 c) Mr. C constantly criticizes doctors.
 d) Mr. _____ is a hypochondriac.

Group 2
  a) Mr. A feels very good.
  b) Mr. B feels neither bad nor good.
  c) Mr. C feels slightly ill.
  d) Mr. _____ feels fair to middling.

Group 3
  a) Mr. A is in excellent physical condition.
  b) Mr. B is in very poor physical condition.
  c) Mr. C is in neither good nor bad physical condition.
  d) Mr. _____ is run-down.

Group 4
  a) Mr. A feels very happy and lively.
  b) Mr. B feels very unhappy and nervous.
  c) Mr. C feels very tired and ill.
  d) Mr. _____ feels very chipper.

Group 5
  a) Mr. A is very easily annoyed.
  b) Mr. B is very easily upset.
  c) Mr. C is very easily hurt.
  d) Mr. _____ is as nervous as a cat.

Group 6
  a) Mr. A says, "I'm hungry as a horse."
  b) Mr. B says, "I'm hungry and tired."
  c) Mr. C says, "I'm hungry as usual."
  d) Mr. _____ is using a cliché.

Group 7
  a) Mr. A is an authority on colds.
  b) Mr. B hates to catch colds.
  c) Mr. C catches colds easily.
  d) Mr. _____ is subject to colds.

Group 8
  a) Mr. A looks very well but isn't.
  b) Mr. B doesn't look very well but is.
  c) Mr. C looks very well.
  d) Mr. _____ looks the picture of health.

Group 9
  a) Mr. A thinks it is his turn to become ill.
  b) Mr. B thinks it is his turn to die.
  c) Mr. C thinks it is his turn to talk.
  d) Mr. _____ thinks his time has come

Group 10
  a) Mr. A didn't sleep at all.
  b) Mr. B didn't sleep very well.
  c) Mr. C didn't sleep very long.
  d) Mr. _____ didn't get a wink of sleep.

COMPREHENSION QUESTIONS

DIRECTIONS   *Answer the questions briefly according to your understanding of the author's intention, whether or not you agree with him.*

1. What is a cliché? Give an example.

2. What is Mr. Arbuthnot an expert in?

3. What is a hypochondriac? Is Mr. Arbuthnot a hypochondriac?

4. What definition does Mr. Arbuthnot give of a bore? Is he a bore by his own definition?

5. What does Mr. Arbuthnot say about his inability to sleep?

6. Has the medicine that Mr. Arbuthnot has taken for his various ailments helped him?

7. What experience did Mr. Arbuthnot have when his appendix was removed?

8. How many doctors has Mr. Arbuthnot seen? What advice have they given him?

9. What did the new doctor on Main Street tell Mr. Arbuthnot? How did he react to the doctor's advice?

10. Mr. Arbuthnot seems to have a bad opinion of modern doctors. Why?

QUESTIONS FOR DISCUSSION AND COMPOSITION

1. Imagine that the cliché expert is a citizen of your country. List and give English equivalents for some of the clichés he might use in talking about the way he feels.

2. Would people in your country be amused by a dialogue consisting of clichés? Why or why not?

3. On what does the humor of the selection depend? Which parts of the selection do you find most amusing? Why?

4. Teachers, particularly teachers of composition, warn students against overuse of clichés. Why? When does use of a cliché seem appropriate? When does it seem out of place? When is the use of the cliché most ineffective?

5. Write a humorous dialogue in which you use some of the clichés found in the selection.

VOCABULARY QUIZ (I)

DIRECTIONS *Substitute the appropriate term from the list below for the boldface term in each sentence. Write in the space provided, using each term only once.*

believed	knocked down	sternly
blond	milky	suddenly
claimed falsely	newly discovered	unkind
cloudy	pale	unusual occurrence
deep	rage	very angry
eager	ran into	wrinkled
friendly	shy	

1. The instructor became **enraged**. _____

2. He always ended up in a **fury**. _____

3. The professor said that the student only **pretended** he couldn't see through a microscope. _____

4. Once in a while he saw a **nebulous** substance through the microscope. _____

5. It was a **phenomenon** of maladjustment. _____

6. The professor spoke **grimly** to the student. _____

7. Bassum was a thin, **timid** man. _____

8. There was a **profound** silence. _____

9. His brow was **furrowed**. _____

10. The professor broke the silence **abruptly**. _____

11. He **bumped into** professors and horizontal bars. _____

12. He was an **amiable** youth. _____

VOCABULARY QUIZ (II)

DIRECTIONS *Place a check mark (√) before the item (a, b, c) that is nearest in meaning to the boldface word or phrase.*

1. The professor returned to the school **brown as a berry**.
   _____*a*) with a good tan
   _____*b*) in very good health
   _____*c*) with an eager spirit

2. Everyone shared the professor's desire that the tackle should **stay abreast of** the class in economics.

____*a*) keep up with

____*b*) keep ahead of

____*c*) stay not far behind

3. Most of the professors **were lenient** with him.

____*a*) were very unfair

____*b*) were very impatient

____*c*) were not severe

4. The editor told Haskins to get **the low-down** on the horse barns.

____*a*) the current scandal

____*b*) the information for a good story

____*c*) the general attitude

5. He **went through anguish** in botany.

____*a*) experienced great distress

____*b*) experienced great difficulty

____*c*) experienced great embarrassment

6. He thought he **could fall back on newspaper work.**

____*a*) could return to college to study journalism

____*b*) could resort to newspaper work if he had to

____*c*) could afford to fail in newspaper work

7. The professor tried to give the student **a hint.**

____*a*) a suggestion

____*b*) a fair chance

____*c*) a bad time

8. Haskins **wasn't cut out for** journalism.

____*a*) wasn't suited for

____*b*) wasn't trained for

____*c*) wasn't intelligent enough for

9. The reporter's **"beat"** was the cowbarns and the horse pavilion.

____*a*) best story

____*b*) assigned area

____*c*) difficult assignment

10. The editor told Haskins to **dig up** something interesting on the **horse** pavilion.

____*a*) write about

____*b*) report

____*c*) find

11. The editor asked Haskins why he never got **anything hot** on the horse pavilion.

____*a*) a scandalous story

____*b*) a human-interest story

____*c*) a timely interesting story

12. The general **tried to get** the soldiers all **mixed up.**

____*a*) tried to confuse the soldiers

_____b) tried to make the soldiers feel inferior

_____c) tried to make the soldiers angry

13. The general **popped up** in front of the cadet.

_____a) stood up

_____b) ran up

_____c) appeared suddenly

14. The general **snapped orders at the cadets.**

_____a) gave confusing orders to the cadets

_____b) shouted orders at the cadets in an unpleasant voice

_____c) gave orders to the cadets in an abrupt, harsh manner

15. The general was **swatting** flies.

_____a) catching

_____b) hitting

_____c) watching

16. **By sheer practice,** he became expert at squad manoeuvres.

_____a) by determined effort

_____b) by moderate practice

_____c) by practice alone

VOCABULARY QUIZ (III)

DIRECTIONS   *Complete the sentences below with which-ever meaning (a, b, c) best fits the situation from the standpoint of meaning.*

1. Juan is making fun of Ahmed's pronunciation. Ben overhears the conversation and remarks to a friend, "Juan can dish it out, but he sure can't take it." He means that Juan _____.

   a) is aware of the mistakes of others but overlooks his own

   b) is very critical of others but not critical enough of himself

   c) can do a good job of ridiculing others but can't stand it when others ridicule him

2. If a boy is lanky, he is _____.

   a) tall, thin, and awkward in appearance

   b) very tall and strong in appearance

   c) very thin and awkward in appearance

3. Haskins thought he could always fall back on newspaper work; in other words, he thought he would be able to _____.

   a) give up newspaper work, too

   b) return to college to study journalism

   c) resort to newspaper work in an emergency

4. An arresting sentence is a sentence that _____.

   a) lacks interest

   b) attracts attention

   c) ends abruptly

5. A glum person is usually _____.
    a) silent because he is very angry
    b) silent because he is sad
    c) silent as a result of his low spirits

VOCABULARY QUIZ (IV)

A.

DIRECTIONS

Arrange the following words in lists under the numbered blanks in the sentences below. If the word fits blank 1, it is a noun; if it fits blank 2, it is an adjective; if it fits blank 3, it is an adverb.

fury	timid	severity
furious	timidly	severely
furiously	timidity	severe
vividly	indifferently	lenient
vividness	indifference	leniently
vivid	indifferent	leniency

We were surprised by the man's ___(1)___ .   He was an ___(2)___ man.
    a)   *a)*
    b)   *b)*
    c)   *c)*
    d)   *d)*
    e)   *e)*
    f)   *f)*

He spoke ___(3)___ .
    a)
    b)
    c)
    d)
    e)
    f)

B. Which of the nouns listed under 1 above would be most likely to occur, from the standpoint of meaning, in the following sentences? (It is possible that more than one word from the list will fit the blanks.)
    1. He always ended up in a _____.
    2. The popular professor was noted for his _____.

3. The cadets were not interested in being soldiers. In fact, their attitude was one of complete _____.

C. Which of the adjectives listed under 2 above would be most likely to occur, from the standpoint of meaning, in the following sentences?

1. The hot-tempered professor was _____ when the student drew the picture of his eye.

2. The professors tried to help Bolenciecwcz and were very _____ with him.

3. The cadets were not enthusiastic about military training. They were _____ soldiers.

D. Which of the adverbs listed under 3 above would be most likely to occur, from the standpoint of meaning, in the following sentences?

1. The general spoke _____ to the cadets.

2. The shy professor _____ gave the student a hint.

3. The author remembers his experiences _____.

COMPREHENSION QUESTIONS

DIRECTIONS *Answer the questions briefly according to your understanding of the author's intention, whether or not you agree with him.*

1. Which course was the author unable to pass? Why?

2. What was he supposed to see through the microscope? What did he usually see?

3. Why did he repeat the course?

4. How did the professor greet him at the beginning of the semester?

5. Was he able to see through the microscope this time? What did the professor say they would do?

6. What did the author finally see through the microscope?

7. What did the professor say when he saw what the student had drawn?

1. Why was it important that Bolenciecwcz keep up in his studies?

2. Why was it difficult for Bolenciecwcz to pass his courses?

3. Did the professors try to help him along in his courses? Which professor tried to help him most?

4. What was the question that the economics professor asked Bolenciecwcz?

5. Was Bolenciecwcz able to answer the question? What did the students and the professor do to try to help him?

6. Why was everyone particularly anxious that Bolenciecwcz keep up with the class in economics?

7. How did Bolenciecwcz react when the professor tried to give him a hint by saying, "Ding, dong, ding, dong"?

1. What course caused the author even more distress than botany and economics? Why?

2. In what way was the author handicapped in the gymnasium class?

3. What was one thing the students had to do in order to pass gymnasium?

4. How was the author able to pass the swimming test?

5. What were students made to do the day they registered in gymnasium? Why was the author unhappy about this experience?

1. Why did Haskins decide to take up journalism?

2. Why wasn't Haskins cut out for journalism?

3. What "beat" on the student paper was assigned to him? Why was it a big "beat"?

4. What kind of articles did Haskins write?

5. Why did it take Haskins such a long time to write a story?

6. Why did the editor become annoyed with Haskins? What did he tell him to do?

7. What story did Haskins bring back from the horse pavilion? How did he begin the story?

1. Why was military training compulsory at Ohio State?

2. Did the military training prepare the cadets for the war going on in Europe? Explain.

3. Did the author consider himself a good soldier?

4. How did he become expert at drill?

5. For what reason was he promoted to corporal?

6. Why did General Littlefield summon him to his office? What was the general doing when he got there?

7. What did the general tell him? Did he tell him why he wanted to see him? What reason did he give for sending for him?

QUESTIONS FOR DISCUSSION AND COMPOSITION

A. What is the author's attitude toward college athletics? Do you agree?

B. What criticisms of American education are implied? Do these criticisms apply to education in your homeland?

C. Do you think Thurber was a good student? Why or why not?

D. Why does Thurber write in the first person? Why does he make fun of himself?

E. Discuss the humorous situations in the selection. Explain what makes them humorous to the reader.

F. Write about (or tell about) a humorous experience in high school or college.

G. Compare the classes described in "University Days" with classes you have been enrolled in at your college or university.

VOCABULARY QUIZ (I)

DIRECTIONS *Substitute the appropriate term from the list below for the boldface term in each sentence. Write in the space provided, using each term only once.*

aid	hostile	shelter
aware	neat	small
cautious	predict	tolerant
deadly	put aside	unpopular
put an end to	results	useless
feared	shape	weak

1. The world has a tendency to **dismiss** curiosity. _____

2. Parents do their best to **extinguish** curiosity in their children. _____

3. A historian may say that his study makes it possible to understand the past and **mold** the future. _____

4. The answers which scholars find to their questions often have important **consequences**. _____

5. The medical scholar may have a stronger motivation than the desire to wipe out a **dreaded** disease. _____

6. Scholars are usually **belligerent** toward any threat to restrict curiosity. _____

7. Scholars are **wary** of committing themselves to institutions or beliefs which threaten the free pursuit of truth. _____

8. The **feeble** phrases of academic indecision may be heard around the world. _____

9. Scholars may take **refuge** from the world in a university. _____

10. One should not think that he has found the answer when he has made only a **tidy** list of possible answers. _____

VOCABULARY QUIZ (II)

DIRECTIONS

Place a check mark (√) before the item (a, b, c) that is nearest in meaning to the boldface word or phrase.

1. A scholar may say that his work may, **in some obscure way,** make possible the construction of a space ship.

_____*a)* in a profitable way
_____*b)* in a certain field
_____*c)* in a way not clearly seen

2. A scholar needs **to be tested and probed.**

_____*a)* to be subjected to a test and made to confess that he doesn't know
_____*b)* to be subjected to a test and proved either right or wrong
_____*c)* to be subjected to a test and questioned thoroughly to determine the extent of his knowledge

3. The world calls curiosity **idle.**

_____*a)* pointless
_____*b)* evil
_____*c)* dangerous

4. A scholar **should not become enamored of** his own voice.

_____*a)* should not be captivated by
_____*b)* should not be misled by
_____*c)* should not be afraid of

5. A scholar may speak with confidence of what he knows, but press him far enough and you will find **the gaps.**

_____*a)* the false information he has communicated
_____*b)* the things he doesn't know
_____*c)* the errors he has made

VOCABULARY QUIZ (III)

A.

DIRECTIONS

Arrange the following words in lists under the numbered blanks in the sentences below. If the word fits blank 1, it is a noun; if it fits blank 2, it is an adjective; if it fits blank 3, it is an adverb.

warily	belligerent	compulsively
wary	belligerently	compulsion
wariness	belligerence	compulsive
competence	feebly	tidy
competently	feeble	tidily
competent	feebleness	tidiness

We are aware of his ___(1)___ .   He is a very ___(2)___ person.

a)   a)

b)   b)

c)   c)

d)   d)

e)   e)

f)   f)

He ___(3)___ listed all possible answers.

a)

b)

c)

d)

e)

f)

B. Which of the nouns listed under 1 above would be most likely to occur, from the standpoint of meaning, in the following sentences? (It is possible that more than one word from the list will fit the blanks.)

1. College students are expected to have acquired some _____ in writing.

2. A scholar has a _____ to communicate whatever truth he finds.

3. Extreme _____ may result in academic indecision.

C. Which of the adjectives listed under 2 above would be most likely to occur, from the standpoint of meaning, in the following sentences?

    1. A scholar is usually _____ toward any threat to the free pursuit of curiosity.

    2. The _____ phrases of academic indecision may be heard around the world.

    3. A scholar should be _____ in both speech and writing.

D. Which of the adverbs listed under 3 above would be most likely to occur, from the standpoint of meaning, in the following sentences?

    1. A scholar should be able to write _____.

    2. A scholar may speak out _____ when his free pursuit of curiosity is threatened.

    3. Scholars _____ approach commitment to institutions and beliefs that they believe may impose restrictions on them.

COMPREHENSION QUESTIONS

DIRECTIONS   *Answer the questions briefly according to your understanding of the author's intention, whether or not you agree with him.*

1. How does the world in general feel about curiosity?

2. Why do parents attempt to extinguish curiosity in children?

3. In the eyes of a scholar, what is a university mainly for?

4. When asked why he wants to know the answer to a question, a scientist may give one answer to the outsider and another to a fellow scientist. Why?

5. What is the historian likely to say when asked by an outsider why he studies history? What is the real reason that he studies history?

6. What is the primary function of a scholar?

7. What was Einstein's primary motive in pursuing his field of research?

8. Why is curiosity a dangerous quality?

9. What more "respectable sounding term" is often used in place of "curiosity"? Why is this term more acceptable?

10. The scholar may meet opposition even though it is quite likely that his findings will bring future benefits to mankind. Why?

11. In what way is the search for truth a subversive activity?

12. In what sense may a university be a sanctuary to the scholar?

13. Can excessive caution in committing oneself become a scholarly vice? Explain.

14. After a scholar has learned something, what is he compelled or forced to do?

15. Where does scholarship begin? Where does it end?

16. What are the two methods of communication for scholars? Why are they both important?

17. In what way is communication the discipline of the scholar?

18. Why is it essential that a scholar be constantly in contact with other minds?

19. Students may have various purposes in coming to Yale University, but what does the faculty expect of the students?

20. The kind of curiosity the faculty expects of students "cannot be satisfied by passing examinations or by memorizing other people's answers or other people's questions." Why? What does the faculty want the students to do?

21. The faculty encourages students to follow their minds where curiosity takes them. Does the faculty expect students to find the whole truth? What should happen in the process?

22. What is the student expected to do with whatever truth he may find?

23. Why is it important that a student learn to communicate in writing as well as in speech?

24. How is writing more than an instrument of communication?

25. In what way is communication a two-way process?

QUESTIONS FOR DISCUSSION AND COMPOSITION

A. The two main qualities that the author says a scholar must possess are curiosity and the ability to communicate. Explain.

B. To what extent do you believe that a university should be preserved as a sanctuary where "*any* question can be asked"?

C. The author says that it is very unlikely that one has thought clearly if he cannot express himself clearly in speech and, particularly, in writing. Do you agree? If so, why? If not, why not?

D. Comment on the following: "Finding answers to questions for the sake of the consequences is not the primary function of the scholar."

E. According to the author, the Yale faculty expects the students to be curious about the truth and to communicate whatever truth they find in speech and in writing. In other words, the students are expected to be in a certain sense "scholars." What is your reaction to this idea?

VOCABULARY QUIZ (I)

DIRECTIONS *Substitute the appropriate term from the list below for the boldface term in each sentence. Write in the space provided, using each term only once.*

ancestry	eaten	showed
characteristic	mixture	subject
complex	obtained	support
contradiction	opinionated	unequaled
decline	permanent	unwilling
demanded	reverse	

1. The conclusions drawn from prehistory do not support the views of the **dogmatic** simplifiers of human nature. _____

2. The old question of man's **descent** is quite well settled today. _____

3. Even thousands of years ago men in society **displayed** great variety in behavior. _____

4. Man is **unique** among animals in two general ways. _____

5. Throughout history man has progressively **secured** more food. _____

6. Man's tools have progressed from the very simple to the more **elaborate**. _____

7. History and prehistory do not **back up** the modern theory of racism. _____

8. One gets the **abiding** impression from a study of prehistory of the great range of potentialities in human beings. _____

9. Men are basically **reluctant** to change. _____

10. In studying history and prehistory one becomes aware of the basic **paradox** of human behavior. _____

VOCABULARY QUIZ (II)

DIRECTIONS

Place a check mark (√) before the item (a, b, c) that is nearest in meaning to the bold-face word or phrase.

1. They are cousins **many times removed.**
   ___a) often separated
   ___b) frequently dismissed
   ___c) very distantly related

2. Man is **a mongrel.**
   ___a) a superior animal
   ___b) a mammal
   ___c) a mixture of races

3. **Prehistory** does not support the modern idea of racism.
   ___a) the period before recorded history
   ___b) the period before modern technology
   ___c) the period before modern science

4. Technological improvement may be considered the result of the **adaptation** of means to ends.
   ___a) admission
   ___b) adjustment
   ___c) development

5. There is a great range of **potentialities** in human beings.
   ___a) overdeveloped characteristics
   ___b) undeveloped possibilities
   ___c) well-developed differences

VOCABULARY QUIZ (III)

DIRECTIONS

Complete the sentences below with whichever meaning (a, b, c) best fits the situation from the standpoint of meaning.

1. A millennium is _____.
   a) a period of a thousand years
   b) a period of thousands of years
   c) a period of ten thousand years

2. If man breeds a variant of a standard type, he _____.
   a) behaves differently from the standard type

b) shows a form that differs from the standard type

c) produces a form that differs from the standard type

3. When we say that an argument is invalidated by scientific **evidence,** we mean that _____.

  a) the argument is destroyed

  b) the argument is supported

  c) the argument is neither destroyed nor supported

4. The trained scientist is no longer bothered by the problem of **the** "missing link," that is, the problem no longer _____.

  a) interests him

  b) satisfies him

  c) worries him

5. Variety in human behavior is the despair of people who insist that human nature is simple, not varied and complex. In other words, the great variety in human behavior causes these people _____.

  a) to change their minds

  b) to lose hope

  c) to admit defeat

COMPREHENSION QUESTIONS

DIRECTIONS   *Answer the questions briefly according to your understanding of the authors' intention, whether or not you agree with them.*

1. What is meant by the term "prehistory"?

2. Why is the scientist no longer disturbed by the question of whether man is, or is not, descended from the apes?

3. According to the scientists, what is the relationship between man and the apes?

4. Does placing man in the general evolutionary history of primates destroy the theological argument that man has a soul?

5. In what way is man unique among animals?

6. According to the authors, do history and prehistory show that **man has** made spiritual and moral progress as well as technical progress?

7. Why haven't the races of mankind become separate species?

8. Is it appropriate to call man a mongrel? Why or why not?

9. Are the variations that stand out in human achievement group variations or individual variations? Explain.

10. What is the modern doctrine of racism? Do history and prehistory support this doctrine?

11. What is the abiding impression of man's potentialities that we get from prehistory?

12. In studying history, what is the basic paradox of human behavior that one becomes aware of?

13. What is meant by the statement that "man is the inventive animal"?

14. Do animals other than man seem to be able to change their environment without changing their bodies? Explain.

15. In what way is modern man almost identical with the Magdalenian man of a thousand years ago? In what way is he different?

QUESTIONS FOR DISCUSSION AND COMPOSITION

A. Do you think that man has made moral and spiritual improvements? For example, do you think man today is more honest, more virtuous, more just than man was thousands of years ago? Do you think that modern man has more reverence or respect for life?

B. In what parts of the world today is "racism" a problem? What is the present situation? What is the historical background of the situation?

C. Summarize briefly in your own words the conclusions from a survey of prehistory presented in this selection.

D. Outline the structure of the selection. Then write a composition that follows this organization. You should have a brief introductory paragraph in which you explain what you are going to list and discuss; then you should follow with four or five paragraphs that develop the four or five conclusions or points which you wish to make. The title of your composition might be "Some Conclusions about My Family" or "Some Conclusions about Science."

VOCABULARY QUIZ (I)

DIRECTIONS

Substitute the appropriate term from the list below for the boldface term in each sentence. Write in the space provided, using each term only once.

absolutely
evil
give to
heavy
produce
relentlessly

richness
simple
smoothness
stress
understandably

unhappy
unpleasant
untrustworthy
varied
vulgar

1. Men over thirty in cars look **shifty.** _____

2. Men over thirty in cars also look **gross.** _____

3. The **sleekness** of the cars makes the people riding in them look shabby by comparison. _____

4. The brightness of the new cars makes the people look **sordid.** _____

5. He looked **downright** shabby. _____

6. Cars **bestow** motion **on** people. _____

7. Cars do something **sinister** to people. _____

8. The dog stuck his head out of the car window, inhaling **myriad** smells. _____

9. Cars **accentuate** the baser characteristics of people. _____

10. People in cars are carried **inexorably** in a direction not always of their own choosing. _____

VOCABULARY QUIZ (II)

A.

DIRECTIONS

Arrange the following words in lists under the numbered blanks in the sentences below. If the word fits blank 1, it is a noun; if it fits blank 2, it is an adjective; if it fits blank 3, it is an adverb.

shifty	shabbiness	sordidly
shiftiness	shabbily	sordid
shiftily	shabby	sordidness

We detected a certain ___(1)___ in his manner.

        a)

        b)

        c)

The people looked very ___(2)___ .   The plan was ___(3)___ carried out.

    a)   *a)*

    b)   *b)*

    c)   *c)*

B. Which of the nouns listed under 1 above would be most likely to occur, from the standpoint of meaning, in the following sentences? (It is possible that more than one word from the list will fit the spaces.)

    1. The brightness of the cars accentuates the _____ of the people who ride in them.

    2. _____ in manner signifies dishonesty to many people.

C. Which of the adjectives listed under 2 above would be most likely to occur, from the standpoint of meaning, in the following sentences?

    1. His coat was very _____.

    2. It was a very unpleasant and _____ story.

D. Which of the adverbs listed under 3 above would be most likely to occur, from the standpoint of meaning, in the following sentences?

    1. He looked _____ around the room.

    2. The people were very _____ dressed.

COMPREHENSION QUESTIONS

DIRECTIONS   *Answer the questions briefly according to your understanding of the author's intention, whether or not you agree with her.*

1. In what sense does the car produce a race of half-people?

2. In comparison to the sleekness and brightness of cars, how do people in them look?

3. According to the author, cars accentuate the baser characteristics of the people who ride in them. How do boys under twenty look? How do men over thirty look? How do middle-aged women look? How do young women look?

4. What does the author say about the behavior of children in cars?

5. Does the author feel that dogs look out of place in cars? Why or why not?

6. Why is the author alarmed by the way young couples ride in cars?

7. The author says that cars have given us motion. What does she say they have taken away?

8. Why do cars suggest small prisons to the author?

QUESTIONS FOR DISCUSSION AND COMPOSITION

A. According to the author, cars have done something sinister to the relationship of the sexes. Discuss.

B. Discuss the implications of the author's statement about cars: "And if they have given us one sort of freedom, they have also become small prisons . . ."

C. What does the author mean by the statement that cars carry people along "in a direction which is not always of their choosing"?

D. The author's final words to the reader are: "Get a horse." What does this comment mean to you?

E. Does the author's attack on cars have broader implications? Does her criticism of the car extend to general criticism of the mechanized society of today? Does this mechanized society have a tendency to dehumanize people?

VOCABULARY QUIZ (I)

DIRECTIONS *Substitute the appropriate term from the list below for the boldface term in each sentence. Write in the space provided, using each term only once.*

annoying · disturbing · self-satisfaction
beautiful · forcing · strongly affected
believes · moral principles · uncertainty
challenges · pleased · unplanned
closely examined · pressed · virtues
closely fitted · read · wide

1. The girl's way of rising was not just another **casual** movement.

2. She had tall ideas about **ethics**.

3. At first her ideas seemed **shocking**.

4. Her ideas were like poetry that **defies** the extra-long line.

5. Everything is long yet **compact**.

6. Her getting up **impressed** me at the time.

7. My attitude was one of **smugness**.

8. After you have **scanned** the poem up and down you find a curious kind of unity.

9. My ideas were **squeezed** together.

10. I could reach for an idea now without **straining** everything in me to hold it.

VOCABULARY QUIZ (II)

DIRECTIONS *Place a check mark (√) before the item (a, b, c) that is nearest in meaning to the bold-face word or phrase.*

1. I had **old-fashioned** ideas.
   _____*a*) pure
   _____*b*) traditional
   _____*c*) rigid

176

2. The girl and I did **crazy** things, like running madly down the beach.
_____*a*) wild, unusual
_____*b*) unhealthy, dangerous
_____*c*) insane, psychopathic

3. Once in a while I would take **a radical fling.**
_____*a*) an immoral idea thrown at me
_____*b*) a step in the wrong direction
_____*c*) a wild departure from the customary

4. My friend told me **to pull myself together.**
_____*a*) to get hold of myself
_____*b*) to stop feeling sorry for myself
_____*c*) to avoid worrying about myself

5. Sooner or later everything **ganged up on** me.
_____*a*) came together in
_____*b*) went away from
_____*c*) got together against

VOCABULARY QUIZ (III)

A.

DIRECTIONS

Arrange the following words in lists under the numbered blanks in the sentences below. If the word fits blank 1, it is a noun; if it fits blank 2, it is an adjective; if it fits blank 3, it is an adverb.

casual	smugness	loosely
casually	smug	looseness
casualness	smugly	loose

The _____(1)_____ of the idea disturbed us.   That is a very _____(2)_____ idea.

a)   *a*)

b)   *b*)

c)   *c*)

His ideas are always so _____(3)_____ presented.

a)

b)

c)

B. Which of the nouns listed under 1 above would be most likely to occur, from the standpoint of meaning, in the following sentences? (It is possible that more than one word from the list will fit the blanks.)

1. He always thinks he's right. His _____ annoys me.
2. He never seems to be tense or uneasy in a social situation. His _____ is envied by many.

C. Which of the adjectives listed under 2 above would be most likely to occur, from the standpoint of meaning, in the following sentences?

1. At first I was shocked because her ideas seemed very _____.
2. A self-satisfied person is a _____ person.

D. Which of the adverbs listed under 3 above would be most likely to occur, from the standpoint of meaning, in the following sentences?

1. A person walks into a room in an unconcerned manner. We may say that the person walked into the room _____.
2. A student gets back a paper with the following comments: "This paper is not very well organized. The paper seems _____ put together."

COMPREHENSION QUESTIONS

DIRECTIONS   *Answer the questions briefly according to your understanding of the author's intention, whether or not you agree with him.*

1. When the young man first saw the girl, why did he like her?

2. What features of the girl were not beautiful?

3. Describe the way the girl got up from a table.

4. What kind of ideas did the girl have? What kind of poetry were her ideas like? What kind of music did her ideas make?

5. Why did the girl's getting up impress the young man?

6. What kind of a physical build did the young man have?

7. What kind of ideas did the young man have? What kind of poetry were his ideas like? What kind of music did his ideas make?

8. Why were the tall girl and the young man a funny pair?

9. What reason does the young man give for their falling in love?

10. What crazy kinds of things did the tall girl and the young man do together?

11. Why didn't the girl and the young man get married? What had come between them?

12. How did the young man feel about the end of the romance? How did he feel several years later? What had happened to him? What did his friend tell him to do? Why did he feel happy? What kind of music did he hear in others?

13. After several years had passed, how did the young man feel about the girl? Why didn't she seem tall any longer?

14. In what way do people grow taller? In what way do they grow shorter and more compact?

QUESTIONS FOR DISCUSSION AND COMPOSITION

A. Describe the girl in the story. (Include both physical and mental characteristics.)

B. Describe the young man in the story. (Include both physical and mental characteristics.)

C. Why did the girl and the young man call themselves "wonderful people"? What was unusual about their falling in love?

D. Do you think that two very different people who fall in love and part may grow more like each other in time? Discuss.

E. Does the selection tell us anything about people in general? Do you agree? Explain.

VOCABULARY QUIZ (I)

DIRECTIONS — *Substitute the appropriate term from the list below for the boldface term in each sentence. Write in the space provided, using each term only once.*

blossomed	lovely	small stream
crawled quickly	moved quietly	strange
dried up	not dangerous	struck
give	not poisonous	sudden stream
inhabitant	seized	water specialist

1. Uncle Melik **clutched** his nephew's shoulder.
2. The boy **sneaked** up on the horned toad.
3. A horned toad **scrambled** over the earth.
4. The horned toad was **harmless**.
5. There was only a **trickle** of muddy water.
6. Occasionally there would be a **spurt** of water.
7. Uncle Melik decided to **devote** all of his time and energy to the pomegranate trees.
8. Uncle Melik said, "Let no harm come to this strange **dweller** on my land."
9. The orchard in the middle of the desert looked **absurd**.
10. Many of the pomegranate trees **withered**.

VOCABULARY QUIZ (II)

DIRECTIONS — *Place a check mark (√) before the item (a, b, c) that is nearest in meaning to the boldface word or phrase.*

1. My uncle liked to plant trees and watch them grow; **only the trees** wouldn't grow.
  ____*a*) merely
  ____*b*) alone
  ____*c*) but

2. Uncle Melik said, "I'm going to make a garden out of this **awful deso-lation.**"

    ____*a*) terrible rocky soil

    ____*b*) terrible barren land

    ____*c*) terrible desert cactus

3. The land was **worthless.**

    ____*a*) without value

    ____*b*) without water

    ____*c*) without trees

4. The boy said that there were probably three rattlesnakes per acre, **conservatively.**

    ____*a*) guessing wildly

    ____*b*) all in all

    ____*c*) estimating carefully

5. The horned toad is not happy **in captivity.**

    ____*a*) when picked up

    ____*b*) when imprisoned

    ____*c*) when watched

6. The man told Uncle Melik **not to fool with horses.**

    ____*a*) not to bother with horses

    ____*b*) not to annoy horses

    ____*c*) not to buy horses

7. Uncle Melik called the tractor **a modern convenience.**

    ____*a*) a scientific implement used in farming

    ____*b*) a very expensive device for a farmer

    ____*c*) a device to make life more comfortable

8. For two or three years they didn't get any pomegranates **to speak of.**

    ____*a*) worth mentioning

    ____*b*) worth selling

    ____*c*) worth harvesting

9. The trees **didn't fare very well.**

    ____*a*) didn't produce much fruit

    ____*b*) didn't cost very much

    ____*c*) didn't do very well

10. **Nothing ever came of the blossoms.**

    ____*a*) the blossoms didn't develop into fruit

    ____*b*) the blossoms didn't grow very large

    ____*c*) the blossoms didn't last very long

COMPREHENSION QUESTIONS

DIRECTIONS *Answer the questions briefly according to your understanding of the author's intention, whether or not you agree with him.*

1. Was Uncle Melik a good farmer? Why or why not?
2. What kind of land did he buy?
3. How much land did he buy?
4. What did he intend to do with the land?
5. How far was the land from town?
6. What kinds of animals and plants were found on the land?
7. What did Uncle Melik say when he saw the horned toad?
8. How old was the boy at the beginning of the story?
9. Whom did Uncle Melik hire to clear the land?
10. What kinds of trees did Uncle Melik plan to plant on the land?
11. Why did Uncle Melik want to keep the farm a secret?
12. How did the Mexicans first attempt to clear the land? Were they successful?
13. Why did Uncle Melik buy a tractor?
14. Why did Uncle Melik hire the water specialist from Texas? Was the specialist successful in finding water there?
15. Why did Uncle Melik decide to plant only pomegranate trees?
16. After the fourth year, how many pomegranates did Uncle Melik harvest? How many did he harvest after the fifth year?
17. Why did he ask the wholesale dealer in Chicago to return the pomegranates to him express collect?
18. Why did Uncle Melik give up the land? What did he return to the man from whom he had bought the land?
19. What request did Uncle Melik make to the man? Was it granted?
20. Three years after Uncle Melik had given up the land, he and the boy drove out to take a look at it. What did they find?

QUESTIONS FOR DISCUSSION AND COMPOSITION

A. Describe the land that Uncle Melik purchased. Is there similar land in your home country? Where? Describe it?

B. What was Uncle Melik's dream? What were the different steps that Uncle Melik took in attempting to realize his dream? (Answer in one-two-three form, such as *First,* he . . . *Second,* he . . . *Third,* he . . . *Finally,* he . . .) Were the steps that Uncle Melik took reasonable?

C. What kinds of dreams do immigrants have in coming to the United States?

D. Does the author approve of imaginativeness? Do you? If you do, do you like Uncle Melik? Why or why not? Do you know any impractical people?

E. Early in the story, this statement is made: *He was too imaginative and poetic for his own good.* Point out instances in the story that support this statement.

F. What is the place of a dreamer in society? What are the obstacles he faces? What contribution to society does the dreamer make?

G. Saroyan's style of writing is often described as a "free, natural style." Point out features of style in the story that seem to support this description. Are there features which seem to contradict this description? Explain.

H. Does Saroyan's style of writing seem appropriate for the story? Discuss.

VOCABULARY QUIZ (I)

DIRECTIONS *Substitute the appropriate term from the list below for the boldface term in each sentence. Write in the space provided, using each term only once.*

brown and dry	hot and red	rocks
cheerful	hurt	shaking
concerned	lake	small stream
containers	loose	sunny
coughing	piles	unfortunate
dizzy	removed	without leaves
frozen		

1. He was **shivering** with cold. _____

2. His legs **ached** so much that it was difficult to move. _____

3. The medicine was in colored **capsules**. _____

4. The boy lay very still and was **detached** from what was going on around him. _____

5. The boy seemed to be a little **lightheaded** as a result of the fever. _____

6. The day was **bright,** but very cold. _____

7. The trees were **bare**. _____

8. The father walked with the dog along the frozen **creek**. _____

9. He jumped on the **mounds** of brush in order to force the quail into the open _____

10. His cheeks were **flushed** with fever. _____

VOCABULARY QUIZ (II)

DIRECTIONS *Place a check mark (√) before the item (a, b, c) that is nearest in meaning to the bold-face word or phrase.*

1. The boy asked his father if it **bothered** him to stay in the room with him.
   _____*a*) annoyed
   _____*b*) disturbed
   _____*c*) frightened

2. The quail **scattered** into the brush.
_____*a*) went in all directions
_____*b*) went hurriedly
_____*c*) went straight

3. He **was poised** unsteadily on the icy brush.
_____*a*) was jumping
_____*b*) was balanced
_____*c*) was walking

4. The boy was still **staring** at the foot of the bed.
_____*a*) sitting very rigidly
_____*b*) looking fearfully and suspiciously
_____*c*) looking steadily and fixedly

5. The next day the boy's hold over himself was very **slack.**
_____*a*) relaxed
_____*b*) noticeable
_____*c*) unnoticeable

COMPREHENSION QUESTIONS

DIRECTIONS   *Answer the questions briefly according to your understanding of the author's intention, whether or not you agree with him.*

1. What made the father think the boy was ill?

2. What was the boy's temperature?

3. What kind of medicine did the doctor prescribe for the boy?

4. What kind of epidemic was going on in the community? Was it dangerous?

5. Did the boy show much interest in the story his father read to him? How did he react?

6. Did he want his father to stay with him? What did he say to his father?

7. Where did the father go when he left the boy? What did he do?

8. Why did the boy refuse to let anyone at the house come into the room?

9. What misunderstanding caused the boy to think he was going to die?

10. What explanation did the father give to the boy?

11. How did the boy react when his father finally convinced him that he was not going to die?

12. How did the boy behave the following morning?

QUESTIONS FOR DISCUSSION AND COMPOSITION

A. Although we know that it was a misunderstanding of the expression "one hundred and two" that made the boy think he was going to die, the experience nonetheless was a real crisis for the nine-year-old boy. Do you think he showed courage in meeting this crisis? If so, what instances in the story show his courage?

B. What further illustrations can you give of the significance of misunderstanding a word or an expression? Are your illustrations tragic, funny, or neither?

C. In reading the story, you probably noticed that the author exercised extreme economy in giving details. Only those details which the author thinks essential to an understanding of the story are given. For instance, the author does not tell us the exact relationship of the father and son. He does not tell us whether the boy has brothers and sisters. He does not tell us about the boy's mother. He does not tell us where the story takes place. But the details given may reveal a great deal to the reader. What details, for example, show that the boy had had some contact with European culture? What details show us the relationship of father and son? What details give us an idea of where the story takes place? What details tell us something about the courage of the boy?

D. What do you think the author's purpose was in including the detailed account of the hunting scene?

E. Discuss "A Day's Wait" in relation to one of the following quotations:
  1. "Courage consists, not in blindly overlooking danger, but in seeing and conquering it."—*John Paul Richter* (1763–1825), German author
  2. "No man can answer for his courage who has never been in danger."
  —*La Rochefoucauld* (1613–1680), French author

VOCABULARY QUIZ (I)

DIRECTIONS *Substitute the appropriate term from the list below for the boldface term in each sentence. Write in the space provided, using each term only once.*

abundance   courageously   showed
apologized   feared   stopped
attack   moist   struck
attempt   reprimanded   suspiciously
bit   rubbed   tightly closed
bitterly   seized   unfairly
choked

1. The house was sometimes **damp** and cold. _____
2. The parents eyed the doctor up and down **distrustfully**. _____
3. The child had attractive blonde hair, in **profusion**. _____
4. The father **dreaded** hurting the child. _____
5. The mother **admonished** the child for not obeying the doctor. _____
6. The doctor **grasped** the child's head with his left hand. _____
7. The doctor thought perhaps he should have **desisted** and come back later. _____
8. In a final **assault** the doctor overpowered the child. _____
9. The child **gagged** on the silver spoon. _____
10. The child had fought **valiantly** to keep her secret. _____

VOCABULARY QUIZ (II)

DIRECTIONS *Place a check mark (√) before the item (a, b, c) that is nearest in meaning to the boldface word or phrase.*

1. The doctor **took a trial shot** at it as a point of departure.
   ____*a*) made a guess
   ____*b*) made an experiment
   ____*c*) fired directly

187

2. The parents were **contemptible.**

_____a) deserving of pity

_____b) deserving of scorn

_____c) deserving of consideration

3. The parents grew more **abject** as the struggle continued.

_____a) wretched

_____b) fearful

_____c) cooperative

4. The mother was **apprehensive.**

_____a) uncooperative

_____b) apologetic

_____c) fearful

5. The child was **inwardly quiet.**

_____a) unnaturally calm

_____b) calm in general

_____c) calm inside

6. The child **shrieked** hysterically.

_____a) breathed

_____b) screamed

_____c) fought

7. The doctor **coaxed** the child.

_____a) attempted to force

_____b) attempted to command

_____c) attempted to persuade

8. The parents **turned themselves inside out** in embarrassment and apology.

_____a) outdid themselves

_____b) reversed themselves

_____c) made themselves ridiculous

VOCABULARY QUIZ (III)

A.

DIRECTIONS

Arrange the following words in lists under the numbered blanks in the sentences below. If the word fits blank 1, it is a noun; if it fits blank 2, it is an adjective; if it fits blank 3, it is an adverb.

abjection	desperate	contemptible
abjectly	desperation	contemptibility
abject	desperately	contemptibly
valiant	apprehension	distrustful
valiancy	apprehensively	distrustfully
valiantly	apprehensive	distrustfulness

We were talking about certain aspects of ___(1)___ .

    a)
    b)
    c)
    d)
    e)
    f)

He was very ___(2)___ . He spoke ___(3)___ .

a)	*a)*
b)	*b)*
c)	*c)*
d)	*d)*
e)	*e)*
f)	*f)*

B. Which of the nouns listed under 1 above would be most likely to occur, from the standpoint of meaning, in the following sentences? (It is possible that more than one word from the list will fit the blanks.)

    1. _____ is regarded as a good quality.

    2. Her _____ is apparent in her suspiciousness of others.

    3. He always went to the dentist with a great deal of _____ .

C. Which of the adjectives listed under 2 above would be most likely to occur, from the standpoint of meaning, in the following sentences?

1. He is very _____ of strangers.
2. Everyone disliked him thoroughly. He was a _____ person.
3. He didn't know what was troubling him, but he was very _____.

D. Which of the adverbs listed under 3 above would be most likely to occur, from the standpoint of meaning, in the following sentences?
   1. He fought _____ and was awarded a medal.
   2. He didn't have much of a chance to win, but he tried _____.
   3. She hung her head _____.

COMPREHENSION QUESTIONS

DIRECTIONS *Answer the questions briefly according to your understanding of the author's intention, whether or not you agree with him.*

1. How long had the doctor known the Olson family?

2. How did the child's mother greet the doctor? What did she say?

3. Why was the sick child in the kitchen?

4. What was the child's reaction to the doctor?

5. Describe the physical appearance of the child.

6. How long had the child had a fever?

7. What disease did the doctor and the parents suspect that the child might have?

8. Why did the doctor object to the mother's telling the child that the doctor wouldn't hurt her? How did he react?

9. Under what circumstances would the doctor not insist on an examination?

10. Was the father much help to the doctor? Explain.

11. Why did the doctor finally ask for a smooth-handled spoon?

12. What reason did the doctor give for not waiting until the little girl was calmer before continuing the examination?

13. Why was the doctor ashamed of his behavior in forcing the child to open her mouth?

14. What did the doctor see when he finally succeeded in opening the child's mouth?

15. What did the little girl do after the doctor had forced her to open her mouth?

QUESTIONS FOR DISCUSSION OR COMPOSITION (I)

A. What is the nature of the conflict in this story?

B. Why does the doctor respect the child but find the parents "contemptible"?

C. What does the story tell us about the use of force? How is the doctor affected by resorting to the use of force? How is the child affected by being forced to open her mouth against her will?

QUESTIONS FOR DISCUSSION OR COMPOSITION (II)

A. In "A Day's Wait" the boy's difficulty is caused by the misunderstanding of the expression "a hundred and two." What misunderstandings—perhaps also verbal misunderstandings—cause the girl's reaction in "The Use of Force"?

B. Compare the relationships of parents to children in the two stories.

C. Compare the reactions of the children during their crises in the two stories.

D. Both children (in the two stories) showed courage and developed tension in their particular situations. Discuss the boy and the girl in relation to (1) the type of courage shown, (2) the tension during the crisis, and (3) the physical reactions.

VOCABULARY QUIZ

DIRECTIONS   *Substitute the appropriate term from the list below for the boldface term in each sentence. Write in the space provided, using each term only once.*

argued	gathered	reappearance
carried	gaunt	sharp-witted
chattered	jobs	slow and worthless
cut down	lean and energetic	small pebbles
detected	leaped	strong
factor	looked shyly	threw
fantastic	passed	water plants
fought	periods	

1. He joked with the squirrels that **frisked** around him. _____

2. The squirrels **peeped** at him from the branches of the trees. _____

3. He **sniffed** the seasons. _____

4. He tried to understand the mystery of the **recurrence** of blossoms in Spring. _____

5. He was more than a **rawboned** boy. _____

6. He grew to become **wiry**. _____

7. He **slung** the man over his shoulders and took him to the cabin. _____

8. He was fast, strong, and **keen**. _____

9. He was able to hold his own when he **scuffled** with the other boys. _____

10. Loneliness **filtered** through his body, eye, and brain. _____

11. The **gravel** of the streams toughened his feet. _____

12. The snowdrifts were piled in **whimsical** shapes. _____

13. He rested between **spells** of work. _____

14. When he **felled** trees, it sounded as though three men were at work. _____

15. The **element** of silence was very great in the making of Abraham Lincoln as he was. _____

192

COMPREHENSION QUESTIONS

DIRECTIONS   *Answer the questions briefly according to your understanding of the author's intention, whether or not you agree with him.*

1. How old was Abraham Lincoln when he started to grow tall? How tall was he at seventeen?

2. What kind of work was he doing at seventeen?

3. How was he able to detect the seasons of the year?

4. What comments did neighbors make about his strength?

5. Were the neighbors impressed with his ability to lift heavy objects? How did he demonstrate his lifting power?

6. One cold night Abraham Lincoln and some other boys found a man in a mud puddle beside the road. What did they try to do? How did the man react? After the other boys had left, what did Lincoln do? What did the man say afterwards?

7. What kind of house did Lincoln live in? Where did he sleep? What did the family have to eat?

8. What reputation did Abraham Lincoln have as a wrestler? What other sports did he excel in?

9. How did Lincoln sometimes earn his board, clothes, and lodging? What kind of work did he do?

10. Abraham Lincoln was alone a good deal of the time during the years he grew from a boy to a man. What kind of loneliness did he become acquainted with? How did the loneliness he knew differ from the loneliness of a city boy?

11. During the years he lived in the wilderness, what were his "companions"?

12. What element or factor played a great part in the making of Lincoln as he was?

QUESTIONS FOR DISCUSSION AND COMPOSITION

A. What kind of environment did Abraham Lincoln grow up in? Who were his friends in these early years? How did he spend most of his time?

B. What are some of the feats of strength that Lincoln performed when he was a young man?

C. The author says that Lincoln's early life gave him "a certain chance for a certain growth." Was this growth spiritual as well as physical? Discuss.

D. Discuss the following statement: "In the making of him as he was, the element of silence was immense." What does the statement suggest about the character of Abraham Lincoln?

E. What impression of Abraham Lincoln do you get from the selection? Does the selection reinforce or change your ideas about Lincoln?

F. Does this sketch of Abraham Lincoln remind you of the stories of other famous men? Tell about one of them.

VOCABULARY QUIZ (I)

DIRECTIONS *Substitute the appropriate term from the list below for the boldface term in each sentence. Write in the space provided, using each term only once.*

deeply insignificant screams
definite obstinate sentimentally
eaten up pain and suffering stand
given back perfume true inner nature
greed piling up unbearable
imaginary recalls

1. Man's youth is full of **anguish** and magic. _____

2. Man cannot **bear** to lose his youth. _____

3. Man would not choose to relive his life even though it could be **restored** to him by magic. _____

4. What is the **essence** of life? _____

5. We feel the miracle of life **poignantly**. _____

6. A young man feels the structure of life with an **intolerable** certitude. _____

7. Many of life's barriers are **phantasmal**. _____

8. Man is **devoured** by his own hunger. _____

9. A young man is usually not concerned with the **accumulation** of material possessions. _____

10. The **avarice** of King Midas is legendary. _____

11. Man possesses a greed that makes the greed of King Midas seem **paltry** by comparison. _____

12. Every man **looks back upon** his youth with sorrow and regret. _____

VOCABULARY QUIZ (II)

A.

DIRECTIONS *Arrange the following words in lists under the numbered blanks in the sentences below. If the word fits blank 1, it is a noun; if it fits blank 2, it is an adjective; if it fits blank 3, it is an adverb.*

poignant	greedy
poignancy	greed
poignantly	greedily
magically	avaricious
magical	avariciously
magic	avarice

1. His   (1)   was obvious.   It was a/an   (2)   expression.

   a)   *a)*

   b)   *b)*

   c)   *c)*

   d)   *d)*

He   (3)   remembered the incident.

   a)

   b)

   c)

   d)

B. Which of the nouns listed under 1 above would be most likely to occur, from the standpoint of meaning, in the following sentences? (It is possible that more than one word from the list will fit the blanks.)

   1. King Midas was known for his _____.

   2. We recalled the days of our youth with _____.

C. Which of the adjectives listed under 2 above would be most likely to occur, from the standpoint of meaning, in the following sentences?

   1. King Midas had a/an _____ touch. Everything he touched turned to gold.

   2. King Midas was a/an _____ old man.

D. Which of the adverbs listed under 3 above would be most likely to occur, from the standpoint of meaning, in the following sentences?

   1. He felt the loss of his youth _____.

   2. He _____ counted his money.

COMPREHENSION QUESTIONS

DIRECTIONS   *Answer the questions briefly according to your understanding of the author's intention, whether or not you agree with him.*

1. At what period of his life does man come to understand what youth is?

2. Man watches the passing of his youth with sorrow and regret, and he will grieve over the loss of his youth for the rest of his life. Does he also welcome the passing of his youth?

3. Why would man never willingly relive his youth even if he could?

4. In what way are we rich and at the same time poor? In what way are we mighty and at the same time able to have nothing?

5. As soon as we put our hand on something, what happens? When do we actually see what we are and what our lives will come to?

6. A young man has everything, but how much of it is he able to use?

7. How does a young man waste his strength? Why is the full power of his strength not felt?

8. What does a young man want and what does he finally get? What happens to him in the end?

9. Although a young man is not primarily concerned with money or the accumulation of material possessions, he is defeated in the end by his own greed. What does the word "greed" mean here?

10. Man looks back on the loss of his youth with sorrow and regret. Why does he experience sorrow and regret? What does he know?

QUESTIONS FOR DISCUSSION AND COMPOSITION

A. The selection contains many paradoxes, or pairs of conflicting or contradictory ideas. For example, man feels sorrow and regret as he watches the passing of his youth, yet he welcomes the loss with a sad and secret joy. What are some of the other paradoxes?

B. According to the author, the essence of the strange and bitter miracle of youth is found in the realization that man in youth has everything, but can hold or possess nothing forever. What does this mean to you?

C. Discuss why you may regard life as "magic," or "miraculous."

D. Point out several instances of "figures of speech" in the selection (for example, "the snake is eating at our heart"). Discuss their meanings and explain how the figurative language adds to the total meaning of the selection.

E. Many people who are past their youth often say such things as "Oh, what I might have been if I had not wasted my youth," or "Knowing what I know now, I'd like to be twenty again," or "Oh, what I might have become!" Choose one of these remarks and develop the idea into a short composition. You may interpret the remark on the basis of your understanding of it, or you may discuss the idea in relation to the life of a person you know.

VOCABULARY QUIZ (I)

DIRECTIONS

Substitute the appropriate term from the list below for the boldface term in each sentence. Write in the space provided, using each term only once.

changed
completely
confusion
courageously
decreased
enormous
fiercely

helping
increased
joyful
literary
never satisfied
read
real

searching
suffocated
took hold of
unproductive
wandered about
worthwhile

1. A mad fury **gripped** his life. _____
2. He **prowled** the stacks of the library at night. _____
3. His hunger and thirst remained **insatiate.** _____
4. It meant losing all joy **utterly.** _____
5. He was **groping** for peace and certitude. _____
6. He did not try to separate himself from the **turmoil** of the earth. _____
7. His hunger so **literal**, cruel, and physical that it wanted to devour the earth. _____
8. He felt his spirit would be **smothered.** _____
9. His spirit would be made **sterile** and hopeless. _____
10. His hunger **mounted.** _____
11. He drove himself **savagely** through the streets. _____
12. Sometimes he was **jubilant.** _____

199

VOCABULARY QUIZ (II)

DIRECTIONS
Place a check mark (√) before the item (a, b, c) that is nearest in meaning to the boldface word or phrase.

1. He was **stupefied** at the thought of all the men and objects in the world.
   ____*a*) overcome with amazement
   ____*b*) driven insane
   ____*c*) made miserly

2. He tried to get a **conclusive** picture of what these people were and did.
   ____*a*) total
   ____*b*) decisive
   ____*c*) characteristic

3. He **gloated** over the long lists of books he had read.
   ____*a*) laughed with great satisfaction
   ____*b*) groaned with bitterness
   ____*c*) gazed with great satisfaction

4. He made **stupendous** lists of all the things he had seen and done.
   ____*a*) amazingly large
   ____*b*) amazingly foolish
   ____*c*) amazingly detailed

5. He held the **conviction** that everything would happen as he wished.
   ____*a*) great hope
   ____*b*) strong belief
   ____*c*) mistaken idea

COMPREHENSION QUESTIONS

DIRECTIONS
Answer the questions briefly according to your understanding of the author's intention, whether or not you agree with him.

1. "And from that moment on mad fury seized him . . ." How do you interpret the phrase "mad fury"?

2. The young man knew a hunger and a thirst that could not be satisfied. What kind of hunger and thirst did he experience? Why was it impossible to satisfy this hunger and thirst?

3. He spent ten years in solitude and wandering. Did he seek solitude? Did he try to escape from the chaos and disorder of the earth? In what way was he driven mad by his love of life?

4. At night he would roam the library, pulling books out of shelves and reading in them. Why did the thought of the great number of books in the stacks drive him mad? Did he want to be a scholar? Why was he driven to read so exhaustively and extensively?

5. Sometimes it would seem to him that the time he spent reading books in the library was wasted. Why? What would he do then?

6. All the time the young man was filled with great hope and a wild belief that he could do all he wanted to do. He would make charts, lists, and catalogs. What kinds of lists and catalogs did he make? What was his reaction when he looked over these lists and catalogs?

7. How did he plan to get the money to make his gigantic adventure possible?

8. At night, as he listened to the sounds and silences of the city and the earth, he began to think of the "dark sleeping earth." How did everything seem to him at times like this?

QUESTIONS FOR DISCUSSION AND COMPOSITION

A. Throughout the selection we find passages that speak of the great joy, the wild hope, and the certitude of the youth. Other passages speak of his great despair, bewilderment, and weariness. Find several passages that illustrate these two moods. Do the moments of great joy, hope, and certitude and the moments of bewilderment, despair, and weariness suggest to you the general pulse or rhythm of life? At what period or periods is the contrast less sharp?

B. In what way is life similar to a river that begins as a tiny stream, develops into a swift, raging current, and finally becomes a relatively calm body of water on its way to the sea? Which stage of the river does man's youth most closely resemble?

C. In "Man's Youth" the author says that man would not willingly relive his youth even if he could. Discuss this idea in relation to "Hunger to Devour the Earth."

D. The youth in "Hunger to Devour the Earth" searches blindly and uncertainly, as all men on this earth have searched, for "one face out of a million faces, a wall, a door, a place of certitude and peace and wandering no more." This youth knows what it is "to see a million faces and to be a stranger and an alien to them always." What does the author's general philosophy about man's relationship to other men and to society seem to be? Is man born a stranger and does he die a stranger on this earth? Does he ever really get to know another human being? Discuss.

VOCABULARY QUIZ (I)

DIRECTIONS   *Substitute the appropriate term from the list below for the boldface term in each sentence. Write in the space provided, using each term only once.*

bridge	enlarges	produce
contradicts	experiment	puzzled
crumble	generalize	remarkable
deduce	great	scientific
developed	interested	skip
distinction	meaning	structure
elementary	possibility	transmitted

1. The fourteen scientists represented in the scientific panel **span** the centuries from Hippocrates to Einstein. _____

2. Albert Einstein is the last scientist represented in the gallery of the **illustrious** dead. _____

3. Einstein achieved scientific **eminence** with the publication of his Theory of Relativity in 1905. _____

4. In his last years, Einstein worked on a problem that had **baffled** him for more than a quarter of a century. _____

5. In addition to its scientific **import**, the Theory of Relativity comprises a major philosophical system. _____

6. The similarities between the electromagnetic and the gravitational phenomena are very **striking**. _____

7. Most of the phenomena of our external world seem to be produced by two **primordial** forces. _____

8. Light waves and radio waves are **propagated** in space through the electromagnetic field. _____

9. The Theory of Relativity **augments** and illumines the reflections of such philosophers as Locke, Berkeley, and Hume. _____

10. Under certain conditions magnetic forces can **induce** electrical currents. _____

11. Newton's machine-like universe began to **topple** before the end of the nineteenth century. _____

12. Deviations from Newton's laws of mechanics shook the whole **edifice** of his machine-like universe. _____

VOCABULARY QUIZ (II)

DIRECTIONS
Place a check mark (√) before the item (a, b, c) that is nearest in meaning to the boldface word or phrase.

1. To most newspaper readers Einstein's name is just a synonym for **the abstruse.**
_____*a*) that which is difficult to understand
_____*b*) that which is scientific in nature
_____*c*) that which is great

2. A vast gap in American education has **persisted** for more than the last fifty years.
_____*a*) continued without change
_____*b*) grown steadily
_____*c*) been noticeable

3. Experiments in the nineteenth century showed that a current of electricity is always surrounded by a magnetic field and **conversely** that under certain conditions magnetic forces can cause electrical currents.
_____*a*) in addition
_____*b*) in reverse order
_____*c*) consequently

4. The abyss between the very big and the very little—the macrocosmos and the microcosmos—will probably be bridged by the Unified Field Theory.
_____*a*) the gravitational field
_____*b*) the deep, immeasurable gulf
_____*c*) the puzzling, unsolved mystery

5. The Unified Field Theory **promulgated** a set of universal laws designed to cover not only the gravitational and electromagnetic fields but also the tiny field inside the atom.
_____*a*) proved
_____*b*) promised
_____*c*) set forth

6. The certainty that science can explain how things happen began to **dim** about twenty years ago.
_____*a*) fall over
_____*b*) increase
_____*c*) grow less

COMPREHENSION QUESTIONS

DIRECTIONS *Answer the questions briefly according to your understanding of the author's intention, whether or not you agree with him.*

1. What period of time is covered by the fourteen men represented in the panel honoring geniuses of science? Who is the earliest scientist represented? Who is the latest?

2. How were the fourteen scientists selected for the panel? Who was the unanimous choice? Which other scientists were frequently mentioned?

3. According to the author, we may measure a gap in American education by two events. What are the two events?

4. What baffling problem did Einstein work on during the last years of his life?

5. The Unified Field Theory attempts to set forth laws governing two fundamental forces of the universe. What are they?

6. Most of the external phenomena of our universe seem to be produced by two primordial forces. What are they?

7. What discovery came from the experiments of Oersted and Faraday in the nineteenth century?

8. Nearly all forces in the material universe, except gravitation and meson, are of what origin? Why?

9. Have the attempts to identify gravitational attraction as an electromagnetic effect been successful? What progress did Einstein make?

10. What is the general aim of science?

11. What progress have modern scientists made in explaining the ultimate nature of electricity, magnetism, and gravitation? Are contemporary physicists confident that man can discover the nature of these forces?

12. What does Bertrand Russell say that electricity is and is not?

13. By what process did Aristotle believe that man could arrive at understanding of ultimate reality?

14. If it is a self-evident principle that everything in the universe has its place, how can we arrive at the conclusion that smoke goes up?

15. When was modern science born? What method forms the basis of modern scientific investigation?

16. A mechanical universe of forces, pressures, tensions, oscillations, and waves evolved as a result of the discoveries of two scientists. Who were they?

17. When did the structure of Newton's mechanical universe begin to topple?

18. Are scientists today confident that science can explain *how* things happen? Explain.

QUESTIONS FOR DISCUSSION AND COMPOSITION

A. The article stresses the importance of understanding as much as possible about Einstein's theories. Why?

B. What does the Unified Field Theory attempt to do? Why is it significant?

C. What examples does the author use to illustrate the similarities between gravitational and electromagnetic phenomena?

D. The aim of science is to describe and explain the world we live in. The meaning of the word "explain" is increasingly restricted, however, as man continues his search for reality. Discuss.

E. How do the goals of Aristotelian science and modern science differ?

F. After the discoveries of Galileo and Newton there was an increasing hope and belief that the processes of nature could be described in terms of ordinary experience or predicted by Newton's accurate laws of mechanics. What is the situation today?

G. There seems to be general agreement today on the importance of science in the school curriculum. Some people feel, however, that an increased emphasis on science may result in the neglect of other fields of study. Discuss.

VOCABULARY QUIZ (I)

DIRECTIONS *Substitute the appropriate term from the list below for the boldface term in each sentence. Write in the space provided, using each term only once.*

absorbed
cracks
dangerous
devised
directed
endless
evidences

forced out
great numbers
matched
periods
pounding
produced
rocks

rough
smelled
started
unfair
violent outbursts
were covered

1. The waters were stormy and **treacherous.** _____

2. The darkness **sucked up** the searchlight. _____

3. The rock provided protection against an **interminable** sea. _____

4. The word "California" has **routed** all other names from the scene.

5. The crabs go into **paroxysms** of rage. _____

6. They saw **hordes** of hermit crabs. _____

7. Xantus literally **proliferated** in all directions. _____

8. It was difficult to get the sea urchins out of the **crevices.** _____

9. Tiny attacked the Sally Lightfoots with every **foul** means he could think of.

10. We **pitted** our superior intelligence against the physical superiority of the Sally Lightfoots. _____

11. Tiny **contrived** several plans to catch the Sally Light-foots. _____

12. The rocks **swarmed** with Sally Lightfoots. _____

VOCABULARY QUIZ (II)

DIRECTIONS   *Place a check mark (√) before the item (a, b, c) that is nearest in meaning to the boldface word or phrase.*

1. The information was essentially correct; they supplied the **fallacy**.
   _____a) misleading notion
   _____b) missing information
   _____c) important details

2. The name "California" was later **extended** to mean all the peninsula.
   _____a) changed in detail
   _____b) broadened in scope
   _____c) forced out

3. The **conjecture** is believable.
   _____a) fact
   _____b) theory
   _____c) story

4. There has been much **erudite** discussion about the origin of names.
   _____a) interesting
   _____b) unnecessary
   _____c) scholarly

5. The pirates **darted out** in a small boat.
   _____a) came out suddenly
   _____b) sailed out bravely
   _____c) started out courageously

6. The rough and pounding surf seemed to increase the **tenacity** of the animals.
   _____a) number
   _____b) competition
   _____c) persistence

7. The pigs and vultures **browsed** on the beach.
   _____a) slept peacefully
   _____b) moved aimlessly around
   _____c) looked happy

8. It was difficult to **dislodge** the urchins.
   _____a) catch
   _____b) shake loose
   _____c) gather up

9. Some groups **thrive** under varying conditions.
   _____a) grow competitive
   _____b) grow slowly but steadily
   _____c) grow healthy and numerous

10. Our party took a **circuitous** route.
_____*a*) circular
_____*b*) unknown
_____*c*) indirect

VOCABULARY QUIZ (III)

DIRECTIONS

Cross out the one word in the parentheses that is not similar in meaning to the others. Example: He (ran, rushed, hurried, ~~called~~*) to the office.*

1. There were (swarms, droves, hordes, thrives) of crabs on the rocks.

2. It was a/an (erudite, interesting, scholarly, learned) discussion.

3. His explanation was (satisfactory, possible, credible, believable).

4. The modern biologist is usually concerned with (security, promotion, advancement, preferment).

5. There was a/an (exuberant, understandable, excessive, superabundant) fierceness in the shore region.

6. The animals (savagely, fiercely, fearfully, ferociously) fought for their survival.

VOCABULARY QUIZ (IV)

A.

DIRECTIONS

Arrange the following words in lists under the numbered blanks in the sentences below. If the word fits blank 1, it is a noun; if it fits blank 2, it is an adjective; if it fits blank 3, it is an adverb.

ferocity	credibly	ingenuousness
ferociously	credibility	ingenuously
ferocious	credible	ingenuous
fierce	tenacity	nonchalantly
fierceness	tenacious	nonchalant
fiercely	tenaciously	nonchalance
nostalgic	fallaciously	
nostalgically	fallacy	
nostalgia	fallacious	

The   (1)   varied with the situation.   It was a   (2)   gesture.

a)   a)
b)   b)
c)   c)
d)   d)
e)   e)
f)   f)
g)   g)
h)   h)

                She   (3)   argued the point under consideration.

                    a)
                    b)
                    c)
                    d)
                    e)
                    f)
                    g)
                    h)

B. Which of the nouns listed under 1 above would be most likely to occur, from the standpoint of meaning, in the following sentences? (It is possible that more than one word from the list will fit the blanks.)

    1. We approached the crabs with an expression of _____ on our faces.

    2. We look back on the days of Darwin with _____.

C. Which of the adjectives listed under 2 above would be most likely to occur, from the standpoint of meaning, in the following sentences?

    1. The explanation may not be true, but it is _____.

    2. In this region there was _____ competition for survival.

D. Which of the adverbs listed under 3 above would be most likely to occur, from the standpoint of meaning, in the following sentences?

    1. We walked toward the crabs _____.

    2. The guide book did not give us false information; we had reasoned _____ from the information given.

COMPREHENSION QUESTIONS

DIRECTIONS

Answer the questions briefly according to your understanding of the author's intention, whether or not you agree with him.

1. Where does the expedition take place? What is the purpose of the expedition?

2. What are some of the ideas or theories about the origin of the name "California"? How does the author feel about these ideas?

3. How does the author feel about scholarly discussions of the origin of names?

4. In what way does naming a thing make it less dangerous?

5. What preparations did the Mexican officials have to make before coming aboard? Did the men on the ship have to wait long for the arrival of the officials? Why or why not?

6. What characteristics of Mexican officials does the author mention?

7. Why did everyone in Cape San Lucas hate the large black birds called cormorants?

8. In what way did the collecting methods of the author and his group differ from the usual methods of modern collectors? In what way was the method used similar to that of Darwin? In what way was it different?

9. What are Sally Lightfoots? What do they look like? Does the name seem appropriate? Explain.

10. The author and his group decided to match their superior intelligence against the obvious physical superiority of the Sally Lightfoots. What plan did they make to outwit the Sally Lightfoots? Were they successful?

11. The author says that man's attempt to catch the Sally Lightfoot usually ends in complete frustration. What are the typical physical reactions?

12. What did the author say about the few Sally Lightfoots that they finally managed to catch?

QUESTIONS FOR DISCUSSION AND COMPOSITION

A. The author says that names seem to attach themselves to things and then stick or fall into disuse. He also feels that the relationship between thing and name is very close. Discuss these ideas in relation to names of persons or places that you are familiar with.

B. According to the author, some modern scientists and philosophers protect themselves from fear by establishing a taboo-box into which they throw all thoughts that frighten them. What outstanding instances of the establishment of taboo-boxes can we find in modern society? What kinds of taboo-boxes do individuals establish to protect themselves from fear?

C. The author describes the cormorants as radicals and subversive forces that upset "the perfect and God-set balance on Cape San Lucas." He goes on to say that ". . . they are rightly slaughtered as all radicals should be. As one of our number remarked, 'Why, pretty soon they'll want to vote.'" Do these observations apply to certain aspects of our society? Explain.

D. "Perhaps the force of the great surf which beats on this shore has much to do with the tenacity of the animals here. It is noteworthy that the animals, rather than deserting such beaten shores for the safe cove and protected pools, simply increase their toughness and fight back at the sea with a kind of joyous survival." Do you think this observation applies to man as well as the marine life described by the author? Explain.

E. Darwin reversed the modern process of looking quickly at the whole field and then concentrating on a particular part of it. Darwin came out with a sense of the whole after a long consideration of the parts. The author looks back with longing at the slow pace of Darwin, but he says that to imitate today the procedure followed by Darwin would be "romantic and silly." Do you agree? Why or why not?

F. Write an account of an interesting day in your life—for example, a day of travel or a day you remember because of special happenings or events. Include in your account not only what happened, but also what you felt and thought about it at the time.

VOCABULARY QUIZ (I)

DIRECTIONS	*Substitute the appropriate term from the list below for the boldface term in each sentence. Write in the space provided, using each term only once.*

accomplishments	force	risks
advancing	foul	shells
deadly	hidden	slant
eating away	persuaded	slow-moving
expenses	poisonous	suggest
extraordinary	reveal	total
fiery hot		

1. Man has been only partially successful in extracting sea salts in quantities sufficient for commercial purposes, despite the **prodigious** quantity and variety.

2. Vanadium was discovered in the blood of certain **sluggish** sea creatures. _____

3. The **feats** performed by corals, sponges, and oysters as chemists are extraordinary. _____

4. The **aggregate** thickness of salt in the Michigan Basin is approximately 2000 feet. _____

5. In many Norwegian fiords the deep layers of water are **lethal** pools.

6. The lower layers of water in the Black Sea are **stagnant**. _____

7. The earth at one time was a place of **encroaching** deserts. _____

8. Oil seepages in northern Alaska **hint** that this land may be one of the great oil fields in the future. _____

9. The coastal planes **tilt** sharply downward. _____

10. The question is whether the sea can be **induced** to give up some of its oil. _____

11. There are many **hazards** to be faced in drilling for oil in undersea fields. _____

12. The **gnawing** of sea water upon metal structures is a problem to be overcome in undersea oil fields. _____

VOCABULARY QUIZ (II)

DIRECTIONS

Place a check mark (√) before the item (a, b, c) that is nearest in meaning to the boldface word or phrase.

1. Silicon is utilized by the **ubiquitous** plants of the sea.
   _____*a*) various
   _____*b*) omnipresent
   _____*c*) sea cucumber

2. Minerals are added to the sea from **obscure** sources.
   _____*a*) outside
   _____*b*) hidden
   _____*c*) strange

3. The ship had a laboratory for the **sampling** of sea water.
   _____*a*) storing
   _____*b*) testing
   _____*c*) evaporating

4. It is not economically **feasible** to take gold out of sea water.
   _____*a*) practicable
   _____*b*) productive
   _____*c*) impossible

5. The bottom waters of the Black Sea are **devoid** of oxygen.
   _____*a*) somewhat lacking in
   _____*b*) probably without
   _____*c*) completely without

COMPREHENSION QUESTIONS

DIRECTIONS

Answer the questions briefly according to your understanding of the author's intention, whether or not you agree with her.

1. What is the primary source of the ocean's salt? How is this salt carried to the sea? Has the saline content of the sea been increasing or decreasing over the ages?

2. What are some of the differences in the composition of river water and sea water? What are some of the reasons for these differences?

3. Minerals are also added to the sea by volcanoes. Explain.

4. Although the flow of minerals is predominantly seaward, the sea does return some minerals to the land. Explain.

5. Describe the long-distance, large-scale transport of cyclic-salts to the Sambhar Salt Lake in northern India.

6. The plants and animals of the sea are much better chemists than men. Explain.

7. What did the German chemist Fritz Haber attempt to do? Why wasn't he successful?

8. Iodine is considered one of the most mysterious substances in the sea. Why? In what way is man dependent on iodine for proper functioning of the body? How is commercial iodine obtained?

9. Ninety-nine per cent of the world's bromine is concentrated in the sea. How is bromine obtained? What are some of the uses of bromine?

10. How is magnesium obtained today? What are some of the uses of magnesium?

11. There are natural basins where the action of sun, wind, and sea carry on evaporation of salt on a scale larger than modern industry can achieve. The Rann of Cutch, a natural basin on the west coast of India, is an example. Describe the process of evaporation of salt in this basin.

12. How were the famous deposits of salt in Stassfurt and Alsace developed?

13. Searles Lake in the Mohave Desert of California contains one of the greatest stockpiles of minerals in the world. How did this area become an inland sea? What minerals are now taken from this area?

14. According to the article, the Dead Sea will probably repeat the history of Searles Lake. Why? What animals now live in the waters of the Dead Sea?

15. What is the most valuable legacy of the ancient seas? What geologic processes are responsible for this gift?

16. The old inorganic theory of petroleum formation has now been abandoned by most geologists. What is the most likely origin of petroleum formation?

17. The conditions favoring petroleum production are found in the Black Sea and certain Norwegian fiords. What are these conditions?

18. Name some areas where vast oil deposits have been found. What do these areas have in common from the standpoint of geological history?

19. Why do the geologists look for salt domes in exploring for oil in the Gulf of Mexico?

20. What are some of the difficulties to be overcome in obtaining oil from undersea fields?

QUESTIONS FOR DISCUSSION AND COMPOSITION

A. Discuss three important sources of wealth from the salt seas.

B. Man's search for mineral wealth often leads him back to seas of ancient times. Discuss the possibility of man's obtaining these minerals more directly by modern methods of extraction.

C. Tell of some close observations you have made about an aspect of nature: the sky, the ocean, vegetation, or rocks, for example.

D. Describe some of the natural resources or scenic wonders of your country. (You might follow some of the patterns of development used by Miss Carson. Notice that she talks about "the most mysterious," "one of the oldest," and various other superlatives. You may describe the mountains, the deserts, the mines, the lakes, the lands, or any other natural wonders.)

VOCABULARY QUIZ (I)

DIRECTIONS *Substitute the appropriate term from the list below for the boldface term in each sentence. Write in the space provided, using each term only once.*

animal-like	moist and cold	searched busily
busy	obedient	shone
earnestly	oppose	short and fat
get	puffy	spoil
grew less	rejection	went out
horrible	repeatedly	worry
hurried		

1. The story is concerned with the **jilting** of Granny Weatherall. _____

2. Dr. Harry's fingers were **pudgy**. _____

3. Cornelia was a **dutiful** girl. _____

4. Granny tried to **snatch** a bit of sleep before dinner. _____

5. She **rummaged** around in her mind for the idea. _____

6. The hand felt **clammy**. _____

7. The children decided not to **cross** Granny. _____

8. "What was I going to do?" she asked herself **intently**. _____

9. Her eyes were **swollen**. _____

10. She saw a **monstrous** shape. _____

11. They both **hustled** out looking for matches. _____

12. The light flickered and **dwindled**. _____

VOCABULARY QUIZ (II)

DIRECTIONS *Place a check mark (√) before the item (a, b, c) that is nearest in meaning to the boldface word or phrase.*

1. Granny said that she was already on her feet, **morally** speaking.
   _____a) hopefully
   _____b) virtually
   _____c) virtuously

2. Doctor Harry called Granny **a marvel.**

    _____*a*) a courageous old woman

    _____*b*) a marvelous patient

    _____*c*) an amazing person

3. Lydia would ask Granny for advice when one of the children **jumped the track.**

    _____*a*) became tired and cross

    _____*b*) had a serious illness

    _____*c*) got out of control

4. She **vowed** that was as close as he would ever come to looking like a saint.

    _____*a*) said thoughtfully

    _____*b*) said teasingly

    _____*c*) said emphatically

5. Cornelia's voice **staggered** like a cart on a bad road.

    _____*a*) moved unsteadily

    _____*b*) broke down

    _____*c*) moved slowly

COMPREHENSION QUESTIONS

DIRECTIONS   *Answer the questions briefly according to your understanding of the author's intention, whether or not you agree with her.*

1. How does Granny Weatherall react to Doctor Harry? What advice does the doctor give her? How does she take his advice?

2. After the doctor left, Granny began thinking of what she was going to do tomorrow. She thought about going through a box of letters in the attic. Whose letters were these? Why did she want to destroy them?

3. At what period in her life did Granny Weatherall think about dying? Did she continue to think about dying after that?

4. How did her children treat her? Did her children still value her advice?

5. How did she now think of her husband? Why was the idea strange to her?

6. At one point Granny felt that she would start tomorrow and put Cornelia's house in order; then her thoughts turned to her children when they were small. How did the children act during the lighting of the lamps?

7. The pillow seemed to rise about her shoulders and squeeze a memory out of her heart. What was this memory? Why had she prayed against remembering it for sixty years?

8. Which child did Granny want most of all? What had happened to the child?

9. When Cornelia whispered, "Is there anything I can do for you?" Granny thought, "I want you to find George." What did she want George to know?

10. What does the figure who takes the reins in the "cart scene" represent?

11. When the rosary fell from her hands, both Lydia and Jimmy tried to put it back. Granny closed two fingers around Jimmy's thumb. Why did she prefer holding on to Jimmy's thumb rather than the beads?

12. Granny realizes that her children have come to see her die, but she feels that it is not time for her death. She says, "I'm not going, Cornelia." Why does she feel that she can't die yet?

13. What are her thoughts about Hapsy? Why does she keep thinking about her? Why is she trying to find her?

14. As Granny is drawing near her death, what does her life become identified with?

QUESTIONS FOR DISCUSSION AND COMPOSITION

A. What tone or mood is set at the beginning of the story? Does this tone or mood suggest anything about the character of Granny Weatherall? Does the name "Weatherall" seem appropriate for her?

B. Through Granny we learn of the events of the last day of her life as she experiences them and of the events of her past life as these memories occur to her. Which events seem clearer to her? What types of activities and people do her memories center around? What do these memories of the past tell us about her character? What qualities did she have as a young woman? What qualities has her long life added or developed?

C. Granny's memories contain the very painful thought of being jilted on her wedding day. What influence did this event have on her life? Was everything that she had lost given back to her? Why did she keep George's letters as well as John's? Was her life complete and satisfying?

D. In the final paragraph of the story, Granny again experiences a "jilting" just like the rejection on her wedding day sixty years ago. Does this final "jilting" tell us anything about the way she has lived and the way she dies?

VOCABULARY QUIZ (I)

DIRECTIONS

Substitute the appropriate term from the list below for the boldface term in each sentence. Write in the space provided, using each term only once.

appreciation	hindered	protest
boldness	kindness	proud
crazy	monument	questioned
delegation	once-great	reveal
difficult	outwit	shaky
erased	picture	stupid
evil	policeman	surround
high-ranking		

1. Garages and cotton gins had **obliterated** the high-ranking names in the neighborhood. _____

2. A **deputation** came to see Miss Emily about her taxes. _____

3. Some of the ladies had the **temerity** to call on Miss Emily. _____

4. One man came in mild **deprecation.** _____

5. The people thought of Miss Emily and her father as a **tableau.** _____

6. The minister would not **divulge** what Miss Emily had said to him. _____

7. Grierson was one of the **august** names of the neighborhood. _____

8. She looked at the druggist with cold, **haughty** black eyes. _____

9. The people wanted to help Miss Emily **circumvent** the two cousins from Alabama. _____

10. Miss Emily's father had **thwarted** her woman's life many times. _____

11. Miss Emily was **perverse.** _____

12. She had only a **doddering** Negro man to wait on her. _____

VOCABULARY QUIZ (II)

DIRECTIONS   *Place a check mark (√) before the item (a, b, c) that is nearest in meaning to the boldface word or phrase.*

1. Miss Emily **vanquished** the delegation.
_____*a*) defeated
_____*b*) refused to see
_____*c*) scolded

2. The man was **diffident** in making his complaint.
_____*a*) very angry
_____*b*) shy
_____*c*) disinterested

3. Miss Emily was **impervious**.
_____*a*) insane
_____*b*) impenetrable
_____*c*) silent

4. The crayon face of her father **mused** above the funeral bier.
_____*a*) meditated
_____*b*) smiled
_____*c*) hung

5. The room was filled with **pervading dust**.
_____*a*) dust that irritated the nose
_____*b*) dust that smelled of the tomb
_____*c*) dust that spread everywhere

COMPREHENSION QUESTIONS

DIRECTIONS   *Answer the questions briefly according to your understanding of the author's intention, whether or not you agree with him.*

1. Even though Miss Emily had not appeared in public or talked to the townspeople for many years, everyone went to the funeral. Why?

2. What kind of a neighborhood did Miss Emily live in? What had this neighborhood been like at one time?

3. Why had Colonel Sartoris exempted Miss Emily from the payment of taxes? Why did he invent a fancy tale about the matter? When the next generation sent Miss Emily a tax notice, what did she do? When a delegation called on her, how did she receive them?

4. About two years after her father's death and a short time after the disappearance of Homer Barron, the townspeople noticed a very bad smell about the place. What did they attempt to do about it? We are told that it was about this time that the people really began to feel sorry for Miss Emily. Why?

5. The day after Miss Emily's father died, the ladies called on Miss Emily. How did she receive them? Did they understand why she acted as she did? Explain.

6. Miss Emily was very sick after her father's death. How did she look when the people saw her again?

7. When the druggist told Miss Emily that the law required a person buying poison to state what he wanted to use it for, what did Miss Emily do? What did the people think she was going to do with the poison?

8. When Miss Emily was seen with Homer Barron, the Yankee construction foreman, what did the people think? How did Miss Emily conduct herself in public? Did she pay any attention to the glances of disapproval and the gossip?

9. What made the townspeople believe that Miss Emily and Homer Barron were going to be married? Were they sympathetic toward Miss Emily at this time?

10. What was the last the townspeople saw of Homer Barron? When they next saw Miss Emily how did she look?

11. From the time of Homer Barron's disappearance Miss Emily's door remained closed except for a period of six or seven years when she was about forty. What did she do during this period of six or seven years? Why didn't she continue her work after that?

12. How old was Miss Emily when she died? Who took care of her when she became ill? Did the townspeople know she was ill?

13. After Miss Emily's death, the old Negro met the ladies at the front door and let them in. What did he do after that?

14. Whose picture was placed above Miss Emily's funeral bier? How did the old men who came to the funeral talk about Miss Emily?

15. After Miss Emily had been buried the townspeople forced open a room upstairs that no one had seen in forty years. What did they find in the room? What did they find on the second pillow on the bed?

QUESTIONS FOR DISCUSSION AND COMPOSITION (I)

A. What is the significance of the title "A Rose for Emily"?

B. In the introduction to this story, it was pointed out that Miss Emily might be regarded as a symbol of the fading and deteriorization of a once-grand and noble Southern aristocracy. How do the people in the story regard the fading and decay of this aristocracy? What is their attitude toward the Grierson family? Support your statements with examples and illustrations from the story.

C. When members of the Board of Aldermen called on Miss Emily about her taxes, she told them that she owed no taxes and called her servant to show them out. When the people gossiped about her relationship with Homer Barron, she made no attempt to explain her actions or to defend herself. When the druggist questioned her about the poison she wanted to buy, she stared at him as if he had no right to question her. What do these incidents tell us about her character? What qualities did she possess?

D. What was the relationship between Miss Emily and her father? How had her father "thwarted her woman's life"? Does the picture ("We had long thought of them as a tableau") the townspeople had of Miss Emily and her father symbolize the father-daughter relationship? When the Board of Aldermen called on Miss Emily some years before, they saw a crayon portrait of her father on a tarnished gilt easel. At Miss Emily's funeral, the crayon face of her father is placed above the bier. What is the significance of these two details?

E. For three days after her father's death, Miss Emily continued to tell the ladies who called that her father was not dead. The statement is made that she had to do that. "We all knew that with nothing left, she would have to cling to that which had robbed her, as people will." What else does she cling to in the same way?

F. Was it cold, violent anger that motivated Miss Emily to deal with Homer Barron in the way she did, or was it something much more than that?

G. From what we know of the character of Miss Emily it is unlikely that fear of discovery alone drove her into seclusion for so many years. Is there a more likely explanation for her seclusion? Even at her death she apparently felt no need to explain her behavior to anyone. Why had she remained silent all these years?

H. Describe an old person of your acquaintance.

QUESTIONS FOR DISCUSSION AND COMPOSITION (II)

A. Granny Weatherall and Miss Emily are both women from the South. Compare societies or groups of people they represented.

B. Compare the difficulties and the problems that they had in their lives.

C. Compare the way they met these difficulties and problems.

D. Compare the strong points and the weaknesses that each possessed.

E. Compare the way they lived and the way they met death.

F. Compare the "old order" and the new of your homeland.

VOCABULARY QUIZ (I)

DIRECTIONS *Substitute the appropriate term from the list below for the boldface term in each sentence. Write in the space provided, using each term only once.*

correctness	improve	purposeless
debasing	make poor	specifying
discouraging	meanness	unbecoming
discrediting	mental powers	unlikely
exercises	need	urgent needs
extreme dislike	not serious	urging
harshness	outmoded	worthwhile

1. Much of our energy is consumed by the **exigencies** of life. _____

2. Play, in one sense, is a **disparaging** term. _____

3. Our energy should not be wasted in **aimless** activity. _____

4. Play is **unseemly** in manhood. _____

5. Play is essentially **frivolous.** _____

6. Many people have felt an **aversion** to classifying social pleasures, art, and religion as play. _____

7. Elimination of the ornaments of life will **impoverish** our nature. _____

8. There is some **propriety** in calling all the liberal and imaginative activities of man play. _____

9. Man finds happiness in the spontaneous play of his **faculties.** _____

10. Slavery is the most **degrading** condition of man. _____

11. Man is often a slave to the **niggardliness** of the earth. _____

12. Man is also a slave to the **inclemency** of heaven. _____

13. Work is everything that is done unwillingly and under the **spur** of necessity. _____

14. By play we are **designating** that which is done spontaneously and for its own sake. _____

15. Play as spontaneous activity done for its own sake would never become **obsolete.** _____

224

VOCABULARY QUIZ (II)

DIRECTIONS

Complete the following sentences with the term that best fits the situation from the standpoint of meaning.

1. If one is not able to cope with his environment, he is _____.
   a) not able to stand it
   b) not a match for it
   c) not able to change it
   d) not satisfied with it

2. Play in old age marks an atrophy of human nature, that is, _____.
   a) a failure of man to grow
   b) a tendency of man to be frivolous
   c) an inclination of man to waste time
   d) a refusal of man to accept responsibility

3. Imaginative activities of man may or may not have ulterior utility. In other words, imaginative activities may or may not have _____.
   a) a worthwhile aim
   b) a realistic outlook
   c) a scientific value
   d) a future usefulness

4. Work, meaning activity done unwillingly and through necessity, would tend to be abolished. This means that work would tend to be _____.
   a) made illegal
   b) done away with
   c) left undone
   d) made easier

5. If man does something that conduces to his welfare, he does something that _____.
   a) buys him security
   b) is harmful to his well-being
   c) adds to his well-being
   d) makes him prosperous

COMPREHENSION QUESTIONS

DIRECTIONS

Answer the questions briefly according to your understanding of the author's intention, whether or not you agree with him.

1. The importance of the terms "work" and "play" may differ in moral classification. What does their relative importance depend on?

2. If we call all useless activity play, what is work?

3. If we mean by play all useless action, is play then a disparaging term or a eulogistic one?

4. Why is play, distinguished as useless activity, considered appropriate for children but not for adults?

5. Persons who think of play as frivolous are unwilling to classify social pleasures, art, and religion as play. Why?

6. Why does the author say that our barbarous ancestors perhaps lived better lives than their well-adapted descendants?

7. What does the author hope may survive in even the most serviceable brain?

8. By what may we measure the degree of happiness and civilization which any race has attained?

9. In what does man find himself and his happiness?

10. What is the most degrading condition that man is capable of?

11. A man may be a slave to a master or to an institution. In what other ways may he be a slave?

12. If work and play take on different meanings and become equivalent to servitude and freedom, what do we mean by work? What do we mean by play? From what point of view is this distinction made?

13. Would play, meaning all that is done spontaneously and for its own sake, tend to be abolished? Why or why not?

14. Under what circumstances should man be able to live safely and prosperously without external stimulus or restraint?

QUESTIONS FOR DISCUSSION AND COMPOSITION

A. What is the meaning attached to the terms "work" and "play" at the beginning of the essay? What is the meaning attached to the terms at the end of the essay? What is the author's purpose in showing us how the terms may be used in different senses?

B. What do the terms "work" and "play" mean to you? How do the distinctions made by the author fit into your ideas of work and play?

C. What does the author mean when he says that play may be our most useful occupation? Does he mean that work, as we think of it in the usual sense, should be replaced by play? Explain.

D. The author says that man is "a slave when all his action is imposed from without, and no breath or strength is left him for free enjoyment." Discuss.

E. What comments might the author make about the popular saying, "All work and no play makes Jack a dull boy"?

F. Analyze the meanings of "work" and "play" in modern society. Is what is work for some, play for others? Do we work when we play? Do we play when we work? Is it all right to enjoy work?

LIST OF SELECTIONS FOR FURTHER READING

Students who have enjoyed selections in this book may be interested in other works by these authors or in the writings of other American authors. Titles by authors included in this volume have been mentioned in the headnotes preceding each selection. The list below gives titles by other writers.

This list is just a beginning. We are not trying to offer a bibliography of American literature, but, on the basis of our experience, we are suggesting some books that may interest students who want to know more about literature and thought in the United States. Instructors may suggest other books; students may add suggestions on the endpapers of this book.

AIKEN, CONRAD (1889–   )
>   *Short Stories* (1950). A collection of stories with subtle, imaginative themes. Two stories, "Mr. Arcularis" and "Silent Snow, Secret Snow," are frequently found in anthologies.
>   *Collected Poems* (1953). Winner of the National Book Award as the most distinguished volume of poetry published in 1953.

ANDERSON, SHERWOOD (1876–1941)
>   *Winesburg, Ohio* (1919). Short stories about small-town life.
>   *Home Town* (1940). A collection of essays.
>   *Memoirs* (1942). Autobiography.

BARZUN, JACQUES (1907–   )
>   *God's Country and Mine* (1954). Reflections on life in the United States; the subtitle "A Declaration of Love Spiced with a Few Harsh Words" suggests the author's attitude.

BENEDICT, RUTH (1887–1948)
>   *Patterns of Culture* (1934). A view of modern anthropology through the study of three primitive cultures, by one of the leading American anthropologists.
>   *Race, Science and Politics* (1940). A popular discussion of what scientists know about race, and an examination and refutation of "racial superiority."

CATHER, WILLA (1873–1947)
>   *My Ántonia* (1918). A novel about an immigrant girl, and her heroic life in early Nebraska.
>   *A Lost Lady* (1923). A novel about a cultivated lady who was caught between the world of heroic pioneers and that of the materialistic new generation.
>   *Death Comes for the Archbishop* (1927). A novel of the Southwest in the times of the Spanish missions.

CLARK, WALTER, VAN TILBURG (1909–   )
>   *The Ox-Bow Incident* (1940). A psychological novel about the lynching of a murder suspect in Nevada cattle country.
>   *The Track of the Cat* (1949). A novel about an isolated family and a panther that is symbolic of evil.

CLEMENS, SAMUEL (pseudonym: Mark Twain) (1835–1910)
The Adventures of Tom Sawyer (1876). A novel of the adventures of a boy in a Mississippi River town.

The Adventures of Huckleberry Finn (1884). A humorous and satirical novel about life in the Midwest in the middle of the nineteenth century, as seen through the eyes of an uncorrupted boy.

DAY, CLARENCE (1874–1935)
This Simian World (1920). Depiction of the apelike nature of man, and speculation on what the world would be like if the dominant species had descended from another kind of animal.

Life with Father (1935) and *Life with Mother* (1936). Autobiographical novels, told with humor and affection, about life in an upper class nineteenth-century family.

DREISER, THEODORE (1871–1945)
Sister Carrie (1900). A novel about a working girl who became a famous actress, and of her life as mistress of a man who became a failure as she rose to success.

An American Tragedy (1925). A novel of a young man who became trapped in a series of love and business experiences that led to his execution for murder.

Newspaper Days (1931). Autobiography.

ELIOT, T. S. (1888–   )
Collected Poems, 1909–1935. Verse including "The Waste Land," a long poem in which the poet represents twentieth-century civilization as futile.
Murder in the Cathedral (1935). A play about the murder of Thomas á Becket, which concerns the moral responsibilities of man and the Church.
The Cocktail Party (1950). A play about several modern characters and their concern over sin and salvation.

FISHER, VARDIS (1895–   )
Children of God (1939). A historical novel about the Mormon movement.

FITZGERALD, F. SCOTT (1896–1940)
This Side of Paradise (1920). A novel about the jazz age of the twenties.
The Great Gatsby (1925). The story of Gatsby and his fabulous post-World War I career—symbolizing dreams that were destined to be destroyed.

FROST, ROBERT (1875–   )
Collected Poems (1930, Pulitzer Prize 1931). Verse, typically expressing the poet's individualistic view of life and revealing his observations of the New England environment.

JAMES, HENRY (1843–1916)
The Portrait of a Lady (1881). A psychological novel about the relationship of a young American woman to a group of Europeans and other Americans living in Europe.

The American Scene (1907). Description based upon lengthy travels through the United States.

LERNER, MAX (1902–   )
>   *Ideas Are Weapons* (1939). Essays, expressing a liberal point of view, on a variety of subjects from law to education.
>   *America as a Civilization* (1957). Essays on life and ideas in contemporary United States.

LEWIS, SINCLAIR (1885–1951) (Awarded the Nobel Prize in 1930.)
>   *Main Street* (1920). A realistic novel that contrasts cosmopolitan and small-town life.
>   *Babbitt* (1922). A satirical novel about a "typical" American businessman.
>   *Arrowsmith* (1925, Pulitzer Prize 1926). A novel about the career of a scientist.

LONDON, JACK (1876–1916)
>   *Call of the Wild* (1903). The story of a dog that leads a wolf-pack in the Far North.
>   *White Fang* (1905). A novel about a wild dog that becomes tamed.
>   *The Iron Heel* (1907). A novel that predicts a fascist revolution to be followed by a golden era.

MC CULLERS, CARSON (1917–   )
>   *The Ballad of the Sad Café* (1951). Collection of novels and short stories, mostly set in the South, including "The Member of the Wedding," which the author later made into a successful play.

O'NEILL, EUGENE (1888–1953)
>   *Beyond the Horizon* (1920, Pulitzer Prize). A naturalistic drama about tragic frustration.
>   *Ah, Wilderness!* (1933). A humorous play with a New England setting.

SCHWARTZ, DELMORE (1913–   )
>   *In Dreams Begin Responsibilities* (1939). A collection containing a story, a play, and poems.
>   *The World Is a Wedding* (1948). Short stories, mostly about middle class Jewish family life.

WARREN, ROBERT PENN (1905–   )
>   *All the King's Men* (1946, Pulitzer Prize 1947). A novel about a political boss; it concerns itself with the problem of political morals in modern America.

WHARTON, EDITH (1862–1937)
>   *Ethan Frome* (1911). A short novel about the tragic lives of a few simple New England characters.
>   *The Age of Innocence* (1920). A Pulitzer Prize-winning novel about New York high society.
>   *In Morocco* (1920). A travel book.
>   *A Backward Glance* (1934). Autobiography.

WHITE, E. B. (1899–   )
>   *One Man's Meat* (1942). Essays on the conflicts of life and one man's solution.
>   *The Second Tree from the Corner* (1954). Collection of the author's later essays.

WILDER, THORNTON (1897–   )
   The Bridge of San Luis Rey (1927, Pulitzer Prize 1928). A short novel about the lives of five people who were killed when a bridge collapsed in Peru in 1714. The theme is the problem of the existence of death and suffering in the world.
   The Ides of March (1948). A historical novel about the last days of Julius Caesar that gives insights into the man and his world.

WILSON, EDMUND (1895–   )
   The Shock of Recognition (1943). An anthology showing the development of U.S. literature from 1845–1938.
   Memoirs of Hecate County (1946). Six stories about a group of well-to-do New York suburbanites.

WYLIE, PHILIP (1902–   )
   A Generation of Vipers (1942). A critical survey of American habits and beliefs.

INDEX OF TERMS

The index that follows includes most of the words and phrases footnoted in this book. In general, proper names, localisms, and dialectal expressions are not included. The first number after a word indicates the page number on which the term may be found; the second number, in parentheses, indicates the specific footnote on the page.